WHITMAN'S
Southern Sojourn

Whitman's *Southern Sojourn*

REDISCOVERING THE POET IN NEW ORLEANS, 1848

Stefan Schöberlein

AND

Zachary Turpin

UNIVERSITY OF IOWA PRESS

IOWA CITY

UNIVERSITY OF IOWA PRESS, IOWA CITY 52242

uipress.uiowa.edu

Printed in the United States of America

DESIGN BY TERESA W. WINGFIELD

The publication of this book was generously supported by a subvention grant from the College of Arts & Sciences at Texas A&M University–Central Texas.

Printed on acid-free paper

LIBRARY OF CONGRESS CATALOGING-IN-PUBLICATION DATA

Names: Schoberlein, Stefan author I Turpin, Zachary author

Title: Whitman's Southern Sojourn: Rediscovering the Poet in New Orleans, 1848 / by Stefan Schoberlein and Zachary Turpin.

Description: Iowa City: University oflowa Press, 2025. I Series: The Iowa Whitman series I Includes index.

Identifiers: LCCN 2025013855 (print}! LCCN 2025013856 (ebook) I ISBN 9781685970475 paperback I ISBN 9781685970482 ebook

Subjects: LCSH: Whitman, Walt, 1819-1892-Homes and haunts-Louisiana-New Orleans I New Orleans (La.)-In literature I LCGFT: Literary criticism

Classification: LCC PS3234.S36 2025 (print) I LCC PS3234 (ebook)

LC record available at https://lccn.loc.gov/2025013855

LC ebook record available at https://lccn.loc.gov/2025013856

This book is dedicated to the hundreds of workers at the National Endowment for the Humanities, the National Endowment for the Arts, and the National Institutes of Health who have lost their livelihoods this year, as well as to the countless invaluable programs, institutions, and research efforts they served.

Being now out of a job, I was offer'd impromptu, (it happen'd between the acts one night in the lobby of the old Broadway theatre near Pearl street, New York city,) a good chance to go down to New Orleans on the staff of the "Crescent," a daily to be started there with plenty of capital behind it. One of the owners, who was north buying material, met me walking in the lobby, and though that was our first acquaintance, after fifteen minutes' talk (and a drink) we made a formal bargain, and he paid me two hundred dollars down to bind the contract and bear my expenses to New Orleans. I started two days afterwards; had a good leisurely time, as the paper wasn't to be out in three weeks. I enjoy'd my journey and Louisiana life much.

—WALT WHITMAN, *Specimen Days*, 1882

[S]ome years ago, of the Brooklyn rara avis, his crude and rabid ideas of "progress," together with his conceited egotism, made the royal bird appear in so ridiculous a plight to the "eyes of all beholders," that it was intimated to our unfortunate "animal," from head quarters, he had better go South for the benefit of his health.— To the Crescent City he went accordingly, and, truly, they must have made short work of him, as, after a few months, we had him back again, large as life, but quite as vain, and more radical than ever. From the South he brings the French motto "Liberty, equality, fraternity," and he stands before us a "Freeman."

—*Brooklyn Daily Advertiser*, 1849

Contents

WHITMAN'S
Southern Sojourn

CHRONOLOGY

February 8, 1848	Walt meets McClure in the old Broadway Theatre.
February 10, 1848	Walt and Jeff depart New York City via a Newark mail train after taking a ferry from the "foot of Liberty Street" in Manhattan at 9 a.m. They arrive in Philadelphia about four hours later and take the 4:30 p.m. train from the corner of Eleventh and Market to Baltimore, where they arrive by 10 p.m.
February 11, 1848	Walt and Jeff depart Baltimore by train around 7:30 a.m. They have a late-afternoon dinner in Harpers Ferry, Virginia, and arrive in Cumberland, Maryland, around 5 p.m. At 6 p.m. they board one of four carriages of the National Road and Good Intent Stage Company and begin their crossing of the Alleghenies (tickets were $13 per person).
February 12, 1848	The brothers watch the sunrise around Uniontown, Pennsylvania; by nightfall, they arrive in Wheeling, Virginia, and depart aboard the steamer *St. Cloud* by 10 p.m.
February 16/17, 1848[1]	The *St. Cloud* lands in Cincinnati, and Walt and Jeff walk about town. On the night of February 17, they are hit by a "hard storm."
February 18, 1848	The brothers arrive in Louisville, Kentucky, and depart at 10 a.m., en route to Cairo, Illinois.[2]
February 24, 1848	Walt and Jeff arrive at Poydras Street Wharf, New Orleans, on "Friday night about ten o'clock." They move into a shabby boarding house at Lafayette Square (corner Poydras and St. Charles).
March 2, 1848	Walt pens a letter to the *Brooklyn Daily Eagle* from New Orleans, which is published signed "Brooklynite."

March 4, 1848	Jeff and Walt attend a "grand fireman's procession," one of a few events mentioned in Jeff's letter of March 14.
March 5, 1848	First issue of the *Crescent* appears. Jeff and Walt visit the French Quarter, including the "old Cathilic cemmetery," likely Saint Louis Cemetery, no. 1 ("last Sunday" per Jeff's letter). Whitman likely gets his portrait taken by a French daguerreotypist.
March 7, 1848	Jeff and Walt attend Mardi Gras.
March 8, 1848	First issue of the *Semi-Weekly Crescent* appears.
March 10, 1848	United States ratifies Treaty of Guadalupe Hidalgo.
March 12, 1848	Jeff and Walt again visit the "Old Cathedral," likely St. Louis Cathedral.
March 13, 1848	First installment of "Sketches of the Sidewalks and Levee" appears.
March 14, 1848	Jeff writes "eighth, or ninth letter" home (all previous ones are lost). The Whitmans have by now moved into Tremont House (impressions echoed in "The Habitants of Hotels," of March 10). That evening, Irish comedian John Collins performs *The Pleasures of Life* at Armory Hall Theatre; Jeff and Walt attend.
March 16, 1848	George Gliddon lectures on Ancient Egypt; Walt very likely attends. A mob of French people surrounds the Parish Prison (French Quarter) holding lawyer Pierre Soulé. Whitman comments on it in a later letter.
March 17, 1848	Walt (and probably Jeff) attend a St. Patrick's Day Parade. Pierre Soulé is freed to cheers from Francophone New Orleanians.
March 19, 1848	Would-be balloonist Madame Renard[s] attempts to fly a hot-air balloon at St. Charles and Poydras streets; Jeff and Walt plan to attend.

March 20, 1848	Walt attends the Hebrew Benevolent Association Ball at the St. Louis Hotel.
March 21, 1848	The first appearance of Model Artists performers in New Orleans takes place; Walt very likely attends. Walt pens a letter to the *Sunday Times* signed "Nassau Street," expressing excitement about the performance.
March 27, 1848	Walt sees the Model Artists program at the St. Charles Theatre.
April 1, 1848	All Fool's Day.
April 2, 1848	Jeff and Walt attend the second, still unsuccessful, attempt by Madame Renard[s] to fly a hot-air balloon.
April 3, 1848	Municipal elections held in New Orleans, resulting in a continuation of Whig status quo.
April 11, 1848	Henry Smith, the "Razor Strop Man," visits the *Crescent* offices in the afternoon. Whitman sees Model Artists again.
April 15, 1848	Whitman likely attends a fundraiser held by supporters of the French Revolution of 1848 at the Orleans Ball Room.
May 8, 1848	Gun salutes are fired below the Whitmans' windows to commemorate the two-day battles of Palo Alto and Resaca de la Palma. That evening, Walt sees Major General Pillow and "Old Hero" Zachary Taylor at the St. Charles Theatre during a performance of Model Artists.
May 9, 1848	Rifle shots as on the previous day are repeated.
May 19, 1848	Mexico ratifies Treaty of Guadalupe Hidalgo.
May 21, 1848	Walt pens a letter to the *Sunday Times* signed "W.," indicating his imminent departure from New Orleans.

May 22, 1848	Establishment Democrats hold their National Convention in Baltimore, nominating Lewis Cass for president.
May 24, 1848	Whitman announces his imminent departure at the office; negotiations ensue.
May 26, 1848	The Whitmans pack their bags.
May 27, 1848	At 4 p.m., Jeff and Walt leave town aboard the *Pride of the West* packet boat.
June 3, 1848	The brothers arrive in St. Louis, Missouri by noon and depart northward on the Illinois River on packet boat *Prairie Bird* at 4 p.m.
June 6, 1848	The Whitmans arrive in La Salle, Illinois, in the morning and walk about town.
June 7, 1848	The Whitmans arrive in Chicago at 10 a.m., which was "too late for the steamer." They overnight at the American Temperance hotel. The Whig National Convention begins in Philadelphia.
June 8, 1848	The Whitman brothers board steamship *Griffith* at 9 a.m. to cross the lakes. In Milwaukee, Walt takes a stroll and imagines moving to Wisconsin. Upon their departure, a woman on board commits suicide.
June 9, 1848	The Whitmans are in Mackinaw City, Michigan, where Lake Michigan meets Lake Huron, and visit Fort Mackinac.
June 10, 1848	The *Griffith* passes down Lake Huron in the morning.
June 11, 1848	The *Griffith* is briefly stuck in sand en route to Detroit.
June 12, 1848	By late evening, the steamer arrives in Cleveland, Ohio; the brothers walk Main Street. The Whitmans arrive in Buffalo, New York, at night.

June 13, 1848	After an evening and the next morning spent exploring Buffalo, the brothers take the train to Niagara Falls and in the evening take the train to Albany.
June 14, 1848	The Whitmans arrive in Albany and explore.
June 15, 1848	Walt and Jeff arrive home via the Hudson River in the ship *Alida*.
June 22, 1848	Barnburners meet in Utica, New York, and finalize their split from the Democratic Party.
July 11, 1848	A small group of Brooklyn Free-Soilers meets; agrees to fund the *Freeman* (then still the *Banner of Freedom*), to be edited by Whitman.
July 13, 1848	Walt sends his first correspondence item to the *Crescent*.
July 18, 1848	At City Hall Park, in sight of Tammany Hall, 20,000 Barnburners assemble. Benjamin F. Butler addresses the crowd; Whitman is in attendance. A row between Hunkers and Barnburners ensues, resulting in "bloody noses."
July 19, 1848	Whitman attends a benefit for Messrs. Kipp and Brown at the Chatham Theatre.
July 27, 1848	Whitman likely attends the reception for the New York Volunteers returning from Mexico.
August 5, 1848	The Free-Soilers of Brooklyn meet. Whitman is one of the men addressing the meeting, and he is chosen as a Buffalo delegate, alongside Alden J. Spooner (son of Whitman mentor, editor Alden Spooner), and a number of radical Democrats, anti-slavery Whigs, and abolitionists.
August 9, 1848	Free-Soil National Convention begins in Buffalo; Whitman attends.
August 10, 1848	Final installment of "Sketches of the Sidewalks and Levee" appears.

September 8, 1848	Walt attends a meeting of Brooklyn Free-Soilers.
September 9, 1848	The first issue of the *Brooklyn Daily Freeman* appears.
September 10, 1848	The *Freeman* building burns down.
September 28, 1848	Whitman learns that the filibustering forces near Corpus Christi have disbanded and expresses his frustration to the *Crescent*: "That miserable Mexico must crumble from her present organization, and gradually merge in the United States."
October 7, 1848	Badensian revolutionary Friedrich Hecker is received with pomp and fanfare in front of Tammany Hall; Whitman attends.
October 9, 1848	John Van Buren addresses a Free-Soil mass meeting in front of City Hall; Whitman attends.
October 11, 1848	Whitman attends the Fair at Castle Garden.
October 12, 1848	Whitman's ward committee of the "Free Democracy" calls for a mass meeting at "Langstaff's Long Room, No. 147 Myrtle Avenue"; the main speaker is former Governor Lucius Robinson (1810–91).
November 1, 1848	The *Freeman* is back in print.
November 7, 1848	The federal election for president results in the immediately obvious victory of Whig candidate Zachary Taylor.
late December 1848	Whitman sees Paul Delaroche's painting *Bonaparte Crossing the Alps* at the Art Union.
January 7, 1849	Walt sends his final correspondence item to the *Crescent*.

a sovereign, a "dimocrat," a one of the b'hoys [. . .]
wandering about the streets of New Orleans "to see the elephant"

—"SKETCHES OF THE SIDEWALKS AND LEVEE,"
Daily Crescent, AUGUST 10, 1848

Introduction

Seeing the Elephant

WHAT IS THERE STILL TO SAY about the three short months that Walt Whitman spent in New Orleans in 1848? The story can seem so clear-cut, if short on detail: Whitman and his young brother arrived in February to start up a brand-new newspaper called the *Daily Crescent*. It was an intense trip—Whitman's first foray outside of New York—but a short one; before the summer heat arrived in Brooklyn, the two brothers would already be back home. Out of all of Whitman's posts at various papers, most of them in Brooklyn or New York, his association with the *Crescent* can appear, in many ways, the least mysterious. The basics—the paper, its editors, and Whitman's colleagues in New Orleans—have been well established since the Good Gray Poet was still alive. While many stories about Whitman in New Orleans may differ in style, then, the substance of the biographical narrative has remained nearly unchanged for more than 175 years, its only upheaval being a short period of misguided attempts to locate apocryphal Whitman offspring in the South. None were ever found. Thus, Whitman's Southern sojourn has gradually attained the status of legend as much as of established fact, as generations of scholars have waited for, hoped for, new discoveries to shed light on these three crucial months in early 1848. In this book, we will offer just such discoveries, alongside a wealth of new research that deepens and sometimes alters what we thought we knew.

For a poet who rarely left the hundred-mile radius around New York City, Whitman's 1848 trip is rivalled in its purported impact on his life only by his stint in Washington, DC, during and after the Civil War. Nearly every biography of the poet dedicates a chapter to New Orleans. Later-life trips, on the other hand—to St. Louis, Kansas, or Ontario—are often relegated to the status of afterthoughts. Even so careful a documentary as PBS's *American Experience: Walt Whitman* (2008), which has since become a bit of a pedagogical primer on Whitman, skips these latter altogether, while lingering on speculations about who Whitman may have encountered and what he may have experienced in the Crescent City.

Such an infatuation with Whitman's experience of the American South makes some sense. "It was inevitable that Whitman—and his biographers—would make a great deal of these months," Paul Zweig notes. "The change that was taking place in Whitman's literary ambition was so unprecedented, and apparently so abrupt, that we want to hang it on some event."[1] Although the writings Whitman produced in New Orleans were in many ways typical journalistic fare, with his reporting continuing to occupy this generic lane up until—and beyond—the publication of the first edition of *Leaves of Grass* (1855), his experiences in the South must have had some lasting effect. Supporting such readings, key sections in later editions of *Leaves*, for instance the 1860 "Calamus" cluster (born of Whitman's unpublished "Live-Oak, with Moss" manuscript poems), contain overt echoes of New Orleans. In this way, then, the Southern sojourn "fixes" an issue with the Emersonian theory of there having been a "long foreground" to Whitman's revolutionary poetry by providing it with an external, powerful event in which to ground the seed of literary genius.[2]

In line with this reading, accounts of Whitman's New Orleans period have generally focused on the young journalist's personal experiences, frequently likening his engagement with the city to that of a tourist. Ed Folsom, for instance, quotes travel and tourism guidebooks,[3] Gay Wilson Allen calls New Orleans an "exciting place" that provided "an escape from the frustrations in New York,"[4] and Philip Callow argues that it "symbolized escape from the frantic change and mechanization of the North."[5] New Orleans, one is tempted to read, was the most memorable pleasure trip of Whitman's young life.

Consequently, the young journalist's peripatetic outings, his theater visits, and, above all, his love- and sex-life feature prominently. The poet's own fanciful comments in later life about having fathered children in the city, as well as his erotic poetry about New Orleans, once led to a slew of misrepresentations that plagued Whitman scholarship for several generations. The work of Emory Holloway, an otherwise groundbreaking early scholar of Whitman's journalism, serves as a symptomatic case. "[I]n New Orleans, as truly as in Paris," Holloway vigorously speculated, "the fact of sex was taken as a matter of course and provided for. And New Orleans would be [Whitman's] teacher."[6] Holloway literalized every flirty joke in Whitman's writings in his quest to identify the women he thought had introduced young Whitman to the world of sensual pleasures. (Holloway would also commit scholastic fraud: in transcribing Whitman's heart-wrenching notes to himself to let go of a beloved person, Holloway omits mention that Whitman cautiously erased the *he*s and rewrote them as *she*s.) Thus, in Holloway's account, the Southern sojourn was a coming-of-age story more imagined than actual. "As late as 1960," Justin Kaplan aptly reminds us, "Holloway [. . .], like the bereft whaling ship *Rachel* at the end of *Moby Dick*, was still deviously cruising in search of Whitman's children."[7]

Holloway's colorful obsession can seem absurd from today's vantage point. More often than not, his accounts of "voluptuous lips" and "the lust of man"[8] blur the line between imagining Whitman's encounters with the city and longing for them oneself. New Orleans, later dubbed the "Big Easy," certainly invites such fantasies. Yet even much more somber scholarship than Holloway's on occasion stumbles in the same direction by exoticizing or othering the Crescent City in a way that bypasses academic rigor. This is most notable in accounts of the other key component of Whitman's Southern sojourn: his encounter with the region's "peculiar institution," slavery.

Whitman's objections to slavery in his later poetry, as well as in his journalism of the period, seemingly suggest that he would have been an odd fit in the Deep South's largest city. For the poet of "I Sing the Body Electric," for example—with its powerful condemnation of the slave auction—New Orleans ought to have been a writerly and personal challenge like no other. But was it? Consider the apparent contrast of a Northern antislavery Democrat of Dutch stock living in a Southern metropolis of slave markets, quadroon balls, and Creole citizens sharing the sidewalk with slaveholders. To some scholars, such a bifocal lens makes Whitman more of an abolitionist than ever, and certainly more than, realistically, he ever was, since evidence is difficult to find that the morality of slavery dominated his thinking in the period. As with Holloway's hopes for Whitman's love life, Whitman-as-imagined-abolitionist-in-New-Orleans, while to be hoped for, is likelier a scholarly fancy, one that leads to a number of misrepresentations not unlike Holloway's, especially relating to Whitman's work at the local newspaper, the *Daily Crescent*. An example may be drawn from Zweig, typically a scholarly realist but also one who, like Holloway, sought a neat narrative arc for young Whitman: "It is hard to imagine," he muses, "that 'Free Soiler' Whitman managed to hold his peace at all times about the *Crescent*'s racial policies, and his attitude would have been good reason to exclude him from editorial conferences."[9] Zweig is building on Allen here, his suggestion being that "there was probably a general uncongeniality between the Northern journalist and these Southern newspapermen, whose customs and habits of thought differed from those of the New Yorker."[10] To date, no scholar has carefully examined the evidence for (or lack thereof) this tempting claim. But while it makes for a good story, it is not, as we demonstrate in this book, terribly close to the truth. Indeed, most of Whitman's editorial colleagues in New Orleans were fellow Northeasterners, and the paper itself would later be described as having espoused "Free Soil Doctrine" while nevertheless remaining "pro-Southern."[11] Such an association was not as paradoxical at the time as it might seem today.

Perhaps the best illustration of the outsized effect that New Orleans, and specifically a teleological focus on the issue of slavery in the city, has had on Whitman scholarship, is in the oft-repeated claim that the poet "kept a poster of a slave auction hanging in his room for many years as a reminder that such dehumanizing events occurred regularly in the United States."[12] It is a powerful image: Whitman, at his writing desk, face to face with the stark fact of slavery, even in the free state of New York. (One might additionally imagine that moment that the future poet of America, in New Orleans, defiantly ripped down the poster as a *memento servitutis*.) Unfortunately, the anecdote is apocryphal, and quite literally outsized: In reality, the "poster" is a small newspaper ad from a different state, about 4½ x 1½ inches in size, which Whitman clipped during his work at the *Crescent* and subsequently stored in a daybook. There, it would have been kept among clippings of cake recipes, obituaries, and other print miscellanea. The more fanciful version of the story only came about because the page containing the clipping tumbled to the floor during a late 1880s conversation and thus briefly became a subject of reflection for the aged poet.[13]

In line with such retroactive logic, the absence of abolitionist writings in the *Crescent* has been used to characterize Whitman not as uninterested in slavery as a political issue, but rather as editorially sidelined, marginalized, or overly cautious to offend—only venturing to offend on other topics so as to avoid speaking his truth about slavery. By this logic, Allen concludes that Whitman "was not editor and apparently did not expect to be."[14] Callow adds that "the owners were in effect editors"[15] and Whitman, for all intents and purposes, "a muzzled journalist."[16] None of this, as our book shows, is true. Even recent biographies, like Jerome Loving's *Walt Whitman: The Song of Himself*,[17] have struggled to imagine a more nuanced Whitmanian encounter with the journalistic and political culture of the New Orleans of his time there.

Some biographers have even wondered if Whitman might have welcomed an imagined sidelining at the office. "Leaving New York and coming to New Orleans had given Whitman a chance to stand back and ponder the danger signals [of sectional conflict] for himself," Callow states, before concluding: "[t]emporarily at least he was a man without a party. His slow withdrawal from politics probably began here."[18] This is a creative leap, to say the least, since what is likely Whitman's *most* political period immediately followed New Orleans, when he joined the Free-Soil Party as an organizer and founded his own party paper, the *Brooklyn Freeman*. All this time, unbeknownst to scholars until now, Whitman kept writing for the *Crescent* from afar, updating the allegedly proslavery paper on the goings-on of committed Free-Soilers like himself up North. Equating "political" writings with abolitionist writings has been, as we will show, another academic hurdle, founded on an oversimplification of the antebellum North-South divide.

In addition to assumptions about sex and slavery, a third common generality has long been maintained in much biographical scholarship on Whitman in New Orleans—namely, that his "imagination was permanently liberated from the provincialism of his small corner of the world. His vision of America was enlarged."[19] While such framing is arguably correct in and of itself, its exoticization of the American South has nevertheless obscured historical realities. New Orleans was not merely an experience of startling heterogeneity for the future poet. While Whitman did effectively exploit culture clashes for his comic writings in the *Crescent*, his perhaps most important insights would speak to the opposite realization: that the urban experience across the nation is marked by similarity across difference. Reflecting on what New Orleanians and New Yorkers had in common, Whitman envisioned what he calls a "cosmopolitan influence" later in 1848. On a fundamental level, that is, New Orleans did *not* feel foreign to him. Nor does this insight stop at national boundaries: Welcoming refugees from the failed 1848 revolutions of Europe, Whitman extended the same cosmopolitan identification. His "urban affection," as Ed Folsom has fittingly termed it,[20] was born in New Orleans and would become global in scale. It could be liberatory as well as imperial.

Of course, Whitman biographers have been in a tough spot for more than a century. About Whitman's life prior to the 1860s, fairly little direct, contemporary evidence about his activities has survived. Consequently, nearly all narratives of Whitman's time in New Orleans have had to stake their cases based on a small set of manuscript anecdotes, published sources, and late-life memories: short passages in *Specimen Days* (1882), three homebound letters from his teenage brother Jeff (who accompanied Walt), a few manuscript pages,[21] and a published 1887 article in the *New Orleans Picayune*, based on said notes. Some direct evidence has also been hiding in the footnotes of Joseph Jay Rubin's *The Historic Whitman* and so has never fully entered the scholarly discourse since the 1970s.[22] In *Whitman's Southern Sojourn*, we add several much-needed pieces to this puzzle, aiming to provide more detail and reintroduce nuance to the scholarly understanding of this long-standing documentary record.

Misreadings of Whitman's own descriptions about his office duties have additionally led to a diminishment of the extent and importance of his actual contributions to the *Crescent*, resulting in only a very small corpus of securely attributed primary texts. Of these, most have been treated as fairly negligible and engaged with only when they bear

Whitman's signature or connect prominently to one of the biographical core themes (for instance, sex and race via his "Dusky Grisette" sketch). Accordingly, most accounts spend more time narrating the arrival of the Whitman brothers in town than their actual stay, since the former is provided by a signed travelogue, published in the first issues of the *Crescent*.

Notably, some evidence in Whitman's hand that does not fit these narratives—such as his repeated insistence of an association with New Orleans of more than a year (1848–49)—is dismissed as symptomatic of old age or of attempts to court the post–Reconstruction South. Yet other late-life recollections (like his "New Orleans in 1848" manuscript and *Picayune* article) are not only taken at face value but marshaled to dismiss anything not contained within. In this way, Whitman's recollection, for example, that each day in New Orleans began with "'making up the news' [. . .] both with pen and scissors" has been turned by biographers into an assertion that Whitman was *exclusively* a "scissors editor" at the *Crescent* and that other identifiable writings must therefore be a form of in-paper freelancing and exceedingly rare. Such claims, as our first chapter will show, do not take into consideration the importance of the newspaper exchange (managed by just such "scissors" editors), contemporary periodical contexts, the nature of journalistic positions before the US Civil War (wherein a clear-cut division of labor between specific, named positions was essentially nonexistent), and Whitman's own prestige status as a successful journalist and editor.

A thorough reconsideration of Whitman's time in New Orleans, in other words, is long overdue, especially with the increasing availability of digitized newspapers, online library collections, and invaluable digital sources like the Walt Whitman Archive. With this book, then, we hope to break up the narratives that have ossified around Whitman in New Orleans by reexamining the known evidence about his stay, introducing a slew of new textual discoveries and contexts, and freeing the Southern sojourn from the teleology of the "long foreground" thesis. On the following pages we thus interrogate this period not just as a deeply meaningful personal experience, but also as a professional milestone for a journalist on the rise. As Paul Zweig reminds us, working for the *Crescent* was not (just) an excuse for a fun trip but, above all, a "glamorous opportunity for [a . . .] journalist with large ambitions."[23] It is a professional project worth being taken seriously by scholars and readers of Whitman, and not merely for the ways in which it may have "led" to *Leaves of Grass*. Our book then grows out of a larger push to assert Whitman's importance not just to American poetry, but also to American journalism. Whitman was both an exemplar of and an important innovator in the development of antebellum periodical culture. As such he—and his hitherto forgotten colleagues at the *Crescent*—are worth examining in his respective cultural, political, and professional milieus.

The book at hand, then, functions as a cultural micro-biography of sorts, chronologically following Whitman's ventures up to, through, and after his three months in New Orleans, contextualizing his writings and his experiences within the realities of one of the global nineteenth century's most exciting years: 1848. The first chapter corrects and expands the historical record of Whitman's trip: his departure from the *Brooklyn Daily Eagle,* his transition to the *Crescent*, and the nature of his post there. Rather than marginalize Whitman's contributions as merely a so-called exchange editor, this chapter argues for an expansive understanding of the term *editor*—not as a doer of a mundane set of tasks, but as a crucial, relationship-building position on the nation's expansive newspaper exchange, a job that required tact, cunning, and strategy. To put it plainly, Whitman's post at the *Crescent* was not a sinecure. Whitman held no marginalized role, bereft of any larger imprint on the paper, as biographers often had it: His was, rather, an editorship for an experienced professional, one imported from the cultural center of the country and tasked with helping a promising start-up succeed. To all accounts, Whitman did just that. With his help, the *Crescent* established itself in the rapidly proliferating newspaper ecosystem of New Orleans, and he would thus help shape the local news scene for decades to come.

After following the two Whitman brothers on their trip across Appalachia and down the Mississippi in chapter 2, we focus in chapter 3 on their first encounter with the Southern metropolis and its vibrant street culture. Tracing the perambulations of the Whitman brothers in the two weeks prior to the appearance of the first issue of the *Crescent,* this chapter interrogates the racial attitudes Whitman carried with him to New Orleans and the degree to which local Black and Creole cultures variously challenged, confirmed, and evolved these attitudes. In particular, we consolidate and analyze, for context, Whitman's most salient pre–New Orleans writings on Blackness and slavery. We then discuss Whitman's racial attitudes primarily as they are preserved in the pages of the *Crescent*, attitudes that are both notably expanded, at times, from Whitman's earlier and more stereotypical writings on American Blackness, as well as limited by his inability to see much beyond the supposedly negative economic effect of multiracialism on white working-class labor.

In chapter 4 we introduce, for the first time, Whitman's fellows on the editorial staff and their history prior to the founding of the paper, focusing, in particular, on the two editor-owners of the *Crescent*, Alexander Hamilton Hale and John Eliot McClure. Never previously the subject of any significant scholarship, Hale and McClure have generally been reduced to little more than inaccurate caricatures, the primary being "proslavery Southern editors." These men were more complex than that, meaning their relationship to Whitman was likewise more nuanced, leaving it in greater need of telling. They figure prominently in this chapter, then, as do Whitman's colleagues on the *Crescent*, who were all part of the vibrant masculine culture of New Orleans in 1848—a place brimming with soldiers, traders, and gold rushers, a place whose characteristic forms of male-male association likely inspired Whitman's thinking on what he would later term the "City of Friends."[24] We meet the young men on the make in 1848 New Orleans, moving among erotic theaters, occult fraternities, and contemporary business culture. In the process, Hale and McClure begin to emerge as two men who shared a life inside and outside the profession and who may have served as a model for the "comradeship" Whitman would try to emulate in his later life and poetry.

Beginning in chapter 5 we focus on specific journalism from Whitman's time at the *Crescent*. Here, we discuss his series of gabby, about-town tableaux titled "Sketches of the Sidewalks and Levee," some of them only recently attributed to Whitman. With the true extent of these writings now available for the first time,[25] this chapter explores the role Whitman's humor played in his engagement with American culture—and why, to the end of his life, he would assert his credentials as a humorist even when, as he was the first to admit, his poetry rarely ventures into outright comedy. In assessing this role, we also highlight the political roots of Whitman's humor, part of an idiosyncratic comic theory that puzzled his late-life associates no less than it does Whitman scholars today.

In chapter 6, we analyze another thematically coherent set of texts from Whitman's time at the *Crescent*: writings about the European revolutions of 1848. Introducing Whitman's colleague John Cooper Larue, a Francophile lawyer and radical Democrat, we describe Whitman as one of the lesser voices of revolution on the *Crescent* staff. While Larue provided detailed historical analysis and socialist rhetoric, Whitman (often only when Larue was out of the office) relied mainly on broad ethnographic stereotypes and revolutionary sentiment when discussing European events, especially those in France. Yet, as we reveal, New Orleans—perhaps even more than New York—was a hotbed of revolutionary sympathies, and Whitman was often caught up in the enthusiasm. That said, our analysis reveals that Whitman, surprisingly, took a much more "centrist" view than one might suppose, with revolutions abroad primarily reinforcing his view of the American republic as a self-regulatory mechanism that absorbs public discontent via elections. The flipside of Whitman's global revolutionary sympathies, then, is how easily they became a kind of jingoistic strategy, as illustrated by his editorials rejecting the peace treaty with defeated Mexico and in his calls for the subjugation and (perhaps partial, perhaps full) annexation of Mexico. To Whitman in 1848, Mexican defeat and European liberation were two sides of the same coin.

And just as the US and Mexico exchanged their respective ratifications of the Treaty of Guadalupe Hidalgo in May 1848, the *Crescent*'s first editor left for home. In our penultimate chapter, we discuss the machinations that led up to Whitman's departure, exploring what may or may not have "pushed" Whitman out, before following him and his brother Jeff on their exciting trip back to New York. As during his journey to the South (discussed in chapter 2), the "West" still figured as a politically and personally powerful theme to Whitman during these weeks of travel, with Whitman's fellow passengers embodying the many familiar concerns that now crowded on deck: Taylorites en route to their convention, republican refugees from Europe, and rugged yeomen of the West, all shoulder-to-shoulder with Walt and Jeff as they glided past slave plantations, bustling western (now Midwestern) cities, and the shores of the Great Lakes.

But Whitman's involvement with New Orleans did not end, it turns out, upon his return to New York City. Indeed, he would not only put a decidedly Southern spin on his ensuing period of Free-Soil politicking, but he also kept up correspondence with his former paper, filling *Crescent* columns from afar with dozens of letters that until very recently were not known to be Whitman's. We explore them in chapter 8, and especially Whitman's investment, expressed in those letters, in the presidential politics of 1848. Our final chapter thus brings together two crucial themes of this decisive year—Whitman's love for the South and his activism for Free-Soil—themes that, though they may not seem like it, build from a single political conviction, expressed most forcefully in his letters sent back to the *Crescent.* We contextualize these letters in another example of Whitman's significant editorial engagements in 1848: his editorship of the *Brooklyn Freeman* and his activism on behalf of the Free-Soil Party. We understand *Whitman's Southern Sojourn*, then, as part of a larger movement to take Whitman's prose writings seriously on their own terms.

CHAPTER 1

With the steamship, the electric telegraph, the newspaper,
the wholesale engines of war,
With these and the world-spreading factories he interlinks
all geography, all lands;
What whispers are these O lands, running ahead of you,
passing under the seas?

—WHITMAN, "YEARS OF THE MODERN" (1871)

An editor sits at his desk [. . .]
Exchanges are lying about—
And ponders the things that appear
To be claiming the thoughts of the world—[. . .]
While waiting despatches delayed,
He clips, and he clips, and he clips
And that's how a paper is made.

"HOW A PAPER IS MADE," *Atlanta Constitution*, JULY 13, 1872

Paper Exchanges

ON FEBRUARY 8, 1848,[1] a young Walter Whitman ran into a Southern businessman in the foyer of the Broadway Theatre. It was a Tuesday evening, and the Byronian tragedy *Werner; Or, the Inheritance* had just let out for intermission.[2] Outside, a dusting of snow covered the cobblestones,[3] and the icy breeze creeping in from the front gates sent flickers through the ornate chandeliers, replete with orientalist motifs, that decorated the stately theater's entryway.[4] The other man, John Eliot McClure (1809–69), was "of most quiet and pleasant manners,"[5] but had otherwise much in common with the extroverted Whitman. A native of Vermont, McClure had grown up in the North and considered himself a radical Democrat. Like Walt, he was a printer by trade, having come to New York to purchase materials. The man knew how to make a paper and had recently been involved with some of the leading dailies in a city on the rise: New Orleans. He had ambitious plans and ample funds to support his journalistic endeavors. The men discussed the printing trade; perhaps Whitman mentioned he had just recently ended his editorial employ at the *Brooklyn Daily Eagle*. The two hit it off, shared a drink, and McClure handed over a wad of bills—and in less than forty-eight hours, Walt and his young brother Jeff had packed their bags and set out for New Orleans,[6] eager to help McClure and his partner start their new business venture: a daily paper to be called the *Crescent*.

This moment is typically where descriptions of Whitman's Southern sojourn begin. Sensible enough: it is a rousing story, carefully crafted by Whitman years after the fact. To get a fuller picture, though, it is necessary to rewind a bit. The actual story of Whitman's involvement with the *Daily Crescent* begins months earlier with the splintering of the editorial room at the New Orleans *Daily Delta* in the late summer of 1847—at the height of the *Delta*'s success.

Located on Poydras Street, not far from the boarding house where Whitman would later stay, the *Delta* had grown from a respectable daily of Democratic persuasion to a prime source of war reporting for the nation. Since spring of 1846, the James K. Polk administration had been waging an expansionist war against the Mexican Republic, rather suddenly making New Orleans a major hub for US troop movements and intelligence. Consequently, any significant happenings in the Crescent City made front-page news across the nation. With no telegraph lines extending between the Gulf of Mexico and the industrial centers of the Northeast at the outbreak of the war, editors like Whitman at the *Eagle* eagerly anticipated New Orleans papers—and specifically the *Delta*[7]—arriving directly by mail or in connected coastal hubs like Richmond, from which local contacts could wire Mexican news north to bigger papers in New York. When Whitman met McClure, he had very likely already seen the other man's handiwork in print. Especially after the capture of the port city of Veracruz in early 1847, coverage of the war relied on a strange mix of modern technology, emergent professional journalism, and a jerry-rigged information infrastructure: embedded Louisiana journalists sent letters to their home papers, where they were quickly turned into news items that were then physically transported to where they could be fed into the growing telegraph network. Parts of that network were beginning to get monopolized by larger paper cabals in the Northeast, and the smaller regional papers—the *Eagle*, the *Delta*, and later the upstart *Crescent*—often had to provide local color when actual "scoops" were out of their reach.[8]

At this patchwork game, the *Delta* excelled. As an overtly jingoistic paper that had agitated for the invasion of Mexico early on,[9] it was able to rapidly fill its pages with updates from an impressive roster of journalists and correspondents, often associated with the Anglo papers in the city of Veracruz. It was granted unprecedented access to US forces, serving as a de facto "clearinghouse for the government's official military dispatches."[10] The *Delta* also ran frequent updates from pseudonymous correspondents with names like "Mustang,"[11] "Alpha,"[12] and "Chaparral"[13]—colorful monikers that would quickly rise to fame in the news columns of the American press. A nimble paper, the *Delta* had editors who knew how to stay ahead of the curve. On occasion the *Delta* even printed special editions directly in Veracruz and only distributed in New Orleans, allowing it to stay ahead of the competition.[14] And stay ahead it did. "New Orleans had been our channel and entrepot for everything, going and returning," Whitman recalled late in life. "It had the best news and war correspondents; it had the most to say, through its leading papers, the *Picayune* and *Delta* especially, and its voice was readiest listen'd to."[15]

Around a collage of such news and correspondence items Whitman at the *Eagle* had spun his account of the war, one that perpetuated a narrative of Mexican aggression against a victimized United States—and promoted the ostensible need for a quick, decisive victory by deploying US troops to force a lasting peace. "Mexico has just as surely been the aggriever, for long long years past, towards us, as that God rules in Heaven," Whitman proclaimed in January 1847. Any peace without massive concessions, he clarified, constituted a "prostitution [of] the sacred name of peace."[16] While he opposed *full* annexation for now—including out of fear of introducing a significant non-Anglo population to the United States[17]—he was open to the idea that a reconstituted Mexico might voluntarily join at a later date.[18] Even when Whitman gleefully celebrated toward the conclusion of actual fighting that "very large accessions of fertile territory will be made to our beloved republic," he attempted to couch his rhetoric in an aura of benevolence: at least, the remaining parts of the country ought to stay independent for now.[19] With many New York papers, especially the Whig *New-York Tribune*, agitating against the invasion, Whitman at the Democratic *Eagle* turned news from the front into patriotic, bellicose fare that made war palpable to occasionally skeptical Northeastern audiences. Yes, war was evil, but it was *Mexico's* evil, Whitman suggested via the *Eagle*, arguing that the US invasion would guarantee future peace, a massive land grab, and a remodeling of the *caudillo* neighbor on republican terms. For his colonialist rhetoric at the *Eagle*, Whitman found the news reporting of the *Delta* essential—and it allowed Whitman to continue this rhetoric, without interruption, at the *Crescent*.

For its coverage of the war, the *Delta* had an ace up its sleeve: Alexander Hamilton Hayes (1806–66), one of the founders and a former coproprietor of the *Delta* who had quit the newsroom to join the fight in Mexico "*en amateur*"[20] and now served as a war reporter for the paper. Beginning around August of 1847, Hayes got involved "with handling correspondence, mail, and newspapers from the Mexican port,"[21] and he then decided to meet up with US forces, hoping to witness the capture of Mexico City. While he arrived late, his involvement with the infantry company of a former New Orleans competitor—the Whig *Picayune*'s Christopher M. Haile[22]—allowed Hayes to experience combat and turned him into a celebrated character in New Orleans.[23] Still, Hayes was no longer bound by old obligations to the *Delta*; his work now also appeared in the *Picayune*.[24] This fact constituted less of a professional break than might be expected: Hayes himself had worked for the *Picayune* before founding the *Delta*. The world of New Orleans journalism was a small one; grudges and disagreements were largely performative and built on the foundation of a collegial ethos stretching easily across papers.[25]

Around the same time that Hayes went to Mexico, another foundational figure of the *Delta* left the paper: John Eliot McClure, already introduced via his famous theater meeting with Whitman, which would take place a few months later.[26] McClure and Hayes had been closely associated for years—at least since their time at the *Picayune*, prior to the *Delta*, where McClure worked in accounting[27] and Hayes was the foreman of the newsroom.[28] During their tenure at the *Picayune*, the paper-reprinted some of Whitman's earliest editorial work (from the *Long-Islander*).[29] Most of Hayes and McClure's many shared ventures started and ended in tandem: Both left the *Picayune* (with two other colleagues) in 1845 over political differences to found the *Delta*—Hayes and McClure were both Democrats, the latter even having toyed, like Whitman, with Locofocoism in his youth.[30] Then, in early 1848, they went on to produce the *Crescent*. Both were Northeasterners (McClure hailing from Vermont, Hayes from Pennsylvania) but had shared decades of professional life and friendship in New Orleans.

When Hayes quit the *Delta* and started to travel, so did his close associate McClure. No announcement in the *Delta* informed its readership of any changes in the editorial makeup of the paper in these months. The reason for the departure of the two men somewhat mirrored Whitman's later departure from the *Eagle*: frustrations over the pro-Polk conservative Democratic politics endorsed by their respective outlets. It was the "exuberance of the *Daily Delta*'s campaign in the presidential campaign [that] undoubtedly led to the disagreement of the staff members as to its policy," and following Hayes and McClure's departure, new editors "plunged the *Daily Delta* into the most violently partisan support of [. . .] filibuster activities [. . .] and of the faction that backed the pro-filibuster sentiment."[31] Advocating for an annexation of all of northern Mexico and a long-term occupation to force such concessions on Mexico, the *Delta* endorsed a political program that gave some citizens of the Whig trade city of New Orleans headaches.

"Fear that existing Southern slavery might be threatened by additional free territory," historian B. H. Gilley has noted, "prompted [. . .] opposition to the annexation" of all or significant parts of Mexico.[32] That the new territory would likely be free, the *Delta* itself agreed. With an editorial contribution signed "A Slaveholder," it endorsed the line of later presidential candidate Lewis Cass in noting that the land in newly acquired territory would not be hospitable to an agriculture that supported slavery. Hence it argued that "Texas with slavery was objectionable to one portion of the Union, but was not therefore rejected, and by the same rule, other territories in which there can be no slavery, should not be rejected now, because it is distasteful to us."[33] Yet adding significant new free territory to the nation—and a number of potential

Southern free states with large Hispanic populations—threatened the political balance between free and slave states laid out in the Missouri Compromise of 1820.

Concern over the *Delta*'s nonchalance about the question of slavery preservation and its endorsement of big-government Democratic politics, led to waves of departures from the paper, and the future editors of the *Crescent* were among the first. While by no means acrimonious, this departure indicated that there was political space in the Southern metropolis, dominated by Whig papers (like the *Tropic,* the *Bee*, and the *Picayune*),[34] for another Democratic-leaning daily. "The *Crescent*'s objective," historian Tom Reilly notes in his excellent study of New Orleans newspapers during the Mexican war, "was to take the middle road between the pro-Whig *Picayune* and the pro-Democrat *Delta.*"[35] It would be as "hawkish" as the rest on Mexico[36]—no small thanks to Whitman—but it would do so in opposition to the Polk administration (especially on the peace question).

While the exact date of McClure's departure remains a mystery, he, of course, would be in New York in early February 1848 to meet Whitman. Additionally, we know that *someone* at the *Delta* left for New York City in the same month Hayes went south, likely to purchase the expensive new cylinder steam printing press that the *Delta* bragged about on January 5, 1848—a piece of equipment sold by Hoe & Co, New York, which could "print 6000 impressions per hour."[37] Using a pen name that suggested a relationship to the *Delta,* a newspaperman going by "Beta" was heading toward New York in early August 1847, relying on the same route Whitman would take in the late spring of 1848. "Beta" published two letters about this trip in the *Delta.* While these largely contain travel impressions, they also suggest insider knowledge of the *Delta* newsroom and take the tone of a Southern newspaperman encountering New York.[38]

When McClure met Whitman at the Broadway Theater, then, his purpose likely overlapped with that of "Beta": McClure, too, was purchasing a Hoe press (as well as type from two New York manufactories), but for the *Crescent.*[39] Or as Whitman later put it in his memoir *Specimen Days*: the editor had been "north buying material."[40] Hoe presses were state-of-the-art and priced accordingly. The cheapest model cost almost twice what McClure would later be paid for his share of the *Crescent* when retiring from the news business.[41] Purchasing a Hoe steam press thus required ample funds and in-person travel. The *Crescent's* Hoe press likely traveled to New Orleans via steamer; it is known to have arrived on February 19, 1848,[42] and would have been installed at St. Charles Street soon after permission was granted by the city five days later.[43] Clearly, New York was *the* place to get the best and latest antebellum print culture had to offer—be it a state-of-the-art printing press or a good editor.

If McClure and "Beta" were *not* two different *Delta* men, coincidentally traveling to New York City around the same time to purchase expensive steam printing presses, but indeed the same person, Whitman's well-worn story of a spontaneous trip south begins to fall apart. In its place, the likelihood of an earlier encounter increases substantially. Not only did "Beta" visit some of the very locales Whitman was known to frequent in 1847—the anchored "Chinese Junk," Park Theatre, the Bowery, the exhibition of Hiram Powers's "Greek Slave," etc.—but there was at least one event that "Beta" and Whitman likely attended alongside each other, months before the alleged first meeting at the Broadway Theatre: an honorary reception for a Mexican War hero, one Lieutenant Marin, held by Brooklyn citizens in late August.[44]

Yet, even if Whitman's anecdote about first personally encountering McClure in between theater performances is strictly factual, the two would have already been acquainted with each other through their respective papers, which kept a close relationship via the newspaper exchange. As two local Democratic publications with national ambitions, both of which supported the Mexican war, the *Eagle* and the *Delta* often quoted each other, reminding us that each sent the other copies of their papers by making use of significantly reduced postage rates provided for such exchanges—a fact that Whitman later abused to smuggle his personal correspondence home from New Orleans without having to pay for it by funneling it through the *Eagle* office.

Besides the political-professional closeness of the *Eagle* and the *Delta*, the two papers even shared personnel, in a manner. The Brooklyn poet-painter Theodore A. Gould (1820–c. 1880/82), first "conjectured" by Whitman scholar Thomas Brasher as having had a role in getting

Whitman the New Orleans job,[45] stands out in this context. Whitman, as Brasher notes, appears to mention Gould in a letter to his mother in the 1860s, suggesting him to be an old, ailing friend.[46] In his youth, the amateur poet, painter, and (later) actor was also the darling of the *Eagle* and the *Crescent*, which excessively promoted his fairly banal work both during Whitman's respective tenures and after them. The *Eagle* and the *Crescent* alike print and reprint Gould's poems from the mid-1840s onward, frequently urging their readers to purchase his various works.

In 1849, for instance, the *Eagle* described "our friend Theo A. Gould"[47] as "a resident of Brooklyn, whose poetical effusions have attracted general attention throughout the country by the striking conceptions, and the beautiful and true feeling which pervade them," recommending Brooklynites buy his self-published volume *A Bouquet of Poesy* (1848).[48] The *Crescent*, for its part, even had two of Gould's paintings hanging in the paper's office, where they were available for purchase by citizens of taste: a portrait of Schiller during Whitman's tenure[49] and a painting of Don Quixote after it.[50] Gould, the *Crescent* noted, is "really entitled to a much higher degree of praise than should be awarded to those not above mediocrity."[51] During the late 1840s, bachelor Gould traveled back and forth between Brooklyn and New Orleans, living for months in one or the other city and finding himself supported by the *Crescent* and the *Eagle* to a degree that suggests personal ties; Gould's work rarely appeared outside of these publications. The *Eagle* even printed Gould's New Orleans travelogue of 1846 years after the fact.[52]

To travel alongside the correspondence and exchange network, as figures like Gould and Whitman did, was not an outrageous proposition. Rather, it was far from uncommon at the time. New Orleans papers, of course, had Washington and New York correspondents, and big papers in New York—whether dailies like the *New York Herald*[53] or the *Tribune*[54] or weekend broadsheets like the *Atlas*[55]—now also wanted Crescent City correspondents. New Orleans was not only a major hub for Mexican war news, but was also a rapidly expanding city of major commercial and political consequence. The long leadup to the presidential nomination of Baton Rouge planter Zachary Taylor, so often framed around happenings in New Orleans or letters printed in local papers, serves as one illustration. Over his newspaper career, Walt, too, would send correspondence from either side of this exchange. In this, he was by no means exceptional; one need only think of Abraham Oakey Hall, the future mayor of New York, who while in New Orleans had been the correspondent for the *Herald* but subsequently morphed into correspondent "Hans Yorkel" for the *New-Orleans Commercial Bulletin* upon his return to New York.[56]

The value for a northern paper of having contacts in New Orleans might explain the chumminess the *Eagle* maintained with its former editor. Until now, scholars have tended to describe Whitman as being "fired" from the *Eagle* in Brooklyn,[57] even suggesting specific reasons (such as Whitman's anti-slavery or free-soil leanings) to explain his departure.[58] Still, this narrative of an abrupt firing followed by an auspiciously timed encounter with McClure was likely a strategic embellishment by Whitman—and, if taken at face value, would run counter to the continued support that Whitman received from his old paper while in New Orleans. Journalist Whitman was a strategic planner, not the rash rebel as which he would later cast himself.

Whitman himself notes that he worked for the *Eagle* "till the last of January '48"[59] (so essentially until the Broadway Theatre meeting), and the *Eagle*, after being mocked by the Brooklyn *Daily Advertiser* over Whitman's departure, explains his leaving in a humorous poem in mid-February by stating "We *sent* Whitman away."[60] Later, in a glowing review of the *Crescent*—which expressly highlighted Whitman's "handy work" and wished him luck—that same *Eagle* still referred to Whitman as a former "principal editor" who "went out" to edit the *Crescent*. Whatever clique now ruled the *Eagle*, it still praised Whitman's work and wished him the best.

Outright animosity toward Whitman in the *Eagle* only starts to appear much later, after his eventual return from New Orleans when he began to run a paper in direct local opposition to the *Eagle*: the Free-Soil Brooklyn *Freeman* (see chapter 8). It was only then that the *Eagle* retrospectively claimed they had "found it absolutely necessary to [make changes]. Mr. W. cried persecution, and by this means interested the Advertiser, the Evening Post, the Globe, &c., in his behalf, and through their good offices got a handsome place in New Orleans."[61] Even in this later attack on Whitman, the *Eagle* emphasized Whitman's agency in the process: he was actively looking for a different position, engaged his various newspaper contacts, and, as this note suggests, may have quit on his own.

Whitman's exit was described as a result of *his reaction*—outcry followed by interesting fellow papers on his behalf—to "changes" at the *Eagle*.

Even the fact that some jokes about Whitman's laziness begin to appear in the *Eagle* around the time of his 1848 move (reflecting an image Whitman had carefully crafted for himself) do not contradict that his departure reads more like a "newspaper exchange" of a different kind: namely, Whitman somewhat smoothly transitioning from one publication to another, at his own behest, while remaining on collegial terms with his old paper. The *Eagle* would even reprint Whitman's *Crescent* musings on the weather in New Orleans, which were addressed to "northern friends"; in its clipped form, the *Eagle* appears to suggest that the phrase referred to them.[62] Whitman even sent correspondence to the *Eagle,* which was likewise addressed to "*Friend Eagle*" and printed prominently in his old paper's columns.[63] It was signed "Brooklynite," the same moniker Whitman signed to his fiction in his old paper. If the *Eagle*, indeed, "sent" Whitman, he paid them back with correspondence and a prominent place on the *Crescent*'s exchange. Virtually no contemporary evidence (other than performative mudslinging) indicates that Whitman was outright fired over his supposed anti-slavery attitudes, nor is there anything persuasive to show that the *Eagle* held a lasting grudge. Whitman even continued to mail personal correspondence through at least two different employees in the *Eagle* office, where his family would pick them up. It is a bizarre scenario to imagine, sending one's siblings to pick up personal mail at a former employer from whom one had been "fired"[64] for laziness and political rabble-rousing. Furthermore, as recent discoveries have underscored, Whitman never fully broke off his association with the *Eagle*, occasionally contributing pieces signed "W." as late as the 1850s, even when employed by their direct business competitors.[65]

Instead, Whitman's departure in many ways echoed the departure of McClure and Hayes from the *Delta*. Associated with the prolabor wing of radical Democratic politics—which, in New York state, were referred to as "Barnburners"—his position at the more mainstream, conservative (or "Hunker") *Eagle* had been a measure of big-tent Democratic politics. In his role as the in-house radical, he had advocated for party unity. Until the close of 1847, this had worked well. While personally supportive of measures to curb the extension of slavery (like the Wilmot

Proviso, which we will discuss in a later chapter), Whitman nonetheless considered such issues as "by no means vitally important" and argued for calm on the question. "[W]e have had too much angry excitement in congress," he wrote in March of 1847.[66]

In the lead-up to the New York state election of 1847, Whitman had thus supported the status quo and urged party unity:

> On the one hand we behold that ticket, as we have it at the head of our paper; and on the other hand the whig ticket. There are no others—at least no others except one or two attached to the little temporary *isms* of the day; and these must be thrown out of the account altogether. All minor points, then, subside into comparative insignificance before one: *Shall the democratic ticket succeed, or shall the whig ticket succeed?*[67]

Embracing realpolitik, Whitman had endorsed the conservative Democratic ticket that had been decried by radicals throughout the state.[68] Whitman even served as secretary of the Tammany machine in the run-up to the 1847 state election and worked to elect the Hunker ticket.[69] That state ticket also included judges who were set to be elected in June—among them judge-hopeful Samuel E. Johnson, the man who would later finance Whitman's anti-Hunker *Freeman* paper.[70]

When the 1847 Democratic ticket failed spectacularly, all bets were suddenly off. The day after the election, when a Whig landslide win was already clear, Whitman published a set of "Reflections" in the lead editorial column of the *Eagle* that lambasted the Democratic platform of 1847 and culminated in the call for "Conservatism, in all its aspects, [to] leave the field—and [for] the democracy [to] unite on its boldest and noblest and most radical doctrines."[71] These doctrines, however, increasingly appeared to make their home outside of the Democratic party. Outraged by the political maneuvering that led to the disastrous 1847 platform, the radical faction had already held a separate convention just a month before the state election. Whitman in the *Eagle* had opposed such measures. Now that the Democratic National Convention was on the horizon and the 1848 federal election loomed large, these so-called Barnburners were continuing their organizational split from the conservative mainstream, calling for a meeting of New York radicals in mid-February, which was to be addressed by future Free-Soil organizer John Van Buren (son of eventual Free-Soil candidate, Martin Van Buren).[72]

Whitman's attempts to bend the *Eagle* to support this element failed; the paper maintained its big-tent argument and now cast the Barnburners as Whig-enablers. As it became increasingly clear that this split would lead to a third-party run, Whitman divorced himself from his post and helped build up organizational structures for those anti-mainstream Democrats who would later form the Free-Soil Party—which he would ultimately support not only as a party organizer but as editor of a Free-Soil paper. But that would come after his return from New Orleans. In the meantime, he would help another set of radicals and malcontents get off the ground a new paper that was likewise skeptical of the Democratic party line: the *Crescent.*

At the end of January 1848, then, Whitman ceased his association with the *Eagle* as he was embracing populist, prolabor ideas within (and without) the Democratic party. This shift had less to do with slavery and more with white, workingmen's rights than many modern-day readers of the poet would like. The *Crescent,* which is later described as advocating "Free Soil Doctrine yet [remaining] intensely Southern" must have looked like a natural fit for Whitman's political leanings in these days.[73] They would have also paid better than the *Eagle* (and some of it up front), promised employment for Whitman's brother Jeff, and offered a thrilling trip south, which came with a first-person perspective on the issue that was breaking the Democratic party: the successful American campaign against Mexico (raising the issue of slavery extension), waged out of Louisiana and, especially, the port city of New Orleans.[74]

Fellow New York and Brooklyn papers followed this development closely and reported it in ways that corresponded to their own political vantage point on the intra-Democratic conflict—all, however, served to promote Whitman as a radical editor, looking for a new gig. Most notably, the *Brooklyn Evening Star* smelled what it thought was a political coup at the time: "Mr. Walter Whitman [. . .] is a 'Barnburner,'" it speculated on January 18, 1848; "the 'Old Hunkers' wanted one of their own men there; and Mr. W. has had to give way to one of the other side."[75] An associate of Whitman's echoed this point in the *Atlas*, a weekend paper edited by a former boss of the young journalist:[76]

> A cauldron, not dissimilar to that which, in Macbeth's time, according to Shaksperian legend, frothed "bubble, bubble, toil and trouble," has, during the present week, been in operation among divers of the editorial fraternity of this city. Mr. Walter Whitman [. . .] has been displaced by a clique of individuals, who assume to control that faction and direct its movements, because of his bold denunciations of slavery, and advocacy of the Wilmot Proviso. He is a young man of fine literary attainments, fearless, energetic, and beyond the reach of corrupt political cliques. He is, however, in my humble opinion, much better capacitated for pursuits that have no connection with the strife of party, and which would not require him to prostitute his talents for the advancement of mendacious office-seekers and ambitious demagogues.[77]

These statements were, obviously, not factual reporting but almost read like ads for Whitman, selling the journalist and his skills to fellow newspapermen and political agitators. Public clashes like these were likely a way for Whitman to vie for the kind of celebrity-editor status of a James Gordon Bennett, even when that prospect was beginning to fade in the increasingly white-collar profession of the late 1840s. More concretely, they might have been an attempt to help Whitman get his next big venture off the ground—not the *Crescent*, but a project that sounds a lot like the *Brooklyn Daily Freeman* that Walt would help found in the late summer of 1848.

As Walt's hometown paper put it within a week of his departure from the *Eagle*: "We are informed from the best authority that the Barnburners of Brooklyn are about starting a new daily paper—as, it is said, the *Eagle* has returned to Old Hunkerism again. Mr. Walter Whitman [. . .] is to have charge of the new enterprize."[78] A piece in the New York *Evening Post* from Whitman's last week at the *Eagle* (late January 1848) echoed the sentiment, reporting that "the radicals of Kings county are now anxious to have a press of their own—and the late editor of the

Eagle [. . .] is to engage in such an enterprise."[79] The *Tribune* confirmed this reporting.[80] Perhaps Walt was lacking the financial means to realize these ambitious plans. He was notoriously strapped for cash, and his later benefactor, the young soon-to-be judge Samuel Evan Johnson (1816–70),[81] was experiencing fiscal troubles, with the city threatening to confiscate three of his properties for nonpayment of taxes.[82] (He was then suing his competitor for the judgeship, who had claimed victory by one vote because election officials had discarded Johnson votes over misspellings; Johnson would not win his post until the Supreme Court ruled in his favor in October 1848).[83]

Whitman's future editorial post following his employ at the *Crescent*, then, appears to have been in the works even before he left for New Orleans. It seems more and more likely, therefore, that the New Orleans trip may have been planned, all along, to fill a short gap between his *Eagle* and *Freeman* tenures. His performative "beef" with the *Eagle*, then, likely had much to do with keeping his name in the partisan press until the *Freeman* could get off the ground. Said plans for the *Freeman* were much more advanced prior to his departure than Whitman's biographies have acknowledged and continued through his stay in the Crescent City.

Indeed, Whitman's future coworker at the *Freeman*[84] even notes in a "personal diary kept in chronological order" under the date of March 6: "This day ascertained that Walter Whitman formerly of the Brooklyn Eagle and Kings County, was making arrangements for establishing a new paper in Brooklyn to be called The Brooklyn Freeman. I am to have a place upon it." While the dating is factually incorrect (and the diary a haphazard manuscript reconstructed decades later),[85] it does suggest that efforts by the radicals of King County to establish a "press of their own" had been well underway and staffing may already have been considered. In that colleague's misdated reworking of contemporaneous diary notes, Whitman transitioned from *Eagle* to *Freeman* without a New Orleans interlude, the long 1848 genesis of the radical paper shortened from months to weeks. Yet, as contemporary press rumors confirm, it nonetheless appears that the brothers Whitman may never have intended to remain in the Crescent City for long. Whitman's Southern sojourn was likely always intended to be a gig—a short detour on Walt's way back into a radical editorship in

Brooklyn. Like many northerners overwintering in New Orleans, they likely anticipated a return before the hot summer months, when the national political contest would start to heat up and Free-Soilers would need a party organ in Brooklyn.

This information does not, of course, diminish the import of Whitman's time in New Orleans. Instead, it serves to underscore not only Whitman's own, shrewd maneuvering—he did not just bumble into opportunities, nor did he make decisions on a whim—but also his high standing among newspapermen in the late 1840s: If you wanted your new paper to cause a splash, you hired Walter Whitman. Even newspapermen thousands of miles away were well aware of that.

Over a century and a half after Whitman's much mythologized trip, historical newspaper echoes underscore that his Southern sojourn was enabled, to a degree at least, by ready-at-hand structures of professional and sentimental exchanges between newspapermen in both cities. These organizational structures cast the editorial tenure at the *Crescent* as a transition, not a rupture, in Whitman's writerly biography and deserve closer scrutiny before we follow the poet-journalist south. As Jerome Loving rightly notes, Whitman may have "heard about the new journalistic venture through the grapevine of exchange papers"—though the connection may have been less indirect than that biographer thinks.[86] The newspaper exchange functioned "in effect [like] a nonprofit news cooperative [operating] without central management and formal contract and instead by virtue of custom and convention [. . .]. In these ways, the newspaper exchange had much in common with radical-republican conceptions of [. . .] worker citizens."[87] Walt Whitman, that future "network poet,"[88] tuned into this exchange and communication system of fellow newsmen regularly and in ways that speak to the conceptual power of the exchange.

While the brothers Whitman would be quite bold in manipulating the newspaper exchange into a familial messaging system, they were by no means pioneers in the matter. Even nonjournalists got in on the action: because of newspaper postal laws, "it was so much cheaper to mail a newspaper," writes communications historian John Nerone, "that ordinary families began writing personal letters in the margins of newspapers."[89] The conflation of private mail and publicly printed mass media communication will not only become a central feature of Whitman's late-1848 relationship with the *Crescent*—when he morphs from in-person editor to correspondent from afar—but it was also quite visible in how papers narrated the postal exchange and the reviews they received after entering the exchange.

In effect, one might even think of the newspaper exchange as a kind of analog social network, maintained through the postal service. Indeed, the very stern-wheelers that the Whitmans would use to travel down to New Orleans carried on board the mail destined for their offices, containing both actual correspondence and newspapers sent. Editors like Whitman would cut out items of interest and reuse them in their paper, either directly quoted or paraphrased. This helped small teams of newspapermen fill dense columns, but it also built relationships between artisans. This practice did not subtract from the effect of any "scoop" the item may have constituted in its original paper—by the time it arrived in the inbox of other papers, its news value was essentially zero. It made sense then, especially economically, to share. The "exchange system *produced* local newspapers," literary scholar Ellen Gruber Garvey has rightly observed, "by yoking together scattered producers who shared labor and resources by sending their products to one another for free use."[90] While credit and attribution for reuse in pre-copyright America was unnecessary, it was often provided as a form of social credit, puffing the other paper in the eyes of fellow editors, who were likewise members of this informal exchange. A paper, let's say the *Poughkeepsie Journal*, might see Whitman at the *Eagle* clipping a lot from the *Delta*—and start sending their own paper to the *Delta* editors in the hopes of receiving *Delta* issues in return. Postage was reduced but not free—so the *Delta* might only send papers back if there was enough material worth clipping from the *Poughkeepsie Journal* in turn. Often, editors spoke to their network of exchange editors, directly and through allusion, in little squibs or notes surrounding reused items.

In its very first issue, which would appear on March 5, 1848, the *Crescent* would sound eager to announce its entry into the world of the exchange. "Will our contemporaries by whom this number of the *Crescent* is received," it implored via its editorial column, "oblige us by *promptly* remitting their papers to us in the way of an exchange?"[91] A newspaper on the exchange was both mass-media print object and letter communication at the same time: It spoke to other editors in a different way than to general readers, yet it did so simultaneously. Its tone, then, was almost necessarily performative: personal yet public in a way that anticipates Whitman's later rhetoric in *Leaves of Grass*.[92] Answers to the *Crescent*'s plea for correspondents would come quickly: "Our contemporary of the National has repeatedly supplied us with exchange papers," the *Crescent* would gratefully note in its second week. "Only those who are aware of the inconvenience of getting along without these articles, in the commencement of a daily print, can appreciate the real value of such a courtesy."[93] When the mail failed—which it often did—Whitman specifically bemoaned losing access to the exchange: "We had but a few exchange papers, and they were nothing but dryness and dullness. Yet it was'nt their fault, poor things! Folks cannot make news; at least none but elderly ladies, of unmarried blessedness, have that privilege."[94] Losing access to the exchange equaled emasculation and risked slippage from news "making," in the sense of "assembling," to the spinsterly sphere of "making up."

Aside from the news value of the exchange and its ability to maintain male-male associations over distances, it also generated direct, positive coverage about the paper itself in the form of reviews and puffs. "The Crescent is equal to any," wrote, for instance, the *Texian Advocate*, "and its articles are written with much spirit. If the Editor print a weekly we would thank them for an exchange; if not for an occasional number of the Daily."[95] Since the Whitman brothers would be in charge of the exchange, the *Crescent*'s reply to positive tokens like these must be Walt's: "Really, Gentlemen, some of your compliments quite make us blush."[96]

Snubs, of course, also triggered replies: A Mississippi paper, for instance, once called Whitman's paper a "d—m poor paper anyhow," after its editor felt mistreated on the exchange, having received only a single *Crescent* issue, apparently for the sole purpose of soliciting a puff instead of starting a relationship.[97] "You are down on our list, *sure*," the called-out Whitman playfully snapped back, while reprinting the critique.[98] Literary scholar Leon Jackson goes as far as describing such initial paper exchanges as "a form of courting gift, akin, functionally, to the flirtatious poems written in albums and designed to create bonds."[99]

Unequal emotional investment could thus trigger a reaction similar in kind to that of a scorned lover.

In the print record of the newspaper exchange, two rhetorical conventions rubbed up against each other and disclosed their inevitable overlap: sentimental gifting and professional ethos. In antebellum newspaper culture, these two could not be neatly separated—working the exchange almost inevitably created attachments. Rhetorically, relationship work trumped the pragmatic purpose of the exchange and "editors disavowed [. . .] economic score-keeping, preferring, instead, to belabor the gratuity and goodwill on which their exchanges were based."[100] The exchange was then always also "a means of creating and sustaining relationships" between professional men across the country and, consequently, "most editors monitored their exchange lists carefully, using them as a bellwether for the state of their editorial relationships more generally."[101]

The embodied nature of the exchange—a form of gifting relying on physically mediated touch that could trigger bodily reactions (e.g., blushing)—would carry through into Whitman's daily labors at the *Crescent* office. "I generally went about my work about 9 o'clock," Whitman later recalled, "overhauling the papers rec'd by mail, and 'making up the news,' as it is called, both with pen and scissors."[102] Since the middle of the twentieth century, scholars have applied the job descriptions of "exchange editor" or "scissors editor"[103] to this task, though these were notably not Whitman's words, and marshalling these terms to marginalize his overall contribution to the paper is unfounded. Notably, he emphasized that he was not only clipping but composing news items ("with pen") and that he was merely outlining his morning routine only, not the whole extent of his employ.[104]

Being the "clipping and rewrite man"[105] was not a minor job—it was central to the paper's identity. The newspaper exchange was the engine of antebellum America's "culture of reprinting."[106] Its centrality was plainly visible in the *Crescent*. In the position of being the editor tasked with "making up the news," Whitman produced a significant portion—often about half—of each issue's specifically composed text (that is, not counting recurring front and back matter items, including ads). For a paper whose issues frequently did not feature a more traditional lead editorial (its editorial writer, as we will see in a later chapter, was busy

DAILY CRESCENT.

By HAYES & M'CLURE.

Office—No. 93 St. Charles Street.

THURSDAY MORNING, MARCH 9, 1848.

A Sorry Business.

Five Days Later from Europe.

Vera Cruz Correspondence.

Mr. Collins—the Irish Comedian.

Arrivals at the Principal Hotels Yesterday.

FIGURE 1. Detail of page two of the New Orleans *Daily Crescent* of March 9, 1848, courtesy of the Library of Congress, Chronicling America.

in the legislature, after all), much narrativizing happens in these "pen and scissors" items—ranging from short quips[107] to factual updates on news reported by the captains delivering the mail,[108] to at times lengthy articles framed as reactions to talk in the press.[109]

We might look at one of the first issues of Walt's future paper, that of March 9, 1848, for an illustration of this (see Figure 1). Page two is laid out in typical *Crescent* fashion: on the right we have factually reported breaking-news items from Veracruz and Europe (just arrived by ship). This is where Whitman's paper has the "scoop," so the spin is somewhat minimal.[110] On the left of that we have a Whitmanian "pen and scissors" piece: a scathing attack on the peace process, framed as a reaction to a slew of newspaper updates arriving via "mail from the North." Here, we have content of the original news—that the president might go along with the peace proposal—but heavily colored by Whitman's pen, resuscitating the value of a news item somewhat devalued by transmission delay. The news, Whitman himself underscored, was as much pen-work as scissors-work.

In a very real sense, the "scissors editor" *was* the voice of the *Crescent*, narrating the goings-on in the nation for Southern audiences. Fellow editors at other papers knew as much. Whitman's friends at the New York *Sunday Dispatch*, for instance, would call the paper as "handsome as the reigning *belle* of the city" and attributed the *Crescent*'s success to both its "two experienced and enterprising publishers" as well as "its editorial department [which] is under the direction of Walter Whitman [. . .] a gentleman of taste and talent, and a most capable editor."[111]

As Matt Cohen clarifies: "[E]xchange and reprinting practice[s] created bonds of reciprocity among editors and could shape authors' and publishers' imagination of a writer's marketplace viability."[112] In becoming the voice of the *Crescent* on the exchange, Whitman not only raised the paper's profile but also his own. When editor Whitman, then, served as the *Crescent*'s public interface with newspapers across the country, he did not (only) absentmindedly cut and paste information from one sheet to the other; he was tasked with editorializing for his readers and maintaining relationships with other newspapermen. He brought to the paper a host of crucial contacts in and around New York that quickly started to exchange papers with the fledgling *Crescent,* allowing it to offer strikingly metropolitan newspaper fare to its readers. For a writer who would later emphasize the radical potential of print as intermediary for bodies—"who touches this touches a man"[113]—the task of selecting, physically manipulating, and reframing the words of others was no marginal task. As an embodied node in the newspaper exchange network, Whitman quite literally kept "in touch" with his fellow editors.

The two Whitman brothers made especially sure that the *Eagle* would continue a tight relationship with the *Crescent* on the network: "If you do not get the paper (the 'Crescent') regular," brother Jeff for instance wrote to his parents from New Orleans, "you must send [brothers] Andrew or George down to the Eagle office for it, I always see that two copys go every morning."[114] The Whitmans in Brooklyn thus kept up quasi-daily appearances at the *Eagle* office. From Jeff's letters, we know that the Whitmans, north and south, used the newspaper exchange explicitly in a way that conflated the personal and the professional. "Mr Wilson in the Eagle office sent Walter [a letter] in which he said that he called [on you, father,] and that you were all well," Jeff wrote in another letter surviving from the period, which concluded with a note explaining that "Mr. Tombs, (the man that has or will give you the letter from Walter and

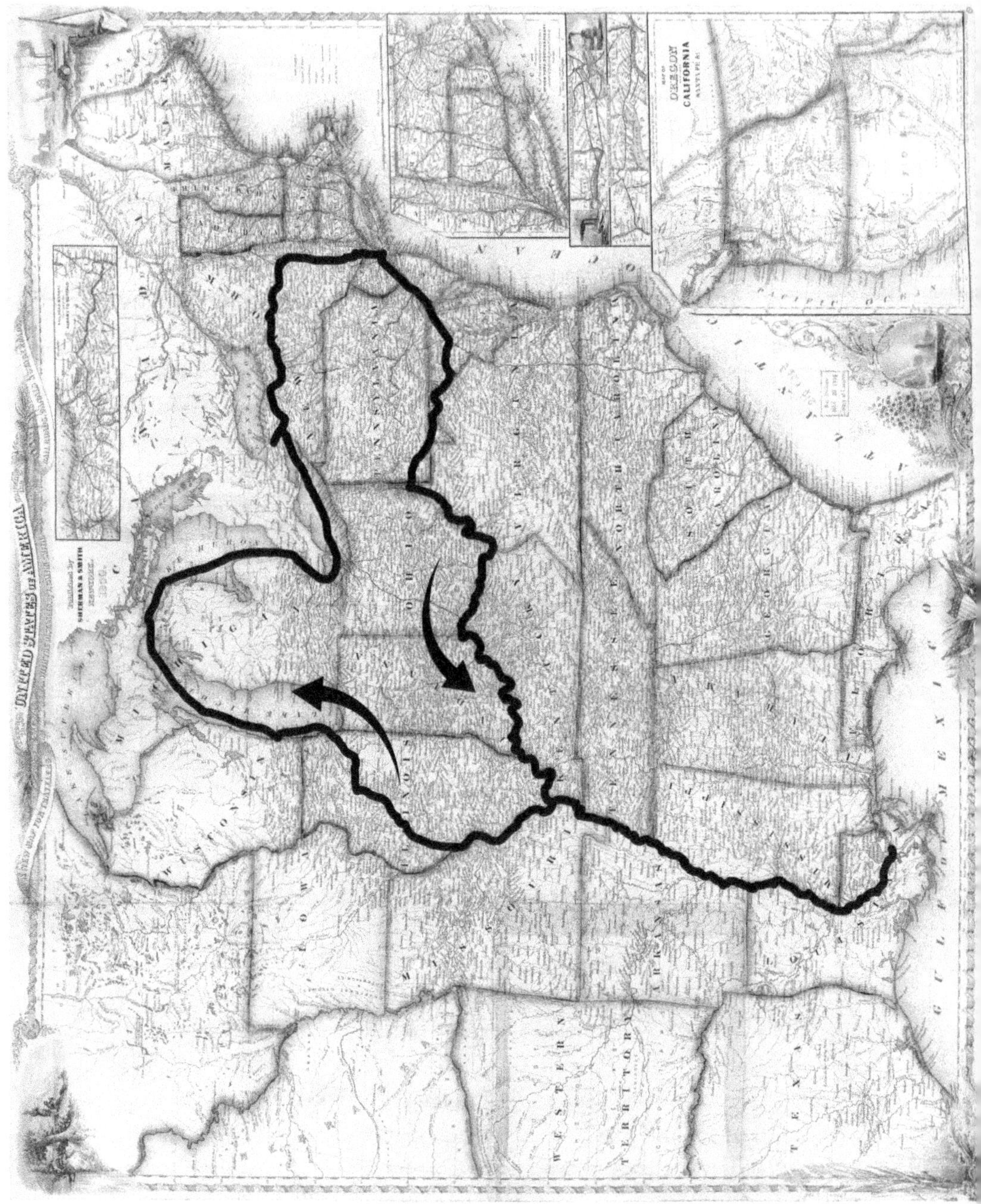

FIGURE 2. "A New Map for Travellers Through the United States of America" (1850), by Calvin J. Smith, courtesy of the Library of Congress. Walt and Jeff's route (indicated here by the authors) stretched over four thousand miles to and fro, and they used all modes of transportation available at the time: trains, carriages, and boats.

the bundle of papers) is a brother of the foreman of the Eagle office."[115] Andrew W. Tombs and Peter W. Wilson were both printers in the *Eagle* office.[116] The former was clearly involved, as Jeff indicated, in smuggling letters through the newspaper exchange; the latter served as the *Crescent*'s New York correspondent under the moniker "P. W. W." before Whitman took over this position upon his return North.[117]

Like the news from Mexico, Whitman's familial communication system relied on newsprint, editor networks, letters, legwork, and professional friendships. These systems were ready-at-hand for the young editor, accompanied by his teenage brother. Whitman's Southern sojourn may have been exceptional in his biography, but it followed the logic of antebellum newspaper networks. On the steamboats, postal routes, and train tracks of the day, news and the makers of news often travelled in tandem. Whitman was one of many journalists transitioning from one node in the network to another—and back. These transitions happened in line with the norms of his trade and were, on the whole, respected by all associated actors. What Whitman did, he did skillfully and with an eye toward professional and political advancement: The Whitmans did not travel the newspaper network as tourists. Yet, while the exchange eased and enabled their transition to the *Crescent*, ample room for novelty remained in store for the pair—not the least of which was the nearly seventeen hundred miles of country they yet had to traverse before they could start their employ at the *Crescent*. It would remain the longest trip of Walt Whitman's life.

CHAPTER 2

The vessel rocked gently to the wind of midnight in that magnificent harbor, around which the gleaming lamps circled, enveloping it in the form of a half moon, and thus justifying to the senses the romantic name of "Crescent City."

—"THE COMBAT OF DEATH," SUNDAY TIMES AND NOAH'S MESSENGER (1849)

New Impressions

FRIDAY, FEBRUARY 10, 1848, would turn out to be a "cold but delightful" day "with clear skies and without wind."[1] But the two Whitman brothers noticed little of it. When they stepped off the Brooklyn Ferry, it was still pitch black. The two had to make their way to the Liberty Street Ferry Terminal to catch their connection across the Hudson, so they could board the 9 a.m. mail drag of the Baltimore and Ohio Railroad. Illuminated only by the eerie haze of gas lamps, they hauled their ample baggage across the tip of Manhattan. Walt knew his way around; these were his old stomping grounds. Newspaper Row lurked in the distance; Wall Street lay to their left. Jeff, a "sagacious" fourteen-year-old who looked up to his brother, stuck close.[2] This was going to be a big trip for both of them. Walt, who had set out on his own at age twelve to apprentice in the printing trade, was certainly the more cosmopolitan of the two—yet he, too, had never ventured far beyond the borders of New York State in all of his twenty-eight years.

Walt and Jeff were following an itinerary that was prominently plastered by a Philadelphia-based company across the New York papers. It promised them to be "Through in Forty-Eight Hours" using postal routes.[3] They would cross the Alleghenies in that time (see Figure 3), relying on trains and coaches before, finally, in the Virginia hinterlands (now West Virginia), switching to a steamer, which would carry them west along the Ohio, then south toward New Orleans on the Mississippi.

THROUGH IN FORTY-EIGHT HOURS FROM NEW YORK TO WHEELING AND PITTSBURG, via PHILADELPHIA, BALTIMORE AND OHIO RAILROAD and from, CUMBERLAND, Md. by 12 daily lines.

TO WESTERN TRAVELLERS—Great United States Mail and Passenger route to Wheeling, Pittsburg, Cincinnati, and the South and West. Passengers going directly through by the U. S. Mail Trains.

Leave New York foot of Liberty street, at 9 A M. daily, and 4½ P. M by Rail road.

Leave Philadelphia, corner of Eleventh and Market sts, at 8½ A. M & 4 P M; arrive in Baltimore at 2 & 10 P. M.

Leave Baltimore at 7½ A M, by the Baltimore and Ohio Railroad, arrive at Cumberland at 5 P M.

Leave Cumberland at 6 P M, by the National Road and Good-Intent Stage Lines, and arrive in Wheeling or Pittsburg, next evening.

Passengers for Pittsburg take the splendid new and modern built steamboats, at Brownsville, and thereby have only 74 miles of staging on the whole route.

First class steamboats leave Wheeling and Pittsburg hourly, and passengers are forwarded without delay to Cincinnati and all other ports in the south and west.

Fare through from Philadelphia to Wheeling $13; to Pittsburg, $12, with the privilege of stopping at Baltimore, and resuming seats at pleasure. For further information apply to J. L. SLEMMER, Agent.

At Adams' & Co's Express Office, No. 16 Wall street, at 11 A. M., or Taylor's Hotel, 28 Cortlandt street.

FOR BALTIMORE.

N. B.—The Mail Lines from Philadelphia to Baltimore leave the Depot, corner of Eleventh and Market streets, Sundays excepted, at 8½ A M. by railroad, 4 P M

☞ Passengers are cautioned against purchasing tickets in New York for Baltimore, Wheeling or Pittsburg, purporting to go by the above mentioned lines, as no one is authorised to sell tickets in New York for these lines.

d1 J L. SLEMMER, Agent for Mail Lines.

FIGURE 3. Advertisement from the New York *Evening Post* detailing the route the Whitmans took from New York to Wheeling, Virginia, courtesy of the Library of Congress, Chronicling America.

As the sun rose across the Manhattan skyline behind them, the brothers' passenger cart rattled south and deposited them in the "City of Brotherly Love" by lunchtime. Their brief visit was not a pleasant experience, it seems. In the *Crescent*, Walt would later bemoan the "lewd and noisy persons" that came creeping out as the shadows grew longer and made Philadelphia's thoroughfares feel decidedly "unsafe."[4] But the two had little time to dilly-dally anyway: by 4 p.m. they would leave America's second capital again—and they still had to haul their heavy trunks over to the corner of Eleventh and Market to purchase their tickets for the rest of the trip. Philadelphia's historical City Hall loomed over the pair as they shivered at the ticket counter. The next stretch of their trip, just to get to their Ohio steamer, would run them a whopping twenty-six dollars. Adjusted for inflation, their southbound trip to Wheeling (in what is now West Virginia) alone equates to over $1,000 today[5]—a significant portion of the *Crescent*'s overall value.[6] McClure, its future proprietor, of course, had footed the bill—$200 up front, as

Whitman later stated[7]—and Walt would be spending much of his time in New Orleans justifying this investment.

If Jeff's first impressions of Philadelphia were a blur, Baltimore likely left even less of an imprint. After another long stretch of rail, the brothers arrived there at 10 p.m., only to depart again before the sun rose the next morning. It is unclear if the two managed to secure lodgings for the night or lingered around the railroad station. In any case, there was little time for rest: by 7:30 a.m. they were already back on the rails, arriving in Cumberland (Maryland) by nightfall. For much of that stretch the rails had followed the Potomac inland. Irritated by the long travel, Whitman bemoaned the empty countryside rushing past the passenger car as bleak and forlorn. Of course "this season of the year," Walt would later write about that part of their trip, "is not remarkably fascinating anywhere," though the "Alp-like loftiness" of the approaching eastern Allegheny foothills had its appeal. They had dined in Harpers Ferry that day, where the Appalachian charm won over the two weary travelers. Here, the "scenery [was] strikingly abrupt and varied" and the charming houses creeping up the hillsides made for the "finest" view. Plus, dinner was only twenty-five cents, for which the Whitmans were even willing to put up with the multiple restaurateurs' undignified quarrels over customers, quarrels that exploded around each new group of visitors who arrived in town.

Where Harpers Ferry was quaint, Cumberland bustled with activity. As an industrial hub connecting the railroad to the nation's first interstate highway—the National Road that led from the Potomac to the Ohio—it was "thriving" on travelers and trade. Whitman was awed by the immense mass of wagons that anticipated their arrival, and he felt them akin to "a caravan of the Steppes" full of "Tartar-looking" men. Even at its halfway point, the trip south was beginning to feel like a trek around the world. "Hundreds and hundreds of these enormous vehicles [. . .] wend their way into Cumberland from all quarters [. . .] with goods to send on eastward, and to take goods brought by the railroad," Whitman observed.

Cumberland was a busy place, and within the hour they were jostled into a horse-drawn carriage to travel the National Road west—toward and through the wild Alleghenies.

> Night now falling down around us like a very large cloak of black broadcloth, (I fancy *that* figure, at least, hasn't been used

> up by the poets,) and the Alleghanies rearing themselves up "some pumpkins," (as they say here,) right before our nasal members, we got into one of the several four horse stage coaches of the "National Road and Good Intent Stage Company," whereby we were to be transported over those big hills. They did the thing systematically, whatever may be said elsewise. All the passengers' names were inscribed on a roll, [. . .] and a clerk stands by and two or three negroes with a patent weighing machine. The clerk calls out your name—your baggage is whipped on the machine, and if it weighs over fifty pounds, you have to pay extra. You are then put in the stage, (literally put in, like a package, unless you move quickly,) your baggage packed on behind—the next name called off—baggage weighed—and so on to the end of the chapter. [. . .] So they boxed us up in our coach, nine precious souls, and we dashed through the town and up the mountains, with an apparent prospect of as comfortable a night as could be expected, considering all things.[8]

Maryland, of course, was a slave state—and Whitman may well be narrating his first encounter with an enslaved person here.[9] If this happenstance impressed him in any way, he was at the very least unwilling to disclose it to his Southern readers.

Instead, Whitman narrates this encounter as another "first": his first meeting with men from the "the West." Stuffed like sardines into their carriage, Walt started chatting with his fellow coach passengers and found himself impressed by an "old gentleman [who] resided on a farm in the interior of Ohio" and who regaled the carriage with tales of his maritime exploits during the War of 1812. To Whitman, the man was a specimen of "actual manliness": "the young men, of New York, Philadelphia, Boston, Brooklyn and so on, with all the advantages of compact neighborhood, schools, etc., are not up to the men of the West." Struck by the Ohioan's "sterling vein of common sense," Walt concludes: "A satirical person could no doubt find an ample field for his powers in many of the manners and ways of the West"—setting up, perhaps, the often strikingly "Western" tinge that would characterize his later comical sketches for the *Crescent*.[10]

After little more than twenty-four hours, the National Road had taken the motley group of travelers past snowcapped mountains, across moonlit

FIGURE 4. Engraving of the City of Wheeling (1849), courtesy of the Ohio County Public Library Archives, Wheeling, West Virginia. The National Road crossed the Ohio here, suggesting that one of the stagecoaches on the bridge may be a "Good Intent" coach.

roads framed by heavy timber, and to smoke-filled inns with a great many "strapping drovers" lounging about. Such "picturesque occasions" led Whitman to rhapsodize about the marvels of Creation and the wonders the western landscape had in store for American artists. He was perhaps thinking of Western painters like George Caleb Bingham (1811–79) here, whose work Whitman had recently seen in New York.[11] All of these rugged backcountry sights, though, paled in comparison to what the next stretch of their trip had in store: the romance of steamboat travel.

As the National Road snaked into Wheeling from the north, the two brothers could see the steam bellowing up from the funnels of the docked river steamers long before the boats themselves came into view. The Ohio lay nestled below the small industrial town, down a steep embankment. It was 10 p.m. and the *St. Cloud* already had its "steam all up,"[12] ready to depart quickly; passengers and freight were hastened on board. The captain, a colorful, seasoned Appalachian riverman by the name of Samuel Mason (1803–83)[13] was eager to depart. The *St. Cloud*, which he co-owned, was his treasure, and he was determined to make good time and establish himself as a reliable connection on the mail route down to New Orleans. Whitman also suspected the captain, a "clever little" man in his estimation, to run a number of deals on the side, leading to unpleasant stops in "all sorts of places."[14] In any case, the *St. Cloud* was only about two years old and advertised itself as "new, splendid, and fast running" and offering "unsurpassed accommodations."[15] This was no mere puffery: The steamer was making such a good name for itself that even then-president-elect Zachary Taylor would choose the *St. Cloud* to come down to New Orleans in November of that year.[16]

In their estimation of the accommodations, Walt and Jeff couldn't have agreed more: They were mind-boggled by the luxury of steamboat travel. "Mother, you have no idea of the splendor and the comfort of these western river steam-boats," Jeff gushed in a letter home. "Every thing you would find in the Astor house in New York, you find on these boats."[17] Their cabin was on deck, so the brothers could watch the Ohio glide past their windows as they reclined on their cots. That view, however, was increasingly dull in February: The mighty river looked brackish and yellow, and the country was monotone. Yet after the simple backcountry fare of previous days, the culture on board, and especially the food, was mesmerizing. As Jeff informs his mother, "For breakfast we have: coffee, tea, ham and eggs, beef steak, sausages hot cakes, with plenty of good bread sugar &c &c. For dinner: roast beef d[itt]o. mutton d[itt]o. veal boiled ham roast turkey d[itt]o. goose with pie and puddings and for supper every thing that is good to eat." Walt echoed Jeff's youthful enthusiasm: "To all intents and purposes, you are as well supplied with creature comforts on board these boats as while you should be the denizen of a Broadway hotel," he wrote to M. M. Noah's *Sunday Times* in March: "[E]atables, in the utmost freshness and profusion—too much profusion, indeed; good clean beds; a long saloon to promenade in; or, if you prefer it, in fine weather, the outside. All these combine to furnish the passengers with no grounds of complaint about such parts of their ease and satisfactions."[18]

In contrast to the luxuries on board, the cities they visited along the way were somewhat disappointing. The boat stopped in Cincinnati, likely in the late afternoon of February 16, and Walt found it bustling and vivacious—but the appeal of the city that had come to be known as "Porkopolis" for its massive hog markets was seriously undermined by the "ungainly mud" of its banks. He had similar reservations about Louisville: The people were friendly, and the city looked "substantial," but its potential was hampered by the "ugly falls" downriver. Perhaps

Walt was holding a grudge here: Captain Mason had decided to run directly down the falls, which caused some panic and consternation in Walt and giddy excitement in young Jeff.

Overall, Walt looked at what was then the West with an eye for industrial development. Cincinnati might take its rightful place as one of the leading "business places in this republic"[19] next to New York, New Orleans, and Philadelphia. Other towns fared worse. Especially the hamlet of Cairo, Illinois, where the *St. Cloud* transitioned from the Ohio to the Mississippi on February 18, rubbed Whitman the wrong way:

> Immense sums of money have been spent to make Cairo something like what a place with such a name ought to be. But with the exception of its position, which is unrivalled for business purposes, every thing about it seems unfortunate. The point on which it is situated, is low, and liable to be overflowed at every high flood. Besides, it is unwholesomely wet, at the best. It is doubtful whether Cairo will ever be any "great shakes," except in the way of ague.[20]

Cairo, promoted by some papers as a next major trade hub, was nothing but "a few small houses, and one or two untenanted large buildings," with little else providing signs "of its future glories," Whitman would confirm in a later article.[21] A Cairo paper was actually on the newspaper exchange with the *Crescent,* and its staff reacted with outrage when they read this. But Whitman stuck to his guns:

> We are prepared to re-affirm the truth, in every particular, even the minutest. It is well known that an immense "speculating" interest has been at work for several years past, trying to force Cairo "into the market." At present, however, and in spite of the most eminent advantages of position, the appearance of Cairo makes more of a "sorry sight" than ever did Macbeth's bloody pickers and stealers. We speak merely of the simple fact.[22]

Where nature and industry failed Whitman, steamboat life made up for it: From the reading parlor to the bar room, the *St. Cloud* compensated for the unpleasantness of muddy banks, occasional storms, and the bland, yellow river. Indeed, Whitman was so impressed with the peculiarities of steamboat life that it features prominently not only in his accounts of the trip but possibly also in a piece of fiction. It would be published in the summer of 1849, again in the *Sunday Times*. One of two New Orleans pieces in the paper that were first cautiously suggested by John Jay Rubin as potentially from Whitman's pen,[23] "The Combat of Death" is a short prose piece that echoes many of Whitman's fiction tropes and his celebrations of steamboat life (such as the "rich wine," that flowed freely in such vessels' enormous "bar-rooms"). Written at a time when Whitman was ending his association with the *Freeman* and beginning to promote himself via weekend papers,[24] the piece narrates a northerner's trip down to New Orleans and features a familiar meeting with a sage old Ohioan, albeit on deck instead of in a stagecoach. "Combat of Death" also echoes a worry that was at the forefront of Whitman's mind: disease—especially the yellow fever.

"Fly, young man [, h]asten away with all speed, for the black scourge of God is lifted over the land," the Ohioan warns the protagonist, before the story summons up images of "death-carts, rolling from every door" and a "horror-stricken town" ravaged by "human nature [. . .] in its most revolting phases."[25] And, indeed, New Orleans had rightly earned itself the nickname "Necropolis of the South" by the 1840s.[26] Editor Whitman was well aware of that: His *Eagle* had run near-weekly updates on each summer's death statistics in the city, titled "Yellow Fever in New Orleans."[27] Yellow fever season was so devastating to the city, it not only killed thousands, but led to depopulation as tradesmen fled the city, leaving it, as Whitman would later put it, terribly "dull" as all these "'northern birds' [were] fast winging their way towards their native hills."[28] The Whitmans, too, would promptly leave before yellow fever would raise its ugly head in the summer—and just as Jeff was feeling dispirited and sickly.

Yet, Whitman put on a brave face. Writing to the *Sunday Times* upon his arrival in New Orleans, he argued that the city had been falsely maligned as a fever bog, and "the yellow fever, after all, is not more to be dreaded than those pulmonary complaints that sweep away monthly so many thousands of victims in the north."[29] He had read as much in the *New Orleans Medical Journal*, he notes—a publication Whitman perused specifically for yellow fever items, at least one of which he would excerpt in the *Crescent*. On March 25, 1848, he praised a piece from the medical magazine for (rightly) identifying the disease as mosquito-borne.[30] Yet even when occasionally stumbling onto correct views about the disease, Whitman mocks all fear of it as unmanly. In one of his short pieces of fiction, for instance, he caricatures such attitudes via an effeminate dandy who "[w]hen the yellow fever season commences, [. . .] darts like an arrow northward."[31] Whitman, of course, had long been a health quack, who would prescribe diet, exercise, and cleanliness to combat diseases like yellow fever well into the life cycle of *Leaves of Grass*.[32] In the *Crescent*, he would also mock physicians as greedy sawbones.[33] His downplaying of yellow fever here served two main purposes, though: defending the honor of the city that printed his new paper—and persuading his Northern friends and family, and likely himself, that yellow fever constituted no real threat to him and the young brother in his care.

Perhaps this darker notion of the "Necropolis of the South" was on his mind, then, when he first encountered the city, drenched in midnight black, on the late evening of February 24, 1848. After fourteen days of travel, the lights of the Crescent City slowly came into view around a sharp bend in the Mississippi. The *St. Cloud* flowed past the Garden District with its ornate, French buildings, then approached the American Quarter, where the Whitmans would deboard at Poydras Street Wharf. Yet the only account of the arrival that is extant (it is missing from his travelogue) is drenched in Gothic ornament. It is a strikingly somber poetic rumination, much in contrast with Whitman's travelogue and the brothers' letters north. An initial draft of this piece—Whitman's only known contemporaneous poem about New Orleans—cast the city in an even darker hue than the published version.

> Sailing down the Mississippi, of a Cloudy Midnight—
> Vast and black starless, the pall of heaven
> Laps on the trailing pall below
> And plunging athwart the solemn darkness
> As if to the Sea of the Lost we go.—[34]

Whitman's nighttime musings (which include the line "Like Earth O river, you offer us burial") suggest an element of concern, perhaps fear, in how Walt experienced his arrival in New Orleans. This mood is absent in many of his other accounts—save, perhaps, the morbid "Combat of Death." The Mississippi might drag the Whitmans to a prosperous future, or it might ferry them like Lethe to a town of the dead.

Not surprisingly, Whitman reverts to a much more chipper tone

FIGURE 5. Detail of *Birds eye view of New-Orleans* (1851), by John Bachmann, courtesy of the Library of Congress. The wide street in the center is Canal Street. The domed building to its center-left is the St. Charles Hotel in the American Quarter, prior to the 1851 fire. To its left is Lafayette Square. At the far right side of the image is the French Quarter and Cathedral Chartres & Orleans.

when writing home. His first impressions as recorded in a letter to the *Brooklyn Daily Eagle*, signed "Brooklynite,"[35] read:

> "Life" in New Orleans is not much different from "life" in New York. Money flies a little faster, perhaps; more work is done by negroes; the bar-rooms are immensely larger—and the soil is not so dry. With these points of difference, one may sum up all. Perhaps the greatest "want" in New Orleans is the want of a score or so of cleanly, well-kept boarding houses. One of those nice places in Brooklyn, now, transposed to here, might make the owner's fortune in a very little time.

The striking similarity of life between New York and New Orleans (two cities sharing a "freedom from all provincialism and the gossip of second-rate towns"),[36] would be a feature of Whitman's later New Orleans writings as well. Especially the comment by "Brooklynite" on New Orleans's "want of [. . .] cleanly, well-kept boarding houses" echoed Walt's experience—as his teenage brother complained in a letter home: "Mother, I never wanted your cleanliness so much before as I did at our first boarding house, you could not only see the dirt, but you could taste it, and you had to too if you ate anything at all. And the rooms too, were covered with dirt an inch thick."[37]

Memories of their "long cabin, neatly carpeted, and lit with clusters of handsome lamps" aboard the *St. Cloud* steamer must have only exacerbated the horrors the Whitmans experienced at laying eyes (and noses) on their first New Orleans boarding house.[38] It is clear that the two didn't keep their moaning to just written complaints. It seems their new employer heard about it, too, and set them up with new rooms: "[W]e are now living at the Tremont house, next door to the Theatre, and directly opposite the office," Jeff jovially informed his family quickly thereafter.[39] Their new landlord was Patrick Irwin (1810–78), a well-respected Irish-Catholic businessman,[40] card-carrying Democrat,[41] and friend to the *Crescent* owners.[42] Below the Whitmans' quarters, Irwin welcomed guests to dine and drink at all hours of the night, likely keeping young Jeff and his brother up on more than one night. As Irwin announced in an ad: "*Meals at all hours*—to suit all occupations. . . . The BAR is supplied with choice Liquors. ☞ THE RESTAURANT will be open until a late hour in the evening. OYSTERS served up in every style."[43] For the rate of five dollars a week, the Whitmans' meal was included with their lodgings,[44] allowing Walt, as he put it in a later *Crescent* piece, to keep his "'mouth fairly watered' as his eye and his appetite were both feasted upon the savory dishes before him."[45]

Tremont House wasn't alone in offering an opulent eatery. The so-called American Quarter the Whitmans now called their home was known for its long, cavernous ground-level establishments: from shooting galleries, to bowling alleys, to enormous barrooms. As Whitman explained it to his friends at the New York *Sunday Times*,

> one of the most striking features to a stranger in New Orleans consists in the immense bar-rooms—some of them as big as the rotunda in the Merchant's Exchange in Wall street. From eleven to one o'clock every day an ample banquet of provisions is set out free at these places, and the common custom is to "take a drink" and something more between those hours. The taking of drinks, however, is by no means confined to those periods. Perhaps, if New Orleans has an evil that may be called *the* bad one of all, it is this drinking practice. Almost everybody of the male genus above the age of fifteen is in the daily habit of "imbibing," and that pretty frequently. Now you know I am not *ultra* in these matters, but it isn't good to drink spiritous compounds at this rate in hot climate.[46]

Certainly, Whitman had once been more "ultra" in his positions on drink. Undoubtedly influenced by his father's alcoholism, he had famously written a whole anti-alcohol novella less than six years prior, titled *Franklin Evans; Or, The Inebriate*. Figures from his former crusading days in Manhattan even showed up in the office at times, for instance in the form of the "Razor Strop Man" Henry Smith (1815–89), who stopped by on his way to the Temperance Hall in the same building.[47] In New Orleans, however, Walt was not above imbibing a julep or two. Still, concern lingered for his young brother, Jeff, quickly approaching "the age of fifteen," as Walt mentioned in his letter to his *Sunday Times* colleagues, disclosing, perhaps, a slightly more "ultra" attitude toward drink in the younger Whitman.

At first glance, New Orleans did not disappoint. While snow and ice was still haunting the Northeast, New Orleans was already "quite warm," as Jeff wrote. "I saw a good many peach trees in blossom to day," he exclaimed excitedly.[48] His brother Walt also marveled at the lush spectacle: "Our Northern friends would not be a little surprised to witness the appearance of things, in the vegetable world, that characterizes the neighborhood of our 'Crescent City,'" he observed in one of the first issues of the *Crescent*: "[V]egetation is hereabouts as far advanced as it is in the latitude of New York by May [. . . .] The beautiful green of our orange trees strike the stranger always with a pleasant feeling—and particularly when he sees them growing, now in full verdure in the open grounds."[49]

Indeed, the warm welcome would make Walt rethink his attitude to the South almost right away. "New Orleans itself has also been much slandered abroad," he informed New Yorkers via the *Sunday Times*. "One at the north invariably connects it with the ideas of duelling, bowie-knives, yellow fever, and bogs"—none of it, he wrote, was truer here than up North. "Besides," he added, "we have none of that abominable evil, so prevalent in New York, of groups congregating at the corners of the streets, and, with their obscene talk or direct impudence insulting females and others who pass them."[50] In his defense of the Crescent City, Whitman at times sounded quite a bit older than his late twenties; Southern customs and habits, somewhat ironically, appealed to the New Yorker of Dutch Quaker stock.

Between the Whitmans' late-night arrival on February 24 and the first issue of the *Crescent* on March 5, 1848, the two brothers explored the exotic city. They attended "two or three procession[s]"—including the Fireman's Celebration on March 4, which Walt would cover for the *Crescent*. They went on extended walks through the surprisingly flat city and soaked in some of its exotic sights, including an "old Cathilic cemmetery" and "the old French church" (St. Louis Cathedral), which allowed Jeff to express his disgust over locals, who "would go up and dip their fingers in the holy water and then go home and <u>whip</u> their <u>slaves</u>."[51] In the resulting newspaper coverage of their walks, however, published on March 6 in the *Crescent*, no echoes of Black culture or Jeff's outrage survive. Walt, on the other hand, seemed fascinated with Catholic ritual, often dropping in on Sunday mass at the St. Louis Cathedral.[52]

FIGURE 6. A French-style 1848 daguerreotype of Walt Whitman, very likely created in New Orleans, courtesy of Walt Whitman House. Courtesy of Walt Whitman House, Camden, New Jersey.

Their first days in town were spent as tourists. On Sundays, the Whitmans headed toward the First Municipality, leaving the American Quarter for a slice of French life that they found thrilling. On March 5, during one of their first outings, the two visited St. Louis Cemetery No. 1, where Jeff was struck by the flowers on display, noting the tombs covered with "large white roses and red ones too [that] were all along the walk from one end to the other."[53] Afterward, Walt must have stopped at one of the French daguerreotype studios clustered in the center of the French Quarter, where he had his portrait taken. As Denise B. Bethel has noted, the resulting picture not only echoes European custom but includes French-language newspaper stuffing.[54] The French "daguerrians" of New Orleans in 1845 (C. Peyroux, P. Laglumé, and A. D. Lansot)[55] all offered their services within eyeshot of the Place d'Armes (today's Jackson Square), framed by St. Louis Cathedral to the north and the busy French Market (where Walt liked to get his coffee) by the riverbank to its south. In one of the first issues of the *Crescent*, a short humor piece, likely by Whitman, playfully riffed on the contrast between the artistic marvels of the photographic technology and the mundane wishes of its working-class customers.[56]

Right across the street from St. Louis Cemetery No. 1 was another major site of New Orleans life—one that Whitman could hardly have avoided: Congo Square, the center of Black life in the Crescent City. It is mentioned in passing in "The Combat of Death" but features more prominently in the second piece of New Orleans fiction to be found in the pages of the *Sunday Times* in 1849. Apparently written by the same author as "Combat of Death," the short story again transposes a number of sentimental plots and characters onto a typical New Orleans scene. In the story, titled "Cantatrice," the protagonist, Peter Ellis, strolls—like Whitman did—from his lodgings by the St. Charles over to the French Quarter and finds himself mesmerized by the strange spectacle he discovers there:

> A huge negro, taller, blacker, and uglier than any found in the immense concourse, had been chosen general director for the day. He was called indifferently "King of Congo," or "King of the Wake," and bore on his head, as a crown, a great pyramid of painted paper boxes fastened together, which had the effect of nearly doubling his natural height. This monarch and all his subjects were tricked out in a manner so inconceivably grotesque that it was impossible to behold them without laughter. Here was one furnished with hoofs. There went another brandishing enormous horns. A third clapped his wings, crowing like a chanticleer. A fourth strutted majestically, spreading behind him the plumes of the peacock; while a fifth displayed the tail of a monkey. Their noble sable features were flecked with all the colors of the rainbow; and their necks, waists, arms, ancles [*sic*], literally bristled with innumerable little bells that jingled and chimed as they moved, like millions of fairy tongues.
>
> The dancers imitated the different cries of every animal described in natural history. They crowed, barked, bellowed, neighed, bleated, squalled, hooted and howled, while still ever without ceasing, the little bells jingled and chimed. And, as if this deafening din were not sufficient to keep pace with the whirlwind of their passionate excitement, they called in the aid

> of all sorts of musical and un-musical instruments. The fiddle uttered its silvery laugh; the drum thundered; the trumpet roared; the fife squealed; while the boatman's bugle, like an angel of gladness, flung its winding notes into the sky; and still the little bells jingled and chimed. They increased the clamor by thumping pans, kettles, tubs, and empty barrels. They shuffled, waltzed, and flew the *polka*; but yet, over all the new evolutions, the genuine original Congo dance maintained its undisputed pre-eminence.
>
> It was the *saturnalia* of animal passion—the jubilee of joyous instinct. Every eye gleamed with rapture; every countenance was radiant with wild light. The whole burning, heaving mass of vitality was worked up to a height of feeling, intense as the emotions of madness. Even many of the spectators caught the contagious fury and joined in the savage glee [. . . .][57]

In what is likely the first literary account of New Orleans's so-called "Mardi Gras Indians,"[58] we perhaps also get what may be Whitman's only, though fictionalized, engagement with Black life in New Orleans beyond mere servitude. Congo Green had been a place of Sabbath celebrations for the enslaved population of the city since the eighteenth century, and it was the only place legally permitted (indeed, designated) for Black gatherings. It featured market stalls, food, dance, and song—and attracted troves of white spectators from across the city and the nation. Whitman, undoubtedly, was one of them. Whether or not Whitman wrote the piece, then, it does disclose the only surviving account of the locale around the time of his visit.

Walt's first *Crescent* piece dedicated to his impressions of New Orleans appears a week into the paper's print run. It disguised itself as being written by a local, but its reference to the city's "pleasant [. . .] Southern summer" made it clear that whoever wrote this piece, had yet to experience the New Orleans heat. The article itself tells a great deal about how Walt spent his first days in the Southern metropolis:

> . . . Does the gentleman desire to see an Attakapas bull (just imported from Havana) speared by an artiste of celebrity? If so, his wish can be fulfilled by visiting Algiers and the Third

Municipality, in the pleasant season of our Southern summer. As for masquerade Balls, we can only be beaten by gay, gallant, chivalrous Paris: and in the way of operas, we can't be beaten at all. There's the French opera at the Orleans Theatre, with its magnificent troupe; and occasionally we have those addicted to music from the "Father-land," who sing to our uneducated ears, strains of the most mysterious sweetness.—Again, once or twice in the course of the theatrical season, we have gems of genius in the way of vocalists from the "sunny skies of fair, classic Italy," who sing as if their very blood had been intermixed with the red currents that flow through the hearts of nightingales. . . .

If a person wishes to perforate his intimate friend or insolent enemy, he has only to go to some one of the numerous shooting-galleries in New Orleans, and by the joint aid of a few dimes and three days' practice, he can be taught to split a bullet against the edge of a pen-knife, at the distance of ten paces. Those, too, who are fond of playing with edged tools, will, by applying to some of our fencing-masters, be taught how to "pink" a gentleman in a manner that Chevalier Bayard would have wept at. More than this could not be desired.

Now, as for our National Drama, we have all the materials necessary. Stars from Europe, from Britain, and, aye, sometimes from our own wild Western States, appear week after week at the different Theatres—which "temples of the drama" are, we suppose, better patronized than any others in "the land of the free and the home of the brave." Those who come to visit us, albeit for a season, must never think that the Queen City of the South is deficient in amusements—for they can enjoy themselves at any thing in the way of drinking, from a glass of the waters of the muddy Mississippi, up to a golden goblet filled with Roman punch:—in the way of eating, from a mouldy sea-biscuit with a slice of rusty bacon, up to broiled, pompano with terrapin eggs and asparagus; and in the way of music, from the tooting of a penny whistle, up to a soul-entrancing strain of a silver bugle, in the still, solemn hours of night.

The fact is, that in this goodly city, we can go through the whole alphabet of enjoyment, and, as they say in the West, "not miss a letter from A to Izzard."[59]

Many Whitmanian giveaways are here: his infatuation with opera, his fascination with German music ("music from the 'Father-land'"), his new-found love for all things "West."

More striking, however, is the passing reference to those "who come to visit us, albeit for a season." Considering that Whitman would only spend the spring in New Orleans while plans for the *Freeman* were being set in motion, this suggests that Walt may have been hired with a short tenure in mind. He would not be an exception in that regard: Over the winter months the city swelled with Northern businessmen, only to grind to a halt again come summer. "The streets of this enchanting place begin to look gloomy, quiet, and deserted," a correspondent of a New York paper complains by late April: "Every boat that leaves for 'up the river' is crowded with the speculative northerners, who have been sojourning among us during the past winter."[60] Whitman would be one of them. After all, Whitman did not have a reputation for hard work—perhaps unjustly so—but he *was* well-known for attracting readers and had ample experience with helping papers get off the ground. While Whitman's late-life comments obfuscate his likely motivations, it is clear that Whitman's period in New Orleans was one characterized by much more forethought and planning than later narratives of fights, fallouts, and spontaneous departures (coming and going) suggest.

As much as Whitman played it off to his Northern readers, New Orleans *did* feel strikingly different in a number of ways to the two Brooklynites. In emphasizing the city's similarity to New York, Walt was not attempting to obfuscate that difference but to elevate the Crescent City to readers in the North. To Walt, so much was clear: The city was equal to the best the country had to offer. Yet it was brimming with obvious and subtle diversities that the two brothers would only slowly come to terms with during bar-room meetings, outings in the French Quarter, and rowdy nights at the St. Charles. Mardi Gras was on the horizon, suggesting, in its devilish play with identity, a thrilling encounter with the multitudes of the Crescent City. Glancing at the festivities at Congo Square—either echoed in "Cantatrice" or exemplified by it—Walt and Jeff would have inevitably begun to realize that the dynamics around race in their new city far exceeded their narrow frame of reference. Walking through the crowded thoroughfares of the Crescent City in those pleasant days of late February, the Empire State, in a number of ways, would have felt far off.

CHAPTER 3

*Such a variety of white humans,
and black humans, and yaller humans!*

—WHITMAN, "SKETCHES OF THE SIDEWALKS AND LEVEE" (1848)

Slavery in the Creole City

WHEREVER WALT AND JEFF went in their first days in New Orleans, one thing immediately became clear: the Crescent City was bustling with people. As a crucial hub for trade and war, its population had ballooned to over 120,000 by 1848,[1] an almost 15 percent increase over the previous three years, placing it among the five most populous cities in the United States. Still, it would not have felt like a typical US metropolis. "Society, as at present constituted in New Orleans, has very little resemblance to that of any other city in the Union," wrote Moore Norman in his 1845 travel guide. "It is made up of a heterogeneous mixture of almost all nations,"[2] specifically European immigrants, Creoles, "emigrants from the sister states [. . .] and the mighty West," as well as "nondescript watermen."[3]

The 1850 US Census lists the state of Louisiana as having, within a total population of around 518,000 people, about 262,000 residents of color, most of them enslaved (245,000). By comparison, "free colored" residents, while substantial relative to many other states, still totaled only 17,462.[4] Over half of those free Blacks lived in New Orleans, a city famed for its variously intermixed Creole culture, which, in population numbers, equated to about 20 percent of the white population. The term *Creole* could variously signify the admixture of French and American cultures, multiple races, or both, and was applied indiscriminately in New Orleans throughout the period. But one thing is certain: The New Orleans that Whitman arrived in, with a booming economy thanks to its position as a major trade depot with the South and gateway to Mexico, was not only one of the largest slave-market locales in the world, it was simultaneously a hub of racially mixed life, where white, Black, Creole, and mulatto populations lived side by side and interacted on the streets—a sight that would have been completely new to Whitman.

Walt's and Jeff's home state of New York had a population of three million, only about fifty thousand (1.6 percent) of whom were Black Freedpeople. By contrast, New Orleans positively teemed with both Freedpeople and enslaved Blacks, who comprised nearly a quarter of the city's population. The boundaries between the races were consequently significantly blurred in the Crescent City: in the 1850 US Census, one of the first to tabulate mixed-race persons among populations of color, New Orleans had one of the highest ratios of mulattoes among Black residents: 46 percent.[5] This means that when Whitman arrived, he faced more than merely the possibility of seeing a few Black Americans, free and enslaved, living their lives in front of him. He saw thousands of people of color, leading real lives all around him: working hard, reading, sporting, raising families, or being sold into slavery. For the first time in his life, Whitman saw up close what multiracial life really looked like, felt like, and how it operated in the South, a part of the American nation that he had been championing as an editor. To Whitman's vision of urban life, New Orleans proved a challenge.

To understand how New Orleans may have (re)shaped Whitman's thinking about race and slavery, it is important to contextualize it against the poet-journalist's previous encounters with the issue. Whitman's early attitudes toward slavery, prior to his trip to New Orleans, are largely known from newspaper editorials he wrote for the *New York Aurora* (1842) and the *Brooklyn Daily Eagle* (1846–48) and from his temperance novella *Franklin Evans* (1842). The earliest writing regarding American slavery thought to be Whitman's is titled "Black and White Slaves" and appeared in the *Aurora* on April 2, 1842.[6] Whitman took as his subject a copy of an eponymous lithograph he'd been sent that depicts an impoverished family of white English laborers dying of starvation (and being harassed by a fat-cat capitalist, to boot), next to a contrasting image of Black American Southern slaves—all of them well-fed and smiling,

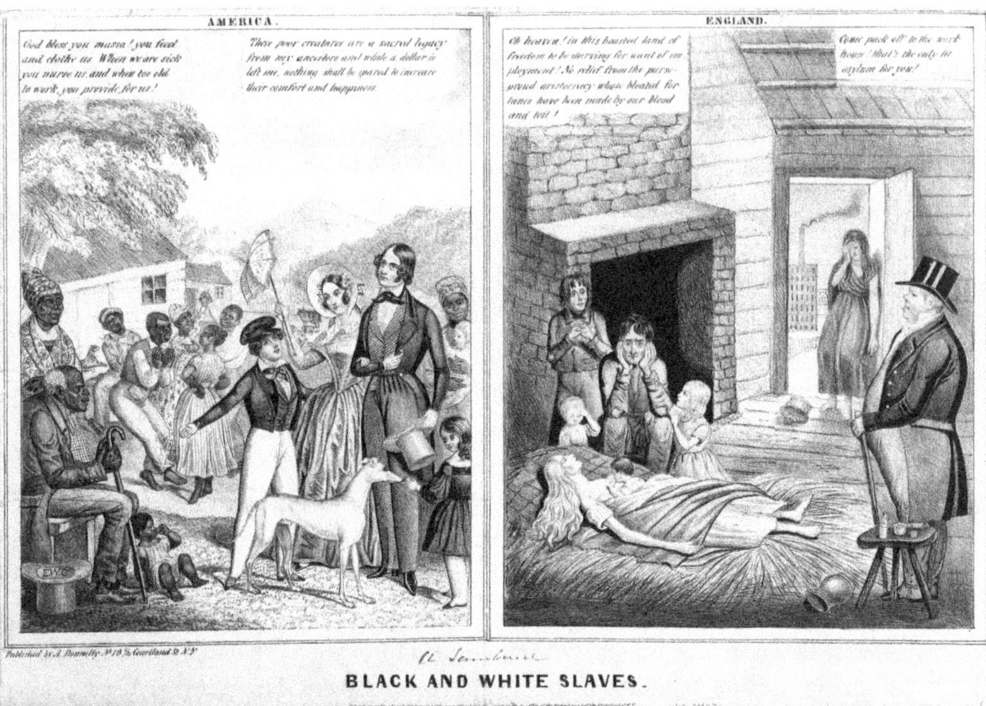

FIGURE 7. *Black and White Slaves* (c. 1846), by Edward Williams Clay, courtesy of the Division of Home and Community Life, National Museum of American History, Smithsonian Institution.

some of them dancing in the background, the whole group being visited by a white "gentleman and lady, with two children," who have, as Whitman described it, "come to pay a call at the shanty of a family of their slaves" (see Figure 7). "Every thing," he added, "bears the impress of cheerfulness and content."

The lithograph, which Whitman had evidently been sent in the mail, was created by Edward Williams Clay, a Northern anti-abolitionist. The twenty-two-year-old Whitman's response to it was probably exactly the sort of reaction that Clay, a slavery apologist, hoped for. Whitman, then newly ensconced as editor for an anti-Tammany, somewhat nativist newspaper, wrote that English abolitionists were nothing short of hypocrites. "There is a good moral conveyed in this picture," he said, since the English abolitionist "raises a great bluster and outcry, because of the oppressed condition of the American negroes [. . . a]nd all the while, the British have within the borders of their own country, miseries compared to which those of the southern slaves are as a wart to Ossa." Only when the British have "pull[ed] down the lumbering fabric of monarchy and aristocracy," he concluded, "and destroy[ed] the prevalence of the spectacles of famine, penury and death," can they "send us some of their charity and their sympathy" for the cause of American abolition.[7]

That the American abolitionist movement held no moral ground as long as working-class whites suffered anywhere in the world was a common rationalization, for those who argued in favor of the institution of slavery, as well as for those (like Whitman) who advocated in favor of (white) workers' rights. Yet Whitman also omits from his account some of the more pernicious elements of the illustration: a Black slave saying "God bless you, Massa! You feed and clothe us"; the slave family being depicted as finely dressed and well-fed; and the white plantation owner, hand over his heart, exclaiming, "These poor creatures are a sacred legacy from my ancestors and while a dollar is left me, nothing shall be spared to increase their comfort and happiness." It was the sort of plantation caricature of placid slave life that remained common across the South well into the twentieth century. In any case, Whitman's editorial suggests that early on the young journalist developed a powerful bias in favor of white working Americans and began his life with a rather dim and prejudiced view of Black Americans, whether free or trapped in slavery.

Whitman's other major statement that year on race and slavery was the so-called "Creole episode" of his temperance novella *Franklin Evans*. In the novella, published in a special edition of a literary weekly, Whitman's titular character gradually succumbs to the dangers of intemperance. In a run of chapters that contemporary readers might now label protagonist Evans's "rock bottom," he meets Margaret, a mixed-race Creole slave woman on a Virginia plantation, who at first is described in admiring, if oversexualized, terms:

> She was of that luscious and fascinating appearance often seen in the south, where a slight tinge of the deep color, large, soft voluptuous eyes, and beautifully cut lips, set off a form of faultless proportions—and all is combined with a complexion just sufficiently removed from clear white, to make the spectator doubtful whether he is gazing on a brunette, or one who

has indeed some hue of African blood in her veins. Margaret belonged to the latter class: and she only wanted an opportunity to show, that the fire of her race burnt with all its brightness in her bosom, though smothered by the necessity of circumstances.[8]

In order to have her manumitted, Evans—who later admits to having been blind drunk at the time—marries Margaret and begins an implied sexual relationship with her. After some days of living together, Evans begins to feel "distaste [. . .] toward the creole, my wife, who, I felt sure, had done her best to entrap me into all this. [. . . B]efore, [she, whom] I had looked on with the deepest admiration, was now almost an object of hate to me." Ultimately, Evans falls in love with another woman—a beautiful white woman, whom he admits "is wonderfully fair, not dark and swarthy, which I detest!"—and in a fit of jealousy Margaret strangles her, before killing herself.[9]

More than his editorial on "Black and White Slaves," Whitman's depiction of Margaret the "creole" here adds a number of layers to what critics read as the poet-journalist's early understanding of race, gender, and geopolitics. Literary scholars Stephanie M. Blalock and Nicole Gray have noted that "this segment of the novel participates in a general tendency of temperance literature to compare the state of the inebriate to that of slavery, while also parroting proslavery language and argumentation."[10] Some scholars, like Gretchen Murphy, have interpreted this episode as Whitman's *critique* of the common comparison made between Northern men "enslaved" to alcohol and Southern Blacks trapped in actual chattel slavery. Others, however, read it as Whitman merely making use of patriarchal and racial essentialism, rather than subverting it.[11] Either way, when in late 1846 he adapted the novella for serialization in the *Brooklyn Daily Eagle*, Whitman made a number of changes that may have exemplified a development on the issue of slavery. This time, Margaret is not enslaved at all, alcohol plays no role in her relationship with Evans, and Margaret's race is left undescribed, beyond the multivalent term *Creole*. It is unclear if these changes reflect a personal change in attitudes or an acknowledgement that, by 1846, slavery had become a more aggressively political topic in the newspaper sphere: The question of slavery extension was already on the table, after all, and slavery had lost its appeal as merely an exotic plot point.

By 1846, Whitman still had never left the bounds of New York City and Long Island, so his imagined experiences of Southern plantation life were secondhand at best: gleaned from gossip, news items, and novels. But what *did* approach him more closely in New York were the experiences of Africans aboard slaving vessels who found themselves shipped through New York harbor in the 1840s. Thus, in March 1846 Whitman deplored, in a *Brooklyn Daily Eagle* editorial, "that most abominable of all man's schemes for making money," the transatlantic slave trade. In particular, he abhorred the abysmal, often lethal conditions on board slave ships, which were to his mind "a disgrace and blot on the character of our republic, and on our boasted humanity!" Whitman described the putrid, appallingly inhumane conditions on a recently docked slave ship, the *Pons*, in which 250 of an estimated 900 kidnapped Africans had died by the time they reached New York Harbor. Of his readership, Whitman begged not only sympathy for the captured slaves, but indignation regarding their conditions: "The slave-ship! How few of our readers know the beginning of the horrors involved in that term!" "Imagine a vessel," he wrote, in which space was extraordinarily cramped, the air was close and hot, and every square inch was packed with suffering humanity: seasick, starving, giving birth, dying—"and all this for filthy lucre! Pah! we are almost a misanthrope to our kind when we think they will do such things!"[12]

It was a fiery editorial, which concluded with Whitman's suggestion that what was left of the slave trade, in Brazil for example, be suppressed and ended, through force if necessary. While this editorial represents a step forward in Whitman's understanding of the experience of enslaved Blacks in America, it is important to recognize the limitations of its argument. For one thing, Whitman was still primarily arguing from what he had read or heard, since it is unclear whether he had actually as yet seen a slave ship and its horrors in person.[13] For another, in his editorial Whitman did not technically argue for the abolition of slavery so much as against the *transatlantic trading* of Africans. And, of course, Whitman had long advocated broadly against abuses on sea as well as on prison ships.[14] Like many white Northerners of his day, even those horrified and outraged by the kidnapping of Black Africans, Whitman still did not offer a firm opinion on *domestic* slavery, which often presented itself, propagandistically, as a wholesome, bucolic alternative to the horrors of the triangular trade.

What we *can* say of Whitman's views on slavery prior to his Southern sojourn is that he at least opposed its extension. One may find, for example, editorials of his in the *Brooklyn Daily Eagle* in which he argued slavery should not be allowed in the Oregon territory (while still arguing that each state should be allowed to "evolve their notions [of abolition] as far as they wish"), nor be allowed to expand to the territory promised by future Mexican concessions (more on grounds of recognizing federal powers in early state formation, than on the belief that slavery is inherently wrong).[15] Both of these editorials referred or alluded to the Wilmot Proviso, of course, a proposed rider to an 1846 federal appropriations bill regarding the then newly begun Mexican-American conflict, in which it was proposed that

> as an express and fundamental condition to the acquisition of any territory from the Republic of Mexico by the United States, by virtue of any treaty which may be negotiated between them, and to the use by the Executive of the moneys herein appropriated, neither slavery nor involuntary servitude shall ever exist in any part of said territory, except for crime, whereof the party shall first be duly convicted.[16]

The Proviso, put forward by Representative David Wilmot of Pennsylvania and eventually nicknamed for him, did not pass, not in the form noted nor in its two subsequent iterations in 1847 and 1848, the latter of which was intended as a rider on the war-ending Treaty of Guadalupe Hidalgo. Initially ignored and downplayed by newspaper editors like Whitman, its message of "Free Soil" eventually became a rallying cry for a party formed of anti-extension, pro-worker Democrats, former Liberty Party members, and anti-slavery Whigs. The suggestion by Wilmot and other radical Democrats that slavery not be extended into new territories galvanized not only antislavery advocates but also limited-government populists who, like the Whitman of this period, were concerned with protecting the power of the white working class from anything perceived as a threat to it, be that tariffs, high postage rates, or the undue competition of slave labor in newly acquired American territories.

Little wonder that the Wilmot Proviso prominently appears in Whitman's late-1847 editorial "American Workingmen, Versus Slavery." In this piece, published prior to his trip to New Orleans, Whitman offers perhaps his most comprehensive discourse on "[t]he question whether or no there shall be slavery in new territories"[17] by taking what historian Sean Wilentz describes as a "strong Radical Democrat stance against allowing slavery into newly annexed territory."[18] Whitman's reasons, however, had little to do with the agonies of enslaved Blacks and more to do with his antipathy toward economic elites and quasi-monarchic planters. In other words, there was "*the grand body of white workingmen* [. . .] on the one side—and the interests of the few thousand rich, 'polished,' and aristocratic owners of slaves at the south, on the other side."[19] Between the two, Whitman argued that extending slavery was a bad economic proposition, since it would "bring the dignity of [white] labor down to the level of [Black] slavery," denying white northern mechanics and farmers and laborers of all kinds "*their rights, their honor, and that heritage of getting bread by the sweat of their brow*," because they would be supplanted, ostensibly, by forced Black labor.[20] Whitman concluded that "the course of moral light and human freedom" will go on, and working-class Americans (white ones, anyway) would overcome the institution, once they realized their own political value. The end of slavery, to Whitman, became a commonsense, working-class position born out of self-interest. More often than not, then, Whitman would lean on a position, as he does in his Ephraim Broadhorn sketch for the *Crescent*, that appears counterintuitive from today's perspective: popular sovereignty—i.e., that citizens of a state should decide on the (non-)extension of slavery. Whitman argues that "nine-tenths of the population of the republic"[21] did or ought to oppose slavery on the basis of workingmen's self-interest—and should not be ruled or swayed by a tiny minority of capitalists, even those in Southern states.

That said, Whitman's understanding of slavery and its horrors—before his visit to New Orleans—was still largely confined to its secondary effect on whites. The actual experience of Black Americans does not yet seem to have been in his field of vision, which was instead occupied by widespread misconceptions about Jefferson and fellow Founding Fathers as having been more antislavery than they really were.[22] For the Whitman who was about to head into the South, what defined a good American life was not merely freedom, but the freedom to work hard and earn a living. And that, in his mind, still seems to have been best exemplified by white work. Anything else was ostensibly a slavery of its own for white workers. This perspective shaped his first impressions of the Crescent City.

As Whitman would later recollect, "the city of New Orleans had been our channel and entrepot for everything, going and returning."[23] Hence, he would "remember the crowds of soldiers, the gay young officers, going or coming, the receipt of important news, the many discussions, the returning wounded, and so on [. . .]. The diagonally wedg'd-in boats, the stevedores, the piles of cotton and other merchandise, the carts, mules, negroes, etc., afforded never-ending studies and sights to me."[24] In an earlier letter to the *Sunday Times* dated March 1848, he had phrased the same observation ("mules," then "negroes") in a different language: "The Levee, with Techoupitoulas, Camp, and St. Charles streets, form one perpetual hubbub of moving life, drays, mules, niggers, barrels, bales, and so on."[25]

In particular, Whitman loved watching people—perhaps unsurprising to any reader familiar with the free verse poetry that would appear in New York less than a decade later under the title *Leaves of Grass*. "I made acquaintances among the captains, boatmen, or other characters," Whitman said of his New Orleans days, "and often had long talks with them—sometimes finding a real rough diamond among my chance encounters."[26] Later, Whitman would frame the diversity of New Orleans, especially its racial multitudes, as of particular value to him. For example, he remembered visiting the French Quarter and its Catholic cathedral: "I used to walk a good deal in this arrondissement" and later "deeply regretted [. . .] that I did not cultivate, while I had such a good opportunity, the chance of better knowledge of French and Spanish Creole New Orleans people." He would note, too, his unshakable suspicion that "there is much and of importance about the Latin race['s] contributions to American nationality in the South and Southwest."[27] Simultaneously, of course, Whitman could still decry the "timid, malignant, idle and shiftless Mexican population south of us" and emphasize the need to subjugate it.

Latin Americans were not the only people whose "contributions" were all around him; everywhere in New Orleans, Whitman saw and recorded the faces, words, and lives of Americans of color. They were integral to his budding poetic sense experiences of the bustling city, its sights, sounds, smells, tastes, and bodily temptations—so that it is little wonder that scholars have often attributed to New Orleans both Whitman's sensory and his sexual awakening. There is, for instance, Whitman's late-life recollection of a coffee seller on the streets of New Orleans:

> One of my choice amusements during my stay in New Orleans was going down to the old French Market, especially of a Sunday morning. The show was a varied and curious one; among the rest, the Indian and negro hucksters with their wares. For there were always fine specimens of Indians, both men and women, young and old. I remember I nearly always on these occasions got a large cup of delicious coffee with a biscuit, for my breakfast, from the immense shining copper kettle of a great Creole mulatto woman (I believe she weigh'd 230 pounds.) I never have had such coffee since.[28]

Even so many years later, with the help of only a few manuscript scraps Whitman had kept about his impressions of his Southern sojourn (primarily of his trip down the Mississippi River),[29] these later recollections are of cultural and racial intermixture: Native Americans, Black and mixed-race Americans, and white Americans all intermingling in a hub of market activity, where foods and drinks and wares of all kinds match the faces around him in their diversity and sensuous attraction.

This attraction was gendered. Enslaved men rarely feature—and when they do, it was not necessarily to their benefit. In a late April man-on-the-street article called "A Walk About Town," for which he signed himself "A Pedestrian," Whitman described those perambulating about the markets near his "little room near Lafayette" Square (a comment that clearly identifies him as the author). Among descriptions of sailors, longshoremen, lawyers, and people selling crabs, catfish, and the like, Whitman mentions a scene of animal cruelty: "Saw a negro throw a large stone at the head of his mule, because it would not pull an empty dray—wished I owned the negro—wouldn't treat him as he treated the mule, but make him a present of a cow-skin, and make him whip himself."[30]

It is one of the more startling moments in Whitman's oeuvre. Here the future poet of "I Sing the Body Electric"—who can already be heard in a prose-catalog anticipatory of *Leaves of Grass*[31]—indulges in a slave-owning fantasy, in which his distaste for physical cruelty paradoxically saw him wishing harm on a Black New Orleanian. The passage underscores the vast gulf of difference that could and did exist between abolitionism, anti-extensionism, and calls for the full emancipation of slaves.[32] This tension, of course, existed in Whitman himself. His unwillingness to accept full citizenship for Black Americans as late as the 1870s, which famously led to a falling-out with one of his closest friends,[33] illustrates the point. Yet it was the same ambivalent view held by the eventual presidential candidate of the Free-Soil Party, Martin Van Buren (1782–1862), who was then quite anti-abolitionist *and* famously opposed citizenship for those "of the African race."[34]

Where Black men still largely featured in the context of their labor (among mules, barrels, ships), women, as the coffee huckster memory suggests, were afforded somewhat more complexity by Whitman—especially if they were beautiful and mixed-race. One of the few *Crescent* pieces he wrote about a person of color, just weeks after his tenure began in March 1848, was about a Creole woman, a "Miss Dusky Grisette." This Dusky "is pretty well known as a very pretty *marchande des fleurs*," wrote Whitman, which in practice meant she spends much of the day selling flowers and coffee in the street and much of the night selling sexual services. Even Jeff picked up on the presence of such women, enthusiastically informing his mother (perhaps unaware of the implication): "At night too the streets are filled with women with baskets full of flowers."[35] New Orleans at the time both had the reputation for being and *was* in fact a major center for sex work, with some estimates putting prostitution as second only to the New Orleans shipping port in terms of relative economic value for the city.[36]

Whitman's account of this trade was surprisingly nuanced—certainly more nuanced than some depictions of "fallen women" in his other works (including *Leaves of Grass*). Take for instance these lines, in which Whitman contemplates men's shifting attitudes toward the Grisette character, which, following some punning on her skin color, go on to celebrate her:

> She is only interesting in character and association. Standing at, or reclining against, the door-cheeks of a store, with the brilliancy of the gas-light falling favorably, and perhaps deceptively, upon her features and upon her person, with her basket of

FIGURE 8. *Flower Girls at New Orleans, Ballou's Pictorial,* May 5, 1855, 258. The accompanying article identifies the location of the scene as Rue Royal and Canal Street. There are "two classes of the flower venders, the French and the negro," the piece comments, and many are "quite attractive in appearance."

> tasteful bouquets at her feet, and some of her choicest buds fancifully setting off her own head-dress. As such, she looks in character as a *jolie grisette*, as she is, and will excite the notice of those who, beneath the light of the sun, and in the noontide gaze of men, would spurn and loathe such familiarities.[37]

With the authorial perspective moving in and out of the point of view of a male customer of Grisette, the narrative comments on the racialized attractiveness of the sex worker and acknowledges, but does not endorse, tropes of the "ugly prostitute in daylight." In doing so it seems to point toward the racial double standard of the sexual politics Whitman witnessed around St. Charles—the very racial markings that are so playfully narrated as enticing under flickering gas lamps, serve to trigger loathing in daylight, when Grisette "perhaps" (a striking refusal to take sides) looks less appealing but (as the reader will learn) more pronouncedly African American. Racial mixing, embodied in her and practiced with her, remains unacknowledged and shunned in the harsh light of day.

But the sketch does not end there. Instead, the reader is treated to Grisette's daytime activities, too, and we learn that her nightly labors do not make up the totality of her existence. After a short rest, Grisette dons a headdress and apron to sell cheap coffee to the working class:

> Perhaps, in the morning, she sells coffee at one of the street corners, to the early draymen, who have an appetite for the regaling draught—becoming "all things to all men" in changing *tout a fait* her set of customers. [. . .]
>
> Flowers and fancy for the upper ten thousand, in the glow and excitement of evening and gas-light—but neither airs nor graces attend her, nor do flowers deck her hair as, by day-light, in the cool of the morning, she repairs to her accustomed stand, with her tin coffee-urn upon her head.[38]

We hear echoes here of Whitman's coffee huckster at the French Market in New Orleans, of course.[39] While a similar sketch might aim to elicit disgust in this mixing of food preparation and prostitution, Whitman draws from a pleasant personal memory, cherished until late in life.

Speculations about Grisette's labors do not end with her as a coffee "huckster" in the mornings. Even later that day, she will ("perhaps") work as a respectable washerwoman, helping her mother and cousin, and playfully chatting about her nighttime clientele:

> Instead of degenerating into a mere dawd, as so many beauties become during the unenchanting hours of day-light, lounging the time away, from sofa to rocking-chair, and from rocking-chair back to sofa again, with some trifle of a novel in their idle hands, Grisette, who does not know a letter in the book and, is thence fortunately secure against the seductions of popular *literature*, betakes herself, with hearty good will, to the wash-tubs.[40]

Certainly, the irksome racial punning of the sketch continues here (black coffee, white sheets, "mulatto" sex work). Yet it is worth noting that, with all of her honest labors, Grisette, in a somewhat paradoxical way, is closer to the author's idealized view of working-class womanhood celebrated throughout his fiction—the seductive sex worker herself shielded against the seduction of literature through illiteracy.[41]

In these passages, then, we might discover Whitman's most nuanced depiction of a prostitute. Grisette's sex work is just that: work. It does not define her. Instead, we find her to be an integral part of the city, moving up and down societal ranks and engaging in tabooed and racialized tasks without turning into (just) a caricature—even in an arguably (and to many modern readers uncomfortably) stereotypical humor piece. She is also the hardest worker presented in these sketches, her workday stretching from the early morning hours to late at night without much interruption. Here we find a comparatively positive depiction of a person abjected three-fold—for her gender, race, and trade—especially when contrasted with Whitman's more overtly misogynist portraits in that same series (see chapter 5).

Commentators at the time often described sex work as occurring both behind closed doors (in brothels, bars, ballrooms, and private residences) and more or less out in the open, with female and some male sex workers walking the streets—as "Dusky Grisette" does—or advertising themselves by peering, or flirting, from countless windows. Historian Judith Kelleher Schafer notes that, by one contemporary estimate, three-fifths of all New Orleans homes acted as workspaces for prostitutes, adding that interracial sex and sex work were very much the norm for the city. The racial order of New Orleans, while publicly vilifying "amalgamation" (interracial relations), also quietly approved of it, as evidenced by both interracial prostitution and the *plaçage* system, in which wealthy white men would marry white women while also secretly entering into civil unions with women of color.[42] All of this is to suggest that, during Whitman's tenure in New Orleans, prostitution was very much a part of the city's racial economy, both secretly and openly. Dusky Grisette is sexualized in much the same way as his sole previous "mulatto" character (*Franklin Evans*'s Margaret) or, perhaps, "La Cantatrice" of the unsigned 1849 story, all figuring as a source of magnetic physical power and a sexualized racial stereotype.

For Grisette *is* a racial stereotype: She is a mixed-race Creole, which Whitman implies through references to her skin and hair color (her name is "Dusky," and Whitman calls her "a *brune*, or, more prettily, a *brunette*"), her hair type ("her long glossy hair is *nearly straight*"), and her French-Creole heritage, as well as a brief allusion to the Shakespearean tragedy *Othello*.[43] Much later, Whitman would confirm as much in private conversation, when reminiscing about his time in New Orleans, where

> [t]he octoroon was not a whore, a prostitute, as we call a certain class of women here—and yet *was*, too: a hard class to comprehend: women with splendid bodies—no bustles, no corsets, no enormities of any sort: large, luminous, rich eyes: face a rich olive: habits indolent, yet not lazy as we define laziness North: fascinating, magnetic, sexual, ignorant, illiterate: always more than pretty—"pretty" is too weak a word to apply to them.[44]

One can hear echoes of Dusky Grisette here—particularly of her ambiguous social and racial status—and Whitman's later attempts to avoid questions of his own sexuality by projecting them onto Creole women in New Orleans (and the imagined children he had with them; perhaps anticipated by the fatherhood plot of "Cantatrice").[45]

Because of this ambiguity, it is hard to know what precisely to make of Whitman's "Dusky Grisette," though many scholars have made many things of her. She is independent, even powerful, the daughter of "a highly respectable washer-woman," on the one hand; on the other, she is completely hemmed in by her trade (as well as monitored by her pimp, or "daddy," as Whitman calls him). Dusky is described as arrestingly beautiful, which many early Whitman biographers took to signal Whitman's supposed sexual attraction. And she, like the coffee seller of Whitman's recollection, seems to be a fixture of her neighborhood, someone whom all know and most like. Yet she is also positioned as an economic and sexual trap for the young urban men of New Orleans, "barter[ing] off sweet looks for sweeter money."[46] The trope of the seductive Creole woman, as it is instantiated in Dusky, appears to be one of Whitman's early, pre-*Leaves* attempts to navigate the complex interplay, within a single person, of gender, race, religion, and work in antebellum American culture.

Whitman's seductive-Creole-woman stereotype remained relatively flat and consistent throughout her appearances in Whitman's early writings: a mysterious and inviting, sexually charged, and vaguely dangerous woman. One might look at her appearance in an editorial on "The Old Cathedral" of mid-April: "Our dark-eyed Creole beauties, with their gilt-edged prayer books in their hands, would walk in with an air that seemed to say that beauty was a part of religion."[47] Nevertheless, as an embodiment of three of the most prominent subaltern groups of the period—women, African Americans, and the sexually self-possessed—Dusky stands as one of Whitman's earlier attempts to capture the contradictions inherent in American life, in which one can be both languorous and hard-working, safe and dangerous, poor and prosperous, Black and white. Thus, Dusky Grisette is, as literary scholar Matt Sandler has argued, not only an aestheticized mulatto stereotype, but perhaps also a precursor of Whitman's poetic loafer figure: the "Walt" who would stand with his hand on his hip in the frontispiece of the first edition of *Leaves of Grass*, not too many years after Whitman's New Orleans visit. Sandler suggests that Whitman "saw in the mixed-race women of New Orleans a thick network of signification and later realized his difficulty in articulating what they synthesized for him."[48]

The difficulty Whitman shows over making sense of the realities around race seems to have been true not only of his encounters with New Orleanian Freedpeople, but also of those with enslaved persons, who were bought and sold daily in the city. Jeff's letters home (which Whitman read over and occasionally added to) recorded as much, as do Walt's editorials and later reminiscences, indicating that the Whitmans were, of course, well aware that they were in a slave city. It would have been impossible to ignore: There were slave markets close to Whitman's editorial office, in both Exchange Place and what is now Jackson Square. Whitman and Jeff walked by them often and almost certainly saw slaves on the auction block. Whitman's later abolitionist "A slave at auction!" section of "I Sing the Body Electric!" would appear to draw from these experiences, as did a number of his manuscripts from the 1850s that posit a speakerly stance bestriding both the slaveholding South and the personhood of those sold.

A prime example may be found in Whitman's "Talbot Wilson" notebook, much of the materials from which found their way, in revised form, into the first edition of *Leaves of Grass*. In a passage in which Whitman declares he will not "descend among professors and capitalists ~~and good society~~" but will turn "my cuffs back from my wrists and go ~~among~~ with ~~the rough~~ drivers and boatmen and men ~~who~~ that catch fish or ~~hoe corn,~~ work in the field," he also establishes a democratic, port-city poetics that weighs the slavery question without settling it, while also sounding as if Whitman had just stepped into the middle of a slave auction:

> I am the poet of slaves,
>   and of ^the masters of slaves
> I am the poet of the body
> And I am
>
> I am the poet of the body
> And I am the poet of the soul
> ~~The~~ I go with the slaves ^of the earth ^ equally with the ~~are mine, and~~
>   ~~the~~ masters ~~are equally~~ ~~mine.~~
> And I will stand between
>   the masters and the slaves,
> ~~And I~~ Entering into both, ~~and~~
>   so that both shall understand
>   me alike.[49]

It is a telling interchange, in that Whitman avoids a specific political stance on the issue of slavery (as was often the case in *Crescent* editorials) while also clearly assuming the full personhood and interiority of enslaved people. "This was the paradox of New Orleans for Whitman," Ed Folsom writes, "a place where slavery dominated but black culture was daily infusing the emerging metropolis and altering its music, the appearance of its people, the sense of what it was to be American."[50] To be an American, in body and in spirit, would, for the Whitman of *Leaves of Grass*, become an inherently multiracial identity. Even though Whitman generalized away many of the particulars of the slave/master dynamic—sounding almost biblical in his refusal to specify place, time, gender, or nationality—what readers may glean from his editorial writing, as well as from Whitman's poetic philosophy in *Leaves of*

NEGROES FOR SALE.

HAVE just arrived from Missouri with ten Negroes, which I will sell at a bargain for cash. I have several boys about 21 years of age that are very likely, strictly No. 1. One fine seamstress and house servant, very likely. Those who wish to purchase and will buy the lot I will most certainly give a great bargain. ASA Q. THOMSON.

Forks Road, Natchez, May 2, 1848.

Natchez Free Trader

May 11th '48

FIGURE 9. A May 1848 advertisement from the *Natchez Free Trader* offering Black people for sale, with Whitman's handwriting below, courtesy of the Library of Congress, Charles E. Feinberg Collection.

Grass, is that he refused to ignore the bodies of Black slaves because of the embodied nature of slavery itself. Having seen, as Folsom puts it, "the dystopia of our slave history" in New Orleans, Whitman certainly also saw "the utopia of an urban space that was blending races in previously unimaginable ways."[51] It is difficult to imagine that some of this evolution in attitude did not stem from the sight of slaves and slave auctions in New Orleans—possible proof being that when he returned to New York, Whitman brought with him an early-May slave-sale advertisement from the *Natchez Free Trader*, which he had received on the newspaper exchange and had pasted into a daybook. The notion of auctioning "bargains in human souls" (framed in the language of the ad; see Figure 9) seems to have startled Whitman at least late in his life; when rereading the advertisement four years before his death, the elderly Whitman would remark that "[i]t is a good thing to keep around as a reminder—yes, a warning."[52]

In 1848, the *Daily Crescent* itself occasionally advertised slave auctions, as well as (on rare occasions) posting runaway slave notices and making complaints about "Unruly Negroes" and "vicious slaves" who, apparently, drank in "grog shops" where they made "assignations for nefarious purposes."[53] But for their part, Whitman and his brother Jeff seem to have felt some sympathy for enslaved people, with Jeff writing home to their family, shortly after their arrival in New Orleans, that

> on Sunday morning we took a walk down to the old French church [i.e., St. Louis Cathedral, in what is now Jackson Square] and an old looking thing it is too. Every one would go up and dip their fingers in the holy water and then go home and whip their slaves. One old black took a bottle full home to wash the sins out of her family.[54]

Yet Jeff's oft-quoted recollection also reminds us of the startling complexities of race in New Orleans: the "old black" who hopes to "wash the sins out of her family." St. Louis Cathedral, of course, was racially integrated prior to the Civil War—a remnant of French Creole culture prior to the racial regime of the Confederate period and later Jim Crow laws. A recollection of an 1845 visitor to the church sounded quite Whitmanian in exclaiming: "Never had I seen such a mixture of conditions and colors [. . .] white children and black, with every shade in between, knelt side by side. In the house of prayer they made no distinction of rank or color."[55]

Catholicism in the Crescent City still maintained a strong "interracial character" that would have been surprising to the Whitmans, who were used to segregated church services, which were the norm in American antebellum Protestantism. This led, as historian of religion James B. Bennett reminds us, to "a great deal of sociability between the free colored and the rich whites" in Catholic congregations.[56] Any encounter with Catholicism in the city—during the Whitmans' frequent graveyard visits, their tours of the French Quarter (and Congo Square), their droppings-in at various churches—brought with it an illustration of a multiracial society.

The "tripartite racial structure and racial fluidity" derived from previous French and Spanish rule of New Orleans had created a social cast of *gens de couleur libres* that "legally had many of the same privileges that whites enjoyed" and were often "famous for their wealth, culture, and education." Beginning in the 1830s, this structure slowly tightened into the racial bipartite system (Black versus white) that already dominated the Anglo South elsewhere.[57] Yet when Jeff is decrying hypocrisy here, he appears to be outraged not only by white hypocrisy, but also perhaps by that of "free colored" slave owners. The "old black" that young Jeff sneered at in church might just be a slave owner herself, then, a practice not uncommon among the Creole elite, though hard for historians to quantify.[58] The complexities, and complex hypocrisies, around slavery challenged the simplistic understanding of the institution that Whitman held upon his arrival.

Clearly, the Whitman who in his poem "Blood-Money," one of his first free-verse publications, only two years later would compare the slave sold on the auction block to Christ sold by Judas—who would write in his unpublished pamphlet *The Eighteenth Presidency!* that "you are either to abolish slavery, or it will abolish you"—*this* Whitman understands Black slavery very differently than the Whitman we find in the columns of the *Crescent*.[59] They, of course, wrote to different audiences and therefore required different strategies. Whitman's private letters, notes, etc., from the time are largely lost. Yet we have occasional glimpses, in Whitman's writings of the period, of a potential simmering change of attitudes. In a post-New Orleans letter to his old editors, dated August 17, 1848, Whitman wrote:

> Our city streets present a plentiful sprinkling of well-dressed, bronze-faced personages, from the West Indies—families who have removed hither in consequence of the troubles among the slaves of those regions. A great many hundreds of these West Indians are in town. They must affect lounging in Broadway; and their easy, indolent air, sometimes exemplified in the person of a fine-looking brunette, may be seen on that famous pavement, at almost any hour of the day.[60]

There are many echoes here of Whitman's previous writings regarding people of color in America, both enslaved and Freedpeople, particularly his discourses regarding the physical features and attitudinal characteristics of Black Americans in the South. His description of their faces as "bronze," of the occasional "fine-looking brunette" (gender unspecified), of their "easy, indolent air," much like the "flower girls" he had previously described: all of these details suggest that the Whitman of this period still "aestheticizes the encounter" with Black Americans, as Matt Sandler puts it, as a kind of external reading of typological characteristics: skin color, hair color, beauty, formality of dress, apparent indolence. At the same time, however, there is the suggestion that, for

Whitman, Black Americans could now also embody the same sort of urban "loaferism"—the lounging, lackadaisical, "indolent air"—of the sort that he would shortly celebrate in *Leaves of Grass* and would defend in his late-life descriptions of Creole sex workers. Furthermore, correspondent Whitman seemed pleased to see this newly arrived "plentiful sprinkling of well-dressed, bronze-faced personages, from the West Indies"—a sight that Whitman would have remembered well from New Orleans but not seen nearly so often in Manhattan or small-town Brooklyn. Perhaps, then, Whitman would come to remember his months in New Orleans not only for their sensuousness and self-actualizing catalyzation, but also for the mere fact of seeing people of color among the multitude. As Whitman would later insist in "Song of Myself," "I see not merely that you are polite or whitefaced . . . . married or single . . . . citizens of old states or citizens of new states," but also "the free Utahan, Kansian, or Arkansian," "the free Cuban," and "the slave."[61]

That freedom from slavery also seems to be underscored in his letter; the writer, after all, suggests that these "West Indians [. . .] have removed hither in consequence of the troubles among the slaves of those regions"—probably a reference to the slave revolt of St. Croix, which led to the emancipation of all slaves in the Danish West Indies in 1848. While it is unclear what his position on the rebellion itself may be, it *is* clear from the positively valenced adjectives used to describe them—"well-dressed," "easy," "fine-looking"—that they are a welcome enough presence to Whitman, who may have felt a connection with them that exceeds mere externalities, instead looking inward to the connections between their love of the street, of lounging, of New York, and his own. One of the core tenants of Whitman's beliefs that remained unchanged over time was his unilateral embrace of immigration. His description of these former slaves echoed such attitudes without qualification.

Yet it may do more than that. At the time, emancipation in the (British) West Indies had long been a talking point in the proslavery South, with notorious figures like John C. Calhoun pointing at its "ruinous" effect on the sugar industry "to show that Slavery of the African is a blessing, and a natural condition of society, productive of the greatest prosperity."[62] Whitman, on the other hand, was not evoking immigrants from the West Indies as threats or lessons but, ostensibly, as *neighbors*—a normal part of the urban experience of New York. Speaking in the guise of a typical Manhattanite, Whitman extends his "urban affection" to these "personages." They fit right in, it seems, with all the other loafers, loungers, dandies, and pretty ladies promenading in the North. And, perhaps, "northern bird" Whitman can now see himself in them.

Perhaps it was Whitman's flaneur persona—begun in his earlier journalism and arguably perfected in New Orleans—that seems to enable him to transcend some of his narrower concerns about the political expediency of the "issue" of Black Americans. His writings in and letters to the *Crescent* not only fill in a gap in Whitman's New Orleans record but suggest themselves as a place of journalistic professionalization as well as genre experimentation. In the end, Whitman would pursue this impetus toward typification into the poetic innovation that are his verse catalogs, into which Black life was written from the beginning, further underscoring its centrality to the ongoing American poetic project.

White, working-class men were at the forefront of Whitman's thinking as he arrived in New Orleans in the spring of 1848. They formed the core of his political thinking, his systems of professional and personal friendships, and his sexual identity. Yet racial crossing, embodied by French and Creole societies, and the presence of complex Black cultures in New Orleans's urban space, began increasingly to define the cosmopolitan experience for Whitman. In his first weeks in the office, Whitman mingled with the masses—and found in their various modes of sociability novel ways of negotiating his own identity within and without societally approved systems of belonging. This negotiating takes place in the pages of the *Crescent*—which was ready to publish its first issue on March 5, 1848.

CHAPTER 4

I dream'd that was the new City of Friends;
Nothing was greater there than the quality of robust love—it led the rest;
It was seen every hour in the actions of the men of that city,
And in all their looks and words

—WHITMAN, "I DREAM'D IN A DREAM" (1860)

City of Men

DURING THEIR FIRST MONTH IN THE CITY, the Whitmans would encounter the democratic *en masse* of culturally and racially mixed New Orleans everywhere: at many public events, whether it be a simple Sabbath stroll,[1] St. Patrick's Day,[2] the comedic stylings of Irishman John Collins at the Armory Hall Theatre,[3] or at several failed attempts by a French woman to fly a large balloon at Poydras Street, within earshot of the Whitmans' boarding house.[4] The latter spawned multiple editorials by Walt, ending on the observation that a group of "b'hoys thought they had been fooled too often—and they tore down the boards of the enclosure, and seizing the unfortunate balloon, trailed it through the streets, and tore it into pieces not more than an inch in width."[5]

No festival, though, compared to Mardi Gras. Any "nervous young lady, or a hysterical old grandmamma, would not have been frightened into fits at the sight of the hideous masques," Walt wrote in the third issue of the *Crescent* about the prior day's events. The Catholic festival was a raucous affair, with processions that would start early in the day and pass right below the *Crescent*'s office windows. According to other papers, the day also typically featured "mischievously disposed men and boys, who assaulted the maskers by throwing flour, mud, clubs, stones, and other offensive weapons at them."[6] Whitman, on the other hand, praised the affair, somewhat tongue-in-cheek, for its peacefulness, writing "We do not believe that more than a dozen fights took

FIGURE 10. Photographic view from Lafayette Square (c. 1867), by Theodore Lilienthal, courtesy of the Louisiana State Museum (1979.120.066). The reconstructed St. Charles Hotel (without its dome) can be seen in the center. Tremont House, the boardinghouse where the Whitmans stayed, had likely perished in the flames as well. The *Crescent* office building, however, was still extant and is plainly visible (detail below).

place."[7] At night, masked balls concluded the festivities. Clearly, the Crescent City was rowdy, bustling, and kept the Whitman brothers well entertained.

New Orleans's cosmopolitan flair certainly rang true for the *Crescent* office. The paper was located above a busy dance studio on the second floor of a red brick, four-story building that faced the central thoroughfare of the city's Anglophone sector:[8] St. Charles Street, home to the eponymous theatre with its enormous, marble dome (destroyed by a fire in 1851) and the famed Verandah Hotel, whose influence on New Orleans architecture can still be felt today. To its north clustered oyster bars, theaters, and saloons and to its south lay beautiful Lafayette Square, framed by administrative buildings (including City Hall) and ornate churches and a favorite for civilized Sunday outings. Lafayette Square's majestic, old live oaks may have inspired Whitman's famous "Live-Oak, with Moss" manuscripts.[9]

At the *Crescent*, the bulk of the writing duty was shared between Whitman and two colleagues: George Washington Reeder (c. 1822–48) and John Cooper Larue (1817–56). The former, a Maryland-born Protestant[10] Irish nationalist[11] was the local news and police reporter and likely spent a lot of time at the Recorder's Courts. Reeder was described as a "most lively sketch writer [and] an ardent patriot" who had served with future president Zachary Taylor in Mexico[12] despite a "frail" constitution. He was also an "amateur comedian" of "microscopic size," "not over four feet six inches [with] singularly youthful appearance and given to a pompous, overwhelming, elaborate politeness"—and, in Whitman's memory, a drunkard.[13] Most of Reeder's writings would likely fill the third page of the *Crescent*, with the previous two reserved for Walt and the New Jersey native Larue.[14] The latter was a local defense attorney,[15] Democratic member of the Louisiana Legislature (which met in New Orleans then),[16] and a former military advisor in Mexico; he leaned radical, even communist, in his politics.[17] His caustic style was widely known. Though admired by Whitman, Larue failed to gain popularity as a writer and politician, which his own obituaries connected to a vinegary personality. Larue advocated for a French Republic at public meetings,[18] and "generally prepared the leading editorials" of the *Crescent*, according to Whitman's memory recalled in old age.[19] Considering his extensive political commitments, Larue likely did not show up to the office every day, and much of the editorializing took place via Whitman's news columns—arguably the focus of the *Crescent*. As a result the paper was light on the kind of lead editorials that characterized more traditionally partisan presses, Larue's occasional micro-essay on economic or political philosophy notwithstanding.

Then there was Durant Da Ponte (1829–94), a New York-raised descendent of a famous Italian singer, just four years older than Jeff.[20] Da Ponte was multilingual and was tasked with translation and miscellanea. In addition, he appears to have authored some poems for the *Crescent* as "D." and republished verses by his mother.[21] Other occasional contributions included letters by a solid roster of long-term correspondents as well as poems by the aforementioned Theodore A. Gould, Matt Field (uncle of journalism icon Kate Field), and an Irish sailor going by the name "Jack Waterways," who was said to drop off verses when on shore leave[22] (but who may just have been a fanciful persona adopted by a local journalist).

In the late 1840s, New Orleans had become "a magnet for [. . .] floating population[s], offering a diverse range of employment, from counting rooms to docks. It was a regular army and navy recruiting depot in peacetime and a volunteer depot not only for the American invasion of Mexico but for filibustering campaigns and the wars of the Texas Republic."[23] As a result, many of these men were transitory, young, and unattached: fortune-seekers en route to the goldfields of California, traders, fighters, drifters. Whitman captured their essence in a series of humorous sketches with a noticeably non-native bent. Of his thirteen-part series "Sketches of the Sidewalks and Levee; With Glimpses into the New Orleans Bar (rooms.)," the first installment of which was published on March 13,[24] half of the sketched characters have an explicit migration background. We find there, for instance, an impoverished Philadelphia businessman, a French oyster peddler, an Irish laborer, a Texan cutthroat, a Tennessean clerk, and a flatboatman from Kentucky. Especially the latter, going by the name of "Ephraim Broadhorn," seems to embody more than an inkling of Whitman's own experiences. It certainly echoes his fascination with the "tall, strapping, comely young men" he noted during the *St. Cloud*'s stops in that state.[25]

The Broadhorn piece, the final installment in the "Sketches" series, is a short tale of a country bloke arriving on a Mississippi flatboat and clashing with New Orleans culture and customs. It jibes with a number of future moments in Whitman's writings,[26] among them, of course, the reference to "The flatboatmen mak[ing] fast toward dusk near the cottonwood or pekantrees" in what would later be titled "Song of Myself."[27] Whitman encountered such trade vessels frequently on his way down to New Orleans, but he had also been primed by one of his favorite visual artists of the mid-1840s: George Caleb Bingham—a highly specific instance that can also be located in the Broadhorn sketch. Whitman loved the Missouri painter's famous *The Jolly Flatboatmen* (Figure 11), set on the Mississippi. It was shown in New York City's Art Union in 1846 and made the painter's career as *the* artist to imagine the democratic promise of the West for a Northeastern, urban audience. Whitman had seen the painting before leaving for New Orleans, and it had primed him for his Southern trip.[28] The Broadhorn sketch certainly seems to echo Bingham's vibrant painting:

FIGURE 11. *The Jolly Flatboatmen* (1846), by George Caleb Bingham, courtesy of the National Art Gallery.

> Ephraim became "one of 'em," and at the age of thirty or upwards, was as unsophisticated a double specimen of Yankee and the Hoosier as ever trod the streets of Orleans in a pair of coarse brogans. It was some time during the past spring that Ephraim landed his flatboat at the Levee, and we chanced to see him as he jumped ashore. His dress was in three pieces—shirt, trowsers and straw hat: the former soiled by a fortnight's wear and tear at the oar, amid sweat and sunshine; the second was "more holy than righteous," as he himself expressed it, and his old straw hat was in keeping with the balance of his apparel. He was not only sunburnt but sunbrowned—hair and beard both lank and long, and reddened by exposure.

The outfits, attitude, and suntans are a perfect match, and we can even identify brogans in the painting. *The Jolly Flatboatmen*, like the Broadhorn sketch, depicts a moment of jubilation over a job well done, interpreted as an expressive, natural republicanism.

Perhaps Ephraim, on his "first visit to Orleans," also reflects Whitman's own attitudes during his first weeks in the Southern metropolis, as he marvels at the "renowned *omnium gatherum* [. . .] [of] the crowd[s]" pushing through throughfares and past levees. He, too, saw himself as "a sovereign, a 'dimocrat,' a one of the b'hoys [. . .] wandering about the streets of New Orleans 'to see the elephant.'" Of course, the Kentucky flatboatman is more of a country bumpkin than Long Island native Whitman ever was, so Walt couldn't help but close his sketch with a nod toward the erotic possibilities of the fluid mass of New Orleans —read in a bumbling misunderstanding over French:

> "Qu'est—ce que c'est?" asked the French gentleman in perfect surprise, as much unable to comprehend Ephraim's Kentucky dialect, as the latter was to understand accents of the Parisian vernacular.
>
> "Kiss who, did you say?" said Ephraim. "Why, I'll be darned if I've seed any body in Orleans that a feller would want to kiss—such a variety of white humans, and black humans, and yaller humans!"

Many of Whitman's sketches for the *Crescent* depict such men who were, like himself, "on the make." Historian Brian Luskey has described youths like Whitman, by example of New York City clerks, as a culturally significant, "unsupervised masculine cohort [. . .] living as boarders in the city," on a quest for respectability and financial stability.[29] These men were, summarizes Jason Stacy, "pioneers of a new consumer culture, where work depended upon a modicum of literacy and the ability to present a respectable image without much capital."[30] Propelled by an egalitarian "ideology of self-making" but lacking the "access to the credit, capital and connection" of a burgeoning bourgeois class, these men became conflicted figures in the American urban imagination of the antebellum period.[31] Accused of lounging, womanizing, and dandyism but also lauded for their "self-made" spirit, they naturally become a focus of Whitman's writings in these years.

Whitman's sketch of "John J. Jinglebrain" (published March 28), for instance, embodies all that culture thought amiss about these new urban men. "No man has greater horror of the restraints which a business occupation imposes," Whitman writes of his protagonist, "than this same dandy [. . . .] He has no ostensible occupation, no business office, no fortune that he has inherited, no 'old man' of a father or an uncle who is very rich and very indulgent, and yet he always has a plenty of money."[32] This young man is neither of old wealth, nor a go-getter—he is a "lounging clerk," a paradoxical creature fantasized about in the antebellum press as embodying all the perils of unchecked social mobility in the city.[33] Consequently, Jinglebrain "boards at one of the crack hotels," "*dawdles* about," obsesses over dress, and is full of vain, literary ambition. He may look like a real man, but he is not: beware "those who have no souls, and who regard only the corporeal outside of the living man," Whitman warns.[34]

If clerk culture caused a crisis in the "meaning of class and masculinity,"[35] as Luskey suggests, the itinerant writer Whitman, hanging out nightly at New Orleans's impressive barrooms, was well aware of it. A man like himself had to constantly balance between the rugged masculinity of an Ephraim Broadhorn and the literary dandyism of a Jinglebrain. One of the first writings he likely produced at the *Crescent* was an editorial note on the Boston Mercantile Library Association, praising specifically a speech given by journalist Daniel Haskell that advocated for the grievances of the clerking class. The *Crescent* note called the address "one of the best of the kind we have ever read [. . .] being written in a manly, straightforward, fearless style."[36] In the excerpted text, Haskell bemoans (and the *Crescent* agrees) that "in many departments of business, the compensation allowed to clerks is so small [. . .] it drives away a large and meritorious class of young men," thus granting the "sons of wealthy men [. . .] a monopoly of the places." As the son of an often-penniless carpenter, this resonated with Whitman. Lack of appropriate remuneration, he insisted, was not merely an individual crisis but a structural problem for the fraternity of clerks and for masculinity at large. Instead of toward men on the make, mercantile life was shifting toward men of means, which threatened to "substitute [the] swell manners and flash appearance of the rogue, for the gentlemanly bearing and manly dignity of the good citizen."[37]

For the new, mobile men of New Orleans, the future men's health expert Whitman reminds us,[38] masculinity was not a given, but required effort. His sketch of a "Samuel Sensitive," published in the spring and summer of 1848, demonstrated what this may look like. The two-parter was Whitman's lengthiest fictional piece in the *Crescent* and likely also his most popular one, quickly reprinted across the US. It, too, focused on a typical clerk figure: a young man from the interior of the country (Tennessee) who would end up in the city as the "first clerk in the mercantile house of Messrs. Pork, Produce & Co."[39] Before settling in New Orleans, however, this man, too, falls victim to the temptations of dress and peddles undergarments, "pantaloons, and cravats" for a local tailor. Employing a tried-and-true Shakespearean genital pun,[40] Whitman describes Samuel's descent into the South and the realm of counter jumping as his "descent upon these regions below—these lower regions." Urban, unattached men, this poet-journalist knew, must assert and negotiate their sexuality in the marketplace. A professional apprenticeship always also constituted sexual self-making.

As in Whitman's case, the big city was full of "seductions" for Samuel, the young clerk. "Handsome in person, well grown for the years, skilled in the mystery of dress, and, withal, a real dabster with a steel pen," Whitman quipped, "what could hinder him from making a figure in the world?"[41] Spending all of his money on sensual frivolities, Samuel almost succumbs forever to the dangers of dandyism and depravity. That is, until "the meshes of love, and then [. . .] the web and entanglement of matrimony" save him. Lost in the temptations of a life on the make, only marriage and matrimony rescue sensitive Samuel's soul. "Those who only know women in the haunts and kennels of sensuality," Whitman reminded the young, urban men reading his paper, "are widely ignorant of the real nature of the sex," which served to cultivate men's desires.[42] Obviously, the *Crescent* was not a sporting paper. Matrimony to Whitman constituted necessary chains put on men's proclivities. While he allowed himself to celebrate all manners of masculine enjoyment in the city—from cockfights to prostitution—he knew well enough what sentimental instruction his broad readership required of their daily reading.

In his writings in the *Crescent*, then, Whitman continues his writerly "response to attacks on clerk masculinity,"[43] negotiating his unease over his own journeyman status through newspaper prose. In 1848, Whitman was struggling with the political valence of these questions: If Free-Soilism would form into a party of workingmen, what *kind* of workingmen would those be? At the time, he seemed to favor the rugged men out West: farmers, homesteaders, no-nonsense gruffs. Yet in reality, Whitman was much more closely aligned with the various dandy and sporting characters in the Crescent City whom he satirized. One need only look as far as Whitman's famed New Orleans daguerreotype, in which he aped French urban style—not the rugged American manliness he valorized elsewhere. Yet, at the same time, Whitman was decrying the economic reasons that kept men like him in a contested status of masculinity: the kind of floating freelancing labor that generated masculine urban culture but also made rising within it a dubious prospect at best. Whitman's future politics of "Free Soil, Free Labor, Free Men" would, then, also always be an attempt to "save" American masculinity, culminating in such documents as his "Manly Health and Training" guide—and, one might argue, *Leaves of Grass*.[44]

Of course, Whitman's own journey of self-making in the southern metropolis has long been cast as one of personal crises and sexual awakenings. As underscored by his homoerotically charged sketches of handsome men (Samuel, Ephraim, etc.), which occasionally quoted the notoriously queer poet Fitz-Greene Halleck (and, of course, Byron), Whitman was not just taken by the multitudinous nature of New Orleans but also by its sheer masculine eros. As tour guide Norman wrote, a significant portion of the city's mobile population was made up of "principally males," of which "many are bachelors [. . .] who live at the hotels and boarding houses" and constituted almost half of the "business men of the city."[45] Urban masculine culture was booming in the Crescent City, and Whitman was right in the middle of it. His resulting sketches were boardinghouse fiction.[46] His pen was cruising.

In his late-life recollections, Whitman was notoriously reticent to discuss these experiences, even overcompensating with his famous homophobic fib of having fathered children in the South.[47] But some of his close associates were not. The aforementioned Gould, the Brooklyn transplant frequently puffed by Whitman's *Crescent*, was quite direct about the goings-on around the St. Charles Hotel, close to where Whitman lived. In a later series for the *Brooklyn Daily Eagle*, Gould recounted the local nightlife scene as follows:

> Sitting, standing, walking, talking, smiling, laughing, lolling, leaning, thinking, swearing, strolling and drinking, were representatives from every part of the world. The exemplary and the profligate—priests, pirates, statesmen, fops, fools, gamblers, gold diggers, etc., etc., all mingled in most grotesque confusions. Embryo heroes, en route to Mexico, conversing with pomp of vanity, with old, tired, battle-scarred veterans. Hoosiers, also, with rough coats, gaping mouths, staring eyes, and independent stride. City merchants, in groups discoursing of trade. Little knots of blustering bravos, "mysteriously affectionate."[48]

Even for a faraway Brooklyn paper, the language here appears to have needed no further elaboration. One can almost see confirmed bachelor Gould wink as he placed quotation marks around that last phrase.

Mysterious affections were not confined to Whitman's after-work activities. The young journalist would, for instance, have encountered the relationship of his two employers (McClure and Hayes) as an association that seemed to practice the very concept of comradeship he later celebrated in his writings. Both, of course, were former "men on the make" who actually "made" it. While it is notoriously tricky to ascribe sexual identities or practices to historical figures ostensibly silent on the issue, the documented echoes of the shared life of McClure and Hayes provide more than a little evidence to counter the long-prevailing trend of heterosexualizing the past.[49] Considering that Whitman's time in New Orleans has long been hypothesized as a reckoning with "gay" identity, it becomes prudent, then, to briefly sketch out the shared queer life of John Eliot McClure and Alexander Hamilton Hayes—even where it extended beyond their encounter with Whitman.

McClure likely first met Hayes in his late twenties in the offices of the *Daily Picayune*. Hayes, three years his senior, was a practical printer and served as the foreman;[50] McClure acted as an accounting clerk for the Whig paper. Their respective responsibilities would stay the same throughout their various ventures: the quiet, diligent McClure overseeing finances,[51] and the more adventurous, straightforward typographer Hayes "in charge of the mechanical department."[52] Their journey continued in this way when the two joined other newspapermen to found the *Daily Delta* in 1845 and, finally, the *Crescent* in 1848.

Both were primarily practical businessmen and likely contributed few writings to the paper. One of the few exceptions was McClure's poetic goodbye to his readers, when faced with his own mortality after contracting cholera in late 1848. While we now know that Whitman's association with the *Crescent* outlasted his time in the South, it may have been this poem—and the resignation by McClure that followed—that had Whitman end his continued mail contributions to the paper. Notably, the poem is addressed "to M. of N.Y." Whitman, at that time, was serving as the paper's New York correspondent under the pen name "Manhattan" (which we discuss at greater length in chapter 8).

A NEW YEAR EPISTLE TO M. OF N. Y.

No poet's art directs the willing pen
To guide my fancy's wandering, potent ken—
Parnassus holds the gift of Muse too dear,
To crown with song each scholar's tame career.
Yet will I dedicate this humble lay
To thee, fair friend, an offering of the day,
The natal morn illumes the world's domain!—
The festal season smiles on us again!
'Tis we'l; for Hope, dress'd out in radiant gear,
Is sure to greet us on the glad New Year.
How fares the day with thee? My fancy swells
To thoughts of sleighs, furs, mirth and jingling bells;
Borne furious on, in great o'erteeming joy.
Is't so? then bliss be thine, with unalloy.
This life is made of changeful days and nights,
Therefore, 'tis best be glad while mirth invites;
It matters not, if foul or fair the weather,
We should rejoice that friends *can* meet together.
What tho' old Father Time brings some dark hours
To gloom our days, like transient April showers,
Our brightest joys are born of sorrow's shroud;
As sunniest day is ushered by a cloud.
Well, and what of thy friend? How goes with him
This welcome holyday? Alas! 't would brim
Thine eye-lids, did the capsulate unfold
The panoramic picture Truth doth hold.
The prince of Asiatic scourge e'en drives his car
Triumphant o'er the town—the gods make war
With man; and gloom sits brooding in each breast,
To view the city all in morning dressed.
Our vacant marts, deserted streets, unburnished arms.
Funereal biers, attest the sad alarms.
Yet *fear* exaggerates the real extent,
And many die, whose fate might else relent.
A few, more blessed with hope, cry "peace, 'tis o'er;
Your orisons are faithless if ye murmur more."
For one, I am content to 'bide my destiny,
And calmly wait the end of God's decree.
Meantime, I'll end this unpretending verse—
(Wishing it were better—thankful it's no worse,)
By tendering the courtesies, which time
And leisure bid me render into rhyme.
O may the years that come and go,
So cherish joy and banish wo,
That every smiling New Year's dawn
Shall happier be than seasons gone.
Life, health and peace, e'en be thy lot,
In palace, hall, or lowly cot.
Green be thy path, in thought and dream,
As glides the pure St. Lawrence' stream
Where thousand islands spring to view—
Thus may thy life its course pursue. J.

New Orleans, Jan. 1, 1849.

FIGURE 12. Poem by "J." to "M. of N.Y.," in New Orleans *Daily Crescent* (January 1, 1848), Duke University Rubenstein Rare Book and Manuscript Library. The poem was printed right above the "Correspondence" section.

The poem was printed on the first page, right atop letters by the *Crescent*'s incoming New York correspondent, who would replace Whitman's "Manhattan" under the name "Indicator."[53] McLure's farewell was a moving good-bye "Epistle" from a man anticipating death, printed in the newspaper he created, and sent through the newspaper exchange to New York, where it was received by Whitman, then managing the mails for another daily (the *Freeman*). Reading over the piece, one might even be tempted to accidentally misread the poet's name, suggested by a poorly kerned beginning of a line ("With man").[54]

McClure, however, survived his brush with death. Still, he was experiencing lasting effects, and, on March 7, 1849, his name was dropped from the masthead of the *Crescent*. A note from Hayes explains his departure:

> The continued ill health of Mr. McClure, has made it desirable for him to seek some relaxation from the arduous labors connected with the business of publication, and he has, also, disposed of his interest to Mr. William Walker, of this city. [. . .] That we regret to part with our former associate, it would be idle for us to say. Those who have known the intimate connexion between us, only can appreciate the feeling.[55]

We know, in fact, the amount of the payment from Walker because McClure lost the promissory note (privately operated paper currency) and ran an ad for it as a "lost item" in the *Crescent* a few days later. In total, McClure earned $1,040 for his shares.[56]

The split, even with Hayes emphasizing the "intimate connexion" that existed between the two men, was not merely a professional one. Soon, both separated their lives more fully and instead formed intense attachments with other men: Hayes followed editor William Walker to California in 1850, where the Nicaragua filibuster ultimately abandoned him, after the two founded another newspaper (the *New Eureka*).[57] Walker, of course, has long been described by historians as a man who had sex with men.[58] McClure, on the other hand, became involved with the restaurateur Sam Weir (c. 1817–57) and led a life as his business partner and *de facto* spouse. Together, the two ran a famous oyster saloon on St. Charles Street, just a block away from the *Crescent* office (see Figure 13). When the unmarried Weir died in 1857, McClure was listed as a quasi-next of kin: "His friends, and those of J. E. McClure, are requested to attend" his funeral, the local chapter of the fraternal order of Odd Fellows announced.[59] Following his partner's death, McClure continued to work in the hospitality business—but not before taking on Weir's first name as a nickname. He is still often listed as "'Sam'

FIGURE 13. Ad for Sam's Saloon, in Amos W. Bell's *The State Register: Comprising an Historical and Statistical Account of Louisiana* (Baton Rouge, LA: T. B. R. Hatch, 1855), viii, courtesy of Sam Houston State University. This would have been the view from the Whitmans' boardinghouse, located at 102 St. Charles, just across the street from Sam Weir's saloon.

McClure" in Whitman scholarship, with no acknowledgement of the history encoded into that name.[60]

The story of McClure and Hayes did not end with their split in 1850, however. After a turn of fortune, years of gold-digging in California, adventures in Texas, and (so it was rumored) travels in Japan and China, Hayes appears to have missed New Orleans. In 1860 he stopped for a brief visit: "Time has silvered his hair, but planted no wrinkles, and his eye is as keen and bright as ever," the *Picayune* noted.[61] More visits followed. On November 22, 1866, however, Hayes's trip to the Crescent City was to be his final one, Hayes having decided "to breathe his last in this place, among old friends," as his former paper speculated.[62] Hayes collapsed stepping out of his carriage and "fell into the arms of an accompanying friend"[63] and was transported to a nearby hotel, where he expired. "During his last moments, his devoted friends McClure and Westerfield, were with him."[64] McClure, of course, was also present at Hayes's interment in the crypt of the Typographer's Union in New Orleans's Greenwood Cemetery.[65] Hayes, who had been his partner for two decades, had returned to die by McClure's side.

McClure himself died three years later, at the same age as Hayes, and was buried with full fraternal ritual in a Masonic crypt, within eyesight of Hayes's final resting place (Figure 14). Neither man had ever married or fathered any children. While the intimate details of their relationship have left no historical record, it is clear that it was the longest and, it seems, most meaningful attachment in either of these men's lives.

To McClure and Hayes, the "erotic and emotional institution[s]" of New Orleans business culture[66] afforded them a secular, mercantile vocabulary to emulate the legal conventions of marriage: it was not the *persons* McClure and Hayes that ran the *Crescent*, for instance, but the company "Hayes & M'Clure," operated jointly. Incorporation, it seems, served as another way to ritualize sharing a common name that went beyond what was required of co-owners of, say, a newspaper or an oyster saloon—but all in a manner that did not overtly violate cultural conventions reserved for matrimony.

The *Crescent* did rub up against sexual norms in one particular case and, like Whitman's later brush with censorship of his poems, it initially

FIGURE 14. Photo by the authors, taken in 2024, of the tombs of McClure (Tomb of the Masonic Order, at left) and Hayes (Tomb of the Typographical Union, at right center) in the Greenwood Cemetery, New Orleans. No name inscriptions survive, but the interments of both are confirmed in cemetery records.

had little to do with queer expression. Instead, the controversy focused on female-centric art deemed pornographic: The performance group known as the Model Artists organized by sideshow mesmerist "Dr." Robert Hanham Collyer (1814–91) had caused a major moral panic across the United States, spawned countless seedy imitators, and finally drove its frustrated creator to an early retirement.[67] Now often characterized as a form of burlesque[68] or striptease,[69] the traveling theater show recreated famous statues and paintings in the flesh as *tableaux vivants*, put on by well-proportioned actors who, though not technically nude, presented themselves "cased in flesh-colored silk netting, tight to each person"[70] on rotating platforms, accompanied by music.[71] The effect seemed so believable, Whitman kept referring to the beauty of "the undraped figure" in his writings about these performances.[72]

To add more kindling to the moralists' fires, Collyer's tableaux generally recreated nude originals, often with overt sexual overtones, including a number of themes playing with orientalism and miscegenation. The fact that Collyer was best known to readers for his sensationalist account of the New York underworld *Lights and Shadows of American Life* didn't help quell worries about the indecency of his performances. In New Orleans, for instance, the troupe performed many iterations of the "Circassian Slave" motif (i.e., harem scenes),[73] accompanied by rousing, exotic music, such as a performance by "the celebrated Ethiopian band of SABLE MELODISTS" (shortly after Whitman's tenure).[74] As Ettore Rella put it: "The good doctor was trying to bridge nineteenth[-] century prudery (with its concomitant sentimentality for the old and classical) and the popular demand."[75] "Prurient interest," as historian David Monod called it, clearly was a driving force in the booming success of the enterprise.[76] Consequently, papers across the United States quickly began condemning Collyer and his troupe, especially as more and more risqué imitators began popping up in less respectable parts of town.[77] Even in New Orleans, Collyer was performing at the same time as other "model artists" inspired but not sanctioned by him.

Collyer's reputation clearly preceded him. When he arrived in New Orleans in March of 1848, he had just been barred from any and all future performances in Baltimore by a Joint Committee of Police,[78] and in the deep South the air was similarly charged against him: soon after his arrival, Collyer put a man on trial for threatening to "'cut his thread of life' and to do diverse other things too numerous to mention" but was turned down by the Recorder Courts.[79] And just a few weeks into performing, the group was summarily banned by the mayor of New Orleans after he saw them perform at the St. Charles[80]—even though illustrious figures like Gideon Johnson Pillow and Zachary Taylor came to attend the scandalous performance (alongside Whitman).[81]

"After leaving New Orleans in disgrace," Collyer was then banned from appearing in Vicksburg and Memphis,[82] put on trial in Philadelphia,[83] and called in front of Boston Aldermen to defend his scandalous tenure in New Orleans. The latter effort was led by a group of outraged citizens who had heard that "a woman whom Dr. Collyer called his wife, danced at the [New Orleans] St. Charles Theatre in the nude state and that the Doctor danced with her." The troupe director allegedly countered with a threat to "flog [the outraged citizen] until there was not a grease-spot left to show that such a man ever existed."[84] Perhaps not surprisingly, permission for Collyer to perform in Boston was not granted.

Whitman was thrilled when he heard the Model Artists program was en route to New Orleans. "Dr. Collyer's 'model artists' [. . .] appear to-night at the St. Charles theatre," he wrote to the *Sunday Times*. "Everybody is anxious to *see the one whom Mr. Clay kissed*— 'Psyche.'"

It had been rumored that former US Senator (and perpetual presidential candidate) Henry Clay had fallen for this particular performer during a show in the capital and rushed on stage to kiss her—thrice.[85] Collyer knew what he was doing. One of the tableaux advertised for that night at the St. Charles was titled "Psyche Going to Bathe." It would be a performance "intended especially for the study of the *connoisseurs* and *artists*," the troupe advertised with an italicized wink.[86] At the prudish *Eagle*, Whitman could not have offered his support to such a scandalous troupe,[87] but the *Crescent* was more open-minded.

Whether or not any technically nude dancing took place in New Orleans, Whitman decided to bend the whole weight of his paper to supporting these scandalous performances, in multiple, often lengthy editorials. He lambasted the "sickly prudishness" of the group's critics[88] and countered critiques of the morality of quasi-nude *tableaux vivants* into a full-throated defense of the nude human body:[89]

> The only objection that we conceive of to the undraped figure, arises from an assumption of coarseness and grossness intended. Take away this, and there is no need (in the cases under discussion) of any objection at all. Eve in Paradise—or Adam either—would not be supposed to shock the mind. Neither would the sight of those inhabitants of the Pacific Islands, whose nakedness is, or was, the innocent and usual custom. Neither does the sight of youth, among us or any where else. And, so stern and commanding is the potency of genius, even over the vulgar—neither do copies of the Venus de Medicis; for the prude dare not open his mouth against what the world, for many a year, has pronounced divine. [. . .] Amid all the works of that Power which, in the most stupendous systems and the smallest objects in them, shows such unspeakable harmony and perfection, nothing can compare with the human master-piece, his closing and crowning work! It is a master-piece in itself, not as it is furbelowed off by the milliner and tailor. Nor would it be altogether uninteresting to pursue the inquiry how far artificial ideas on the subject of swaddling this work, so much in vogue among civilized nations—and barring off the contemplation of its noble and beautiful proportions—how far, we say, these

> practices may have aided in the effect of diminishing the average amplitude and majesty of the form, which effect must be confessed to when comparing present times with the age of the old Grecians and Latins.
>
> As for the Model Artists, we know excellent women, and men, too, who have attended their performances with rational gratification [. . .].[90]

The phrase "rational gratification" is, of course, key here as it indicates the crux of the issue: Were the Model Artists undertaking a fundamentally pornographic performance, aimed primarily at the *sexual* gratification of its audiences? Whitman, beginning in March of 1848, had to attend multiple performances to get to the bottom of this question.

While Whitman in the aforementioned piece was quick to point out the "excellent women" in the audience (as moral arbiters), this may have been embellishment. A later piece clarified:

> Last evening the St. Charles theatre was crowded almost to suffocation. The second and third tier of boxes were occupied by gentlemen, and in the first tier we counted among the dense throng one *lady and a half*—that is to say a lady and her young sister. Many persons supposed that there would be an outbreak of popular indignation during the evening; but, on the contrary, the performances went off with the greatest enthusiasm and the most splendid *eclat* [*sic*].[91]

Of course, women may have been present that Whitman could not name: sex workers, who at the time commonly plied their trade in the side boxes of the major theaters of the American South, and who, as Whitman points out in his "Sidewalks" sketches, stationed themselves on St. Charles Street, right outside the theater.

Apparently, the *Crescent*'s broad pitch to "Take the Ladies" to the show[92] did not pan out as intended. Toward the end of his tenure, in a letter to the *Sunday Times*, Whitman noted that Collyer's "models are [still] revolving nightly to very good houses—all men."[93] As a historian summarized, Collyer's troupe "had a great deal of trouble attracting women to the show," which only served to underscore its seedy character in the public eye.[94] Audiences thus became, as a Virginia paper put it, "spectators in the trade of fair women's abasement."[95] When the *Delta* sent a reporter later that summer to inspect the "horrors" Collyer had to offer, it found the audience "full of hard-faced, fat-cheeked, bald-headed, carbuncle-nosed elderly gentlemen, who should have been at home, attending their family affairs."[96] The Model Artists, that paper concluded, was a show for horny old men. A contemporaneous illustration of the Model Artists in New York depicts them as such (see Figure 15): old, bespectacled men with narrow features, loose tufts of sparse, gray hair hanging off their heads, hunched over in exhilaration, and a few occasional young men or boys keeping them company.

The moral panic around the Model Artists reached such heights that papers felt inclined to parody it. The very same *Delta* that would later renounce the show so vividly welcomed it on March 6, 1848, with a humorous first-page sketch depicting an outraged "gentleman with specks" who believed himself to have encountered the troupe in the wild and pleaded with a Recorder Court judge to ban the pornographic show. A police officer tasked with investigating finally reports stumbling upon a line of naked men: "'Why, I'm blow'd—I again axes your Honor's pardon; but I assure you, as I'm a wigilant officer, that they was a jolly-looking raw recruits, every one on 'em a six-footer, that was a undergoin' medical inspection by the doctor.'"[97] The *tableau vivant* in question turned out to be a physical exam of handsome young police officers. Our "gentleman with specks" had been scandalized (or perhaps titillated?) by a display of naked men sanctioned by a medical context. While the choice of male recruits for the punchline may have been intended to add a measure of propriety to the front-page item, it also underscores an important fact about Model Artists: it provided an erotic experience almost exclusively shared between men and that also featured quasi-nude men and boys[98] in its displays.

To Whitman, the experience of seeing Model Artists (as he did at least three times), seemed to have been profound, likely in more than one sense. His defense of the "divine" nature of the acts on display was not only an attempt to couch a proto peep show in respectable metaphors with biblical or neoclassical connotations (as Collyer did) but also underscored his later defense that "[n]ot an inch nor a particle of an inch is vile" when it came to the human body and its various acts,

FIGURE 15. Collyer's Model Artists in New York (James Baillie's "The Three Graces," 1848), courtesy of the American Antiquarian Society.

longings, and excretions.[99] Sharing an erotic experience with men—sensual and en masse, oscillating between urban anonymity and direct, bodily encounter—triggered something in him. So, when Whitman thought through moments like these in his 1860 "Calamus" cluster, he remembered a "City of Orgies"—a wharf city, featuring not only "soiree[s]," "feast[s]," and "processions" but also specifically "shifting tableaus, [and] spectacles."[100] Or in other words: the turning *tableaux vivants* of the Model Artists and the erotic thrill of a room full of male spectators jeering, fantasizing, and, perhaps on occasion, masturbating in the "dense throng" of bodies filling the dark auditorium.[101]

Theater in the antebellum period was not the highbrow affair it has come to be, of course. Instead, the raucous space of the playhouse was perhaps more similar to a modern football stadium. It constituted a "demos that [was] fueled by the dynamic assertions of populist assembly" and thus "posed as a mimetic model for democratic governance."[102] Theatrical performances, as literary scholar Emily Banta has argued, were then a way for audience members to playfully relate to one another and to assert control over the performers via heckling, booing, demanding encores, etc. Theater became a training ground of sorts for Jacksonian America, and discourse on the theater consequently evoked the language of "popular sovereignty" and, in the case of theater riots, the specter of "mob rule."[103] Or to quote Alexis de Tocqueville, theater was the most democratic of the arts and brought "out most of the qualities and nearly all the vices inherent in democratic literatures."[104] Whitman's "Calamus" musings on a republic built on the "institution of the dear love of comrades"[105] may then not only be a utopian, poetic fantasy but also an echo of a bodily experience Whitman had in New Orleans: a masculine demos united by a sexual experience, an erotic push and pull between men at a proto peep show and the scantily clad (if clad at all) performers on stage. Indeed, in the theatrical shows of the Model Artists, Whitman would come the closest to seeing "[s]avage, felon, President, judge, prostitute, farmer, sailor, mechanic, young, old" side by side:[106] On May 8, 1848, future president Zachary Taylor, a hero of the US invasion of Mexico, would join the rowdy crowd of men during the performance of a particularly risqué display by the Model Artists (the "Circassian Slave"). Once he was spotted, the audience broke out in "vociferous cheering," Whitman would recall, and the "Star-Spangled

Banner" was played.[107] Sexual arousal here turned patriotic display as icons of naked antiquity made way for republican emblems.

Male-male fraternizing, of course, did not end with business partnerships or controversial public events. Finding themselves in an urban world wrought by insecurities over class identity and masculinity, men like Whitman and his colleagues longed for new forms of male-male association, on a sliding homosocial spectrum, from sexually charged performance to exuberant but chaste public events. They were by no means alone in this process. Where traditional forms of meaning-making fell flat for cosmopolitan middlemen and business-minded risers without established capital, professional organizations, benevolent orders, and secret societies stepped in.

Most men associated with the *Crescent* newsroom were active in at least one (and often multiple) of these associations, which, as scholars assert, hold "special relevance for the study of institutionalized friendship patterns, and the formation of subgroup identities."[108] Oyster restaurateur Sam Weir was a member of the Independent Order of Odd Fellows,[109] while his partner, editor McClure, served at various times in the Grand Commandery of Knights Templar and Appendant Order of the State of Louisiana,[110] the Order of Heptasophs,[111] and the George Washington Lodge,[112] among many others. Alexander Hayes was active in the fraternal Typographer's Union (which was organized in "chapels")[113] and George W. Reeder agitated for Irish Nationalist secret societies.[114] Editorial writer Larue was the chapter president of the "Sons of Temperance"[115] and an Odd Fellow.[116] The Whitman brothers' landlord managed Odd Fellows' Hall.[117] Whitman himself had been active in the Washingtonian Movement, of course, with its strong fraternal elements that were later taken up by a number of secret societies dedicated to the cause, like the aforementioned Sons of Temperance, who congregated in the *Crescent* building.[118]

"Many of the city's most prominent men, regardless of their political affiliation, belonged to at least one [such] club" in antebellum New Orleans.[119] While membership numbers in secret societies, especially in the antebellum period, are notoriously hard to gauge, New Orleans—so its newspapers suggest—was a hotbed of fraternal association.

The paradoxical success of the anti-Catholic, nativist Know-Nothing Party in Catholic New Orleans over the next decade, may, as one historian has observed, underscore this fact: It presented itself as a broad fraternal reform movement, promoted by leading private clubs and secret orders of the cities.[120] Its success would, in many ways, be precipitated by its deft use of the fraternal infrastructure that operated in the city. The political and social life of men in the Crescent City was organized not primarily by church or family ties but by secret clubs, benevolent societies, and fraternal orders.

These associations answered a societal need not only for the men who participated in them, but also for society at large. Unattached professionals, far away from their families, were a major problem in the nineteenth century. The "lonely bachelor" was not only a common literary trope it was also "a highly problematized social identity."[121] Writing for the *Crescent*, Whitman both declared "I am a bachelor" in a fictionalized peep,[122] while also ruminating in another about "the effeminate man, who develops not the uses of his manhood" and asking in parentheses, "Wouldn't this include old bachelors?"[123] The concern over clerkish bachelordom was not only a moral panic about men having sex with men but also always a fear over un(re)productive elements in society.

Marriage, some suggested, should be forced via punitive taxes on bachelors over the age of thirty.[124] Legislatures in New York, Texas, Wyoming, Louisiana, and Illinois, for instance, debated or passed measures along this line during the century.[125] Whitman on behalf of all bachelordom had previously mocked such proposals in the *Eagle*.[126] Reacting to this debate in New Orleans in spring 1848, an enraged letter to the editor by "A Bachelor" bemoans the shortsightedness of such measures, suggesting that "inequality of fortunes" still leaves "a large portion of the bachelors over 30 unable to support families," a trend that would only be exacerbated by increased taxes.[127] Insecurity over class went hand in hand with sexual insecurity in Whitman and his contemporaries: How did a man on the make avoid being seen as an exemplar of "effeminate man"? Exorcising the specter of impotent bachelordom, fraternal organizations stepped in to emphasize male-male bonding, a sense of masculine tradition, and societal activism through benevolence.

Male association in New Orleans asserted itself against charges of impotence through confident, public displays. In their first month in the city, the brothers Whitman attended a number of parades celebrating the men of the city and their benevolent deeds. "On Saturday the 4th of March we had a grand fireman's procession and I think it was larger than the one (the firemen part) in New York. [T]he engines were very large and are drawn by horses (six or eight)," young Jeff wrote their parents in his earliest surviving letter.[128] The resulting piece in the *Crescent* celebrates the event as a chivalric feast:

> The engines were decked with flowers—the firemen were clad in their gayest suits, and every emblem gave token that it was a day of rejoicing to the philanthropic and the brave.
>
> Oh, how proud it made one feel of this country, to see those stalwart men leading along the engines of peace, not of destruction—engines destined not to batter down the walls, but to preserve the threshold and the household gods of those who were their brothers! Their motto, like that of the ancient chivalry, was "Ready—aye—ready!"[129]

The firefighters in New Orleans, as in many other cities, grew out of the free association of volunteer fire corps, operated here by the Firemen's Charitable & Benevolent Association, which provided many of the staples of fraternal association: mutual insurance, cemetery access, ranks, titles, and festivities. Besides the parade the Whitmans attended, the Firemen's Association would come to host multiday festivities, with masked balls and firefighters dressing up as knights—the archetype of the unmarried man liberated from the social stigma of bachelordom.[130]

For men of the "chivalric" class of Hayes, McClure, and Whitman all across major cities in the United States, "the fraternal order, through the content of its ritual and its formal qualities as an organization, presented a particular concept of the social world, one which idealized hierarchy and promoted an ideology of social mobility and exclusivity."[131] Where church and family failed to provide a sense of belonging, male-male societies stepped in, often organized around ethnic, professional, or reformist markers of identity. Centering on such widely differing activities as unionizing, mutual aid and insurance saving, advocating for teetotalism, or celebrating republicanism, these societies crafted a sense of class and gender solidarity for young professional men, often of middle-class backgrounds,[132] through arcane symbolism, a cultish inflation of ranks and titles, and a mythologized, paternalistic vision of the past as a wellspring of identity formation. In a society like New Orleans in the late 1840s, so marked by urban flux and moral panic over unattached men, fraternalism provided a much-needed veneer of stability.

Whitman was acutely aware of the intense fraternal aura of the Crescent City, updating his former paper regarding the goings-on of the Odd Fellows up north after his return to New York City[133] and integrating fraternal puns into his writings while in New Orleans. His humorous sketch of a French oyster peddler, for instance, introduced its character as "Timothy Goujon, V. O. N. O. (Vender of Oysters in New Orleans)," a joking reference to the common abbreviation of "I.O.O.F." for the Independent Order of Odd Fellows, seeming to poke lighthearted fun at the fantasy of social rising and transcendence of class encoded into fraternalism.[134]

Under Whitman's editorship the *Crescent* dedicated half of its third page to updates of the various "benevolent societies" (largely: IOOF, Masonic Lodges, and Sons of Temperance) and featured fraternal updates in its other pages, including in the editorial column.[135] Some of these pieces express a sense of admiration for the scale of fraternalism in the US and its egalitarian gist. One read: "ODD FELLOWS—There are in the United States more than 1000 Lodges, with 100,000 members [. . .]. Christian, Turk and Jew may enter, but those who declare their disbelief in a Supreme Being are inadmissible."[136] Similar puffs can be found for the "Sons of Temperance."[137] Altogether, the *Crescent* was hardly remarkable here; its coverage was typical of New Orleans papers. Compared to Brooklyn, however, this must have felt like quite an intensification of fraternal sentiment to Whitman. The *Eagle* and its local contemporaries did not feature dedicated sections for secret societies, though Whitman, noticeably, had reviewed Odd Fellows' publications for that paper.[138] Still, Whitman had his nascent reservations about fraternalism, which would, late in life, lead to him condemn "the constitution and nomenclature" of secret societies as

FIGURE 16. Caricature of an Odd Fellows initiation ritual by James Fuller Queen (1840–1860), courtesy of the Library of Congress.

"utterly and damnably feudalistic."[139] Between early inklings of interest and his late-life dismissal, fraternal echoes in Whitman have remained underexplored.

While men may have initially been attracted to these societies for their express beneficial purposes (mutual aid, insurance, unionizing, etc.), it was the ritualistic, identitarian aspect of these communities that ultimately ensured their success. In the late 1840s, fraternalism in the US experienced a "dramatic resurgence in popularity" and focused on self-improvement and "market values" like temperance to combat their old image as dens of vice.[140] With the renewed focus on their mission came a decidedly more involved, darker form of ritual. As fraternalism scholar Mark C. Carnes has noted (citing, in turn, primary sources): "There was something special about certain rituals that 'attracted,' 'charmed,' or 'lured' members, and many men were somehow predisposed to 'crave' or 'desire' them."[141] Homoerotic attraction and bonding are what Carnes suggests but never names. He notes, however, how "themes and symbols of fraternal rituals [were] often laden with [. . .] gender and interfamilial associations." They frequently involved male nudity, graphic depictions of physical violence by and submission to paternal figures, as well as imagery of death and rebirth (see the caricature in Figure 16).[142] As such, they may be read as symbolic attempts to "break a female monopoly on reproductive power" in society.[143]

In his history of the golden age of fraternalism, Carnes presents a vivid narrative retelling of an initiation ritual for a young clerk into the Odd Fellows. It involves mystic chanting, blindfolded men tied up in chains, fake corpses, and a willing surrender to the robed fathers of the lodge and their promise of "Universal Brotherhood."[144] The hours-long process was a multistep humbling of the initiate to symbolically face his mortality, die, and be born again into the order. This final step involves the initiate accepting the historical mythos of the brotherhood: "The foundation stone was laid by our forefather Adam, and remains unsullied."[145] The first patriarch of the Odd Fellows, he learned, was Adam himself and the society was "coeval with the first inhabitants of the earth"—it was an ancient paternal order, older than all of human history.[146]

The Odd Fellows were thus exemplars of male societies identifying as "*enfans d'Adam*"; their vision of society led by homosocial ritual and fraternal feeling overlaps to a striking degree with Whitman's own, from his infatuation with male fitness in "Manly Health" (1858) to his 1860 clusters in *Leaves of Grass* that would echo his New Orleans experience.[147] Associations of men, formed on an equality of (nude) bodies, who recover an Adamic state of athletic purity while exchanging knowing glances and secret hand gestures—these associations were still connected in Whitman's later work to New Orleans. In New Orleans, Whitman encountered a number of different forms of male-male association that attempted to answer the question posed by the problem of clerkdom with a new language, ritual, and, quite often, an air of eroticism. The experiences offered by these new modes of association—from business culture and peep show crazes to secret societies—attempted to provide identity and belonging among men while steering clear, of course, of any overt associations with "sodomy" or "inversion." While historian William D. Moore thus rightly cautions that any overt "references to fornication are lacking in the documentary record" of fraternal orders,[148] it is worth noting that the orders offered members participation in a wide spectrum of men exploring new possibilities of association beyond the modes of belonging offered and sanctioned by mainstream society. In their conceptual openness and masculinist eros (beyond just nudity), they spoke to a writer like Whitman, who would be interrogating like notions from a more expressly queer angle in the "Calamus" cluster.

In his famous "Live-Oak, with Moss" manuscript, which formed the basis for the later "Calamus" and "Children of Adam" groupings (1860), we can see elements of this logic evoked in response to observing "in Louisiana a live-oak growing." Unlike much of Whitman's later poetry, "Live-Oak, with Moss" appears to have a single and clear, personal narrative throughline. Ruminating on the figure of a lonely, scorned lover, Whitman's speaker upscales a feeling of loss into a sense of belonging to other men, with like experiences:

> It seems to me I can look over and behold them, in Germany,
> France, Spain—Or
> far away in China, ‸India, or in
> Russia—talking other dialects,
> And it seems to me if I could know those men ~~better~~ I should
> love them as I love
> men in my own lands[149]

This is Whitman's celebration of a queer cosmopolitanism. It was a lesson learned from an act of cultural triangulation. Whitman, as scholars of cosmopolitanism have observed,[150] did not just enable a global, universalist experience for the readers of his later poetry, but his poetry in turn was enabled by his own critical experience with travel.

Whitman's "city upon the hill"—his Edenic garden to which he hoped to see "the world, anew ascending"—is thus an international city, overflowing with "manly love" and led by acts of brotherly men:

> I dreamed in a dream of a city where all the
> men were like brothers,
> O I saw them tenderly love each other—I
> often saw them, in numbers, walking
> hand in hand;
> I dreamed that was the city of robust
> friends—Nothing was greater there

than ~~the quality of~~ manly love—it led
the rest,
It was seen every hour in the actions of the
men of that city, and in all their looks
and words.—[151]

Given the original manuscript context of the piece ("Live-Oak, with Moss"), this masculine utopia has a decidedly Southern twang to it.

In many of his writings for the *Crescent*, Whitman leveraged his own experience to grapple with what he would, later in 1848, come to term "cosmopolitan influence," "a sort of citizen-of-the-world disposition"[152] that creates a breed of men with "*no* characteristic trait [as all the] peculiarities of all nations are softened and blended in him."[153] Urban men in New Orleans behaved and looked like urban men in New York. Like the Odd Fellows going back to Adam or the Order of Heptasophs to the first Zoroaster, Whitman began to argue for radical renewal—one that goes back to the roots—in the way men relate in the city. While Whitman learned this lesson from his Southern sojourn, his readers need not put in as much effort.

In 1848 Whitman was contemplating a radical politics centered around white, working-class men, urging not just an alleviation of their political grievances, but a revival of Jacksonian culture that fundamentally centered around them. We find these men in his valorizations of the men of "the West" as the real blood of America, in his humorous celebrations of workingmen of common sense in his *Crescent* sketches, and in his concerns over the emasculating effect of the city's clerking culture. His theorizing of how to overcome these effects—short of escaping the city altogether (as he would on occasion contemplate)—was fundamentally focused on restructuring the ways men relate to each other in that space. The Free-Soil Party, full of such "don't-care-a-damnative young men" that were after Whitman's heart, was one such way of organizing. The fraternalism of New Orleans was another.

In his journalism for the *Crescent*, the question of the clerk radiated through Whitman's defenses of the human body ("Eve in Paradise—or Adam either—would not be supposed to shock the mind")[154] in his lambasting of "sanctimonious, long-faced religionist[s]"[155] and in his valorization of the American project as "young, vigorous" and in no danger of dissolution.[156] In New Orleans, Whitman wrestled with how the cultural charge of impotence levelled against bachelors, clerks, and other unattached men might be overcome. What productive forces might be unleashed by these cosmopolitan brothers? How did this new identity—which shows such radical, egalitarian promise—relate to the American project? Here, we see emerge the early fibers of a throughline of Whitmanian thinking: his grappling with how male-male association works within and against mainstream society, what language and ritual it employs to name itself, and what new mode of living may be gleaned from it. Later, he would use the word "comrade" to describe these relationships. For now, observing those bustling around him in New Orleans, Whitman underscored the power of the private and political bonds among men.

CHAPTER 5

They do charge me, as you say, with lacking humor:
it never seemed to me it could be true: but I don't dispute it.
I pride myself on being a real humorist underneath everything else.

—WHITMAN, IN *With Walt Whitman in Camden* (1889)

Sidewalk Humor

IN ITS MULTITUDINOUSNESS, New Orleans often seemed quite funny to the Whitmans. In fact, one of the very first things they did was to go see a comedian. "I am going to night to see Mr[.] Collins," young Jeff wrote to his parents on March 14, "and I expect some fun." He was right to anticipate as much. Walt had positively reviewed the Irish comedian as early as 1846 (when he called Collins a "star"),[1] and for the *Crescent* he eagerly puffed the upcoming performance, his praise noting that Collins's "voice has a splendid compass, and his tones are as varied as the different sounds of the lyre. We hope sincerely that he may have an overflowing house."[2] Indeed, Walt seemed to have taken a keen interest in humor in 1848. "A satirical person could no doubt find an ample field for his powers in many of the manners and ways" of the folks one encounters on a trip down South, he had mused in the first issue of the *Crescent*.[3]

Racial and ethnic typology (as well as gender stereotypes) and the shenanigans that ensue when they mix on busy sidewalks—misunderstandings, mispronunciations, contrasting affectations—unsurprisingly played a key role in how Whitman works as a humorist. A comedian like "Mr. Collins" was funny to him because he embodied, as Whitman wrote in his puff, the "wit, humor and vivacity of his countrymen." Collins's performances didn't always focus on jokes and laughter outright but often reveled in sentimental songs, tears, and heartache.

This attitude very much echoed Whitman's—and less than a week later, he premiered his own series of humorous observations in the paper: "Sketches of the Sidewalks and Levee."

The series, subtitled "Glimpses into the New Orleans Bar (rooms.)" constituted the only thematically coherent, titled corpus that Whitman produced while in New Orleans.[4] Instead of the once-canonical eight, the series is, as we have demonstrated elsewhere,[5] actually made up of thirteen installments that briefly ceased publication in May 1848 (anticipating Whitman's departure later that month) and resumed two weeks after Whitman's return to New York.[6] One "Sketch" was even printed out of order, with the first installment of a two-part piece on "Samuel Sensitive" appearing after the second and following Whitman's return north.

Stretching from his first weeks in New Orleans to the late summer in New York, "Sketches of the Sidewalks and Levee," with its seventeen thousand words total, is in play as one of Whitman's more sustained newspaper endeavors, rivalling his "Letters from a Travelling Bachelor" (nineteen thousand words) and surpassing his "Sun-Down Papers" (ten thousand words). It constitutes the only Whitman series discovered so far that relied fully on fictional characters and humorous microplots and combined those with the piecemeal format of his other journalistic/essayistic newspaper series.

The total outline of this humorous Whitman production looks as follows:

March 13, 1848—Peter Funk, Esq.
Sketch of a "Peter Funk" and the fake auction of a golden watch for which Funk is tasked to drive up the price.

March 16, 1848—Miss Dusky Grisette
Encounter with a mixed-race flower girl and prostitute, leading to speculations about her daytime employments and musings upon the racial dynamics of New Orleans.

March 25, 1848—Daggerdraw Bowieknife, Esq.
Portrait of a criminal and desperado, haunted by his murders.

March 28, 1848—John J. Jinglebrain
Attack on vapid dandyism via a caricature of a soulless, mustachioed pursuer of haircuts and elegant garb.

April 4, 1848—Timothy Goujon
Portrait of a French oyster vendor, relishing French accents and linguistic mixing.
April 12, 1848—Mrs. Giddy Gay Butterfly
Harsh sketch of a woman too vain to be a good housewife and mother.
April 18, 1848—Patrick McDray
Follows the day of a "Paddy" and his unrefined wife, abounding in Irish accents while casting Patrick and his wife as hotheaded but lovable.
May 2, 1848—Samuel Sensitive [Part II, printed out of order]
Depicts Samuel's pursuit of and marriage to Miss Julia Katydid.
June 29, 1848—Doctor Sangrado Snipes
Cautions readers against an overreliance on doctors by depicting them as error-prone, dangerous grifters.
July 12, 1848—Old Benjamin Broekindown
Cautionary tale of a down-on-his-luck merchant who would have squandered all of his wealth, were it not for his prudent wife.
July 15, 1848—Samuel Sensitive [Part I, printed out of order]
Introduces Samuel, a Tennessee-born merchant apprentice who sets out to "make it" in New Orleans but imprudently slips into dandyism—from which love saves him.
July 25, 1848—Miss Virginity Roseblossom
A harsh attack on spinsterism that blames the phenomenon on the unattractive character of certain women, leading the author to muse on physiognomy and the nature of love—and woman's responsibility for instigating the feeling.
August 10, 1848—Ephraim Broadhorn
Celebration of a Connecticut-born, Kentuckian longboat "b'hoy" visiting the big city, feeding his manly appetite on an abundant lunch, and making a fool of himself when mistaking French for English and annoying a local Frenchman in conversation.

Whitman's "The Habitants of Hotels" of March 10, 1848, served as set-up and *de facto* frame for these "Sketches." "Habitants," signed by

"W.," presents us with pithy, on-point snapshots that seem to anticipate the segments that would begin appearing in the pages of the *Crescent* only a few days later. The piece ends by previewing a series to come—and with a view of a bar, likely inspired by the rowdy "bar-room" at the base of the Whitmans' Tremont House lodgings:[7] "The parlor of the hotel we will not enter, but when we have a pen, virgin so far as ink is concerned—any quantity of satin paper with gilded edges, and a few gallons of cologne, we shall endeavor to describe the peculiarities of those chosen mortals who will live above board—or, at least above the bar-room."[8]

Whitman's pen was aching to write about these charming, occasionally sleazy characters, employing similar wordplay (above board / above the bar-room) to create a caricature of lowlifes with an ironic air of respectability as the "bar (rooms)" in the subsequent "Sketches" will. To see what "shall" follow here, readers have to turn to subsequent sketches of "Jinglebrain" who "boards at one of the crack hotels," or the sleepless "Daggerdraw" menacingly pacing the hallways of "boarding-houses," or the crook Peter Funk with whom the author claims to have "boarded a while," etc., etc. A noteworthy degree of vagrancy is a shared trait between sketcher and sketchee in "The Habitants of Hotels." Whitman's newspaper narrator relishes the persona of the "looker in"—a temporary guest who snoops around and quips about the personages brushing past on the street or in the narrow halls of boardinghouses, occasionally lapsing into philosophical musings and what the author calls "moralizing."

What Whitman finds humorous in these sketches was often grounded in the prevalent typologies of the day. There is, for instance, Patrick McDray, an Irishman who sports a thick Fenian drawl, a pock-marked face, and a fiery, often violent wife who nonetheless bore him a sizable litter of children. Whitman had been struck by McDray's type from his earliest days in New Orleans, observing the draymen participate in the "perpetual hubbub of moving life" that transpired daily on the Levee section stretching along "Techoupitoulas [*sic*], Camp, and St. Charles streets."[9] Yet, though its subject is a racial caricature, Whitman's sketch nonetheless elevates McDray. When this "Paddy" becomes the self-respecting "Mr. Patrick McDray," Whitman's sketch both chuckles at that pompous assertion—*and* playfully endorses it. Drawing on popular pseudosciences like phrenology and physiognomy, satirist Whitman finds the truth of characters like McDraw, Broadhorn, or Daggerdraw "legibly fixed on the very lineaments of [their] face."[10] Play with these psychological and physical archetypes is at the core of these sketches. It teases readers to anticipate and recognize types while at the same time celebrating them. Even the politically charged plot of McDray gaining wealth by politicking—and voting as a noncitizen[11]—is ironized, but never outright mocked, as an example of McDray living the American Dream.

Whitman's humorous typologies, and the challenges they pose to modern readers, are perhaps nowhere in these sketches clearer than in their best-known installment: that of the mixed-race sex worker, already discussed in chapter 3. "The jaundiced view of women in 'Miss Dusky Grisette' is uncharacteristic of Whitman's sympathetic depiction of fallen women," a biographer once famously exclaimed, going as far as to deny Whitman's authorship of the piece: "He would never have delighted [. . .] in the young woman who 'has a smile and a wink for every one of the passers-by.'"[12] Of course, worse depictions of sex workers are well-documented in Whitman—even in the Whitman of *Leaves of Grass*, who would come to sing of the "prostitute that draggles her shawl" with her "bonnet bob[bing] on her tipsy and pimpled neck."[13]

"Whitman seems to have loved motherhood more than womanhood, but he praised both in his poetry,"[14] biographer Jerome Loving has stated, ignoring how close Grisette, albeit under heavy layers of irony, comes to Whitman's idealized views of pure womanhood. And, of course, Whitman *was* prone to rhetorically punish violations of nineteenth-century sentimental norms around motherhood, as is illustrated in other installments. One such sketchee, Giddy Gay Butterfly, commits Whitman's cardinal sin: She is vain, excessively so. Butterfly's love of self and dress in middle age renders her children "poor, little, motherless Butterflies." They are orphaned by lack of motherly care:

> There are some people in this world of inhabited creation that supposed—vainly suppose—that if children—little immortals in jackets and trowsers—only have a plenty of bread and meat wherewith to cram their stomachs, and a trifle of clothing withal, that the grand totality of parental duty, in all its length and

> breadth and importance, is abundantly fulfilled. As for the rest—why, the streets and the highways can open wide their arms and receive them.[15]

In de-mothering herself, Giddy Gay Butterfly becomes a spinster: "as years increase she, of course, appears less attractive, and will, no doubt, become soured in temper from such cause."[16] Spinsterhood is a thoroughly established target of Whitman's mockery. From the outright disgust over the "avarice and wretchedness" of a greedy mother who had given up her children in his "Travelling Bachelor"[17] to the "solemn and sour" spinster of Whitman's earlier *Franklin Evans*[18] and the "yellow-faced" spinster of his contemporaneous "Shadow and the Light of a Young Man's Soul,"[19] Whitman had little understanding of, but offered ample ridicule for, women refusing the role of mother.

Spinsterhood is consequently a status that Whitman in these sketches describes as foul and unnatural—a souring that can apparently even be read in the face. "There dwells about the mortal physiognomy of this elderly branch of the virgin tree," the author observes of spinster sketchee Virginity Roseblossom, "nothing but thorns and fish-hooks," going on to compare her appearance to that of a lizard and her voice to an artillery barrage. In her, the "blessedness of a feminine nature is all turned into wormwood and bitterness" and "the sweet milk of human kindness has long since become curdled and sour." Roseblossom becomes a warning to the young as her heartless ambition "spreads its bitterness over [. . .] families, and carries them through the spring and early summer of life with no inhalement of sweets, and no plucking of flowers!"[20] To Whitman in and beyond the "Sidewalks" sketches, womanhood either ripens into blessed motherhood, or spoils, becomes bitter, turns to vinegar, withers on the vine. In this worldview, old mothers are wise, old spinsters are rotten. Much of the sympathy and warmth that livens up Whitman's male-centric sketches turns to mockery in his depictions of these women. A general sense of laughing *with* a protagonist decidedly turns into a laughing *at* in these female-centric sketches.

The sketches also frequently quote from popular British authors Whitman had read and enjoyed, sprinkled into the narrative in a manner similar to other writings by Whitman for the *Crescent* (for instance his "Novelties in New Orleans"). In block quotes strewn throughout these texts, we find Byron, Shakespeare's *Romeo and Juliet*, *Richard II*, *Hamlet*, and *Macbeth*, Richard Brinsley Sheridan, Alexander Pope, plenty of Robert Burns and Thomas Moore, Oliver Goldsmith, and Walter Scott—all literary interlocutors well-documented in the works of 1840s Whitman. Biographer Loving judges these "strained literary allusions" to be "more than slightly condescending," but one can locate them in Whitman from his early reporting to as late as *Specimen Days*.[21] The "Sketches" also include a reference to the *Journals* of British actress Fanny Kemble,[22] who had yet to fully break into stardom in the United States before her first solo tour of the country in 1849. Whitman had become "entranced" with her performances after attending her show at the Park Theatre in 1834.[23]

Besides all of these British authors dear to Whitman, the sole quote from an American poet is from the work of Fitz-Greene Halleck, a writer so admired by the author of "Sketches," that he forces his "Kentucky flatboatsman" to have a narratively pointless childhood in Connecticut, just so he can incorporate the poet's eponymous praise of the state (quoting the Free-Soil poem twice and paraphrasing it at times). Like Halleck, the author of "Ephraim Broadhorn" "admire[s] the plain, blunt, honest, and open character of our Western b'hoys" and finds "pure republicanism" in their manly, rough intelligence.[24] Halleck's Knickerbocker humor ("quiet, faint, and fine" as Lydia Sigourney called it),[25] brimming with local and literary allusions and as "refined as it [was] racy,"[26] formed a template for the style Whitman was playing with in the "Sidewalks" sketches. Certainly, the kind of "mock portrait" humor that Halleck perfected in his famous 1819 "Croaker Papers" series in the New York *Evening Post*, provided a template for a lot of Whitman's own humor pieces.[27] Whitman would later socialize with Halleck at Pfaff's beer cellar,[28] and Halleck's queerness likely had a major impact on the younger man's own poetic and personal development. Halleck biographer John W. M. Hallock claims that "Whitman might never have been able to envision his homosexual theology without the previous work of Halleck," whom he terms the "American Byron."[29] Indeed, Whitman's list of high-cultural English referents was so full of "confirmed bachelors" and flaunters of sexual norms—Burns, Goldsmith, Pope, Shakespeare, and Byron—that they almost read like clever (or subconscious) counter-texts to the heteronormativity the "Sketches" at times espouses on the surface.

If Whitman, then, was so insistent on "being a real humorist"—against the assessment of his old-age companions and many of his modern biographers—it is worth exploring not only what Whitman's own humorous works entailed but also *why* Whitman thought them humorous. While antebellum humor is understudied as it is, the situation looks still more dire for Whitman studies: Even in those rare examinations of Whitman's humor that do exist, the question "What did Whitman find funny" has remained unanswered. This situation is even more puzzling, considering that Whitman himself was fairly up-front about what he believed constituted "good humor."

American humor, Whitman would later explain to Horace Traubel, has too often been misunderstood: that "to misspell or be idiotic or vulgar is to be funny" was a "damnable idea," he maintained. "Humor," then, was distinct from mere "mockery." The word "humor," Whitman told Traubel, always "mystified" him. As he went on to explain:

> I think Shakespeare had it [. . .]. The question is, was Shakespeare's humor good natured? Good nature is the important equation in humor. Look at Heine, for example: I'm not sure of his place: but look at him—consider him: ask yourself whether he was not a mocker as well as a humorist. They do charge me, as you say, with lacking humor: it never seemed to me it could be true: but I don't dispute it: I only see myself from the inside—with the ordinary prejudice a fellow has in favor of himself.[30]

Whitman's assessment of Shakespeare as a good humorist makes sense, considering how many references to the bard he peppered throughout his "Sidewalks" sketches. Like Shakespeare's famous Dogberries or Falstaffs, Whitman heavily relied on stock characters—but unlike aristocratic Shakespeare, his works featured *republican* stock characters: French oyster peddlers, vain dandies, and manly country bumpkins. They were "humorous" in the sense that they constituted a light-hearted, somewhat heightened version of the American commonplace: These figures were archetypes who could have jumped right out of a George Caleb Bingham painting, circulating in popular parlance and illustrating a kind of humorous condition that lay at the heart of the American experiment. Whitman's was a Jacksonian "good humor," found in placing Jinglebrains, Daggerdraws, Samuel Sensitives, and, perhaps, even Grisettes at the base of popular sovereignty and not despairing over the resulting absurdities but reveling in them.

In a separate conversation with Traubel, Whitman expanded on the notion of Shakespearean humor, echoing one of the staunchest defenders of his own, his long-time friend William Douglas O'Connor. "The humor in the Shakespearean comedies is very broad, obvious, often brutal, coarse: but in some of the tragedies—take Lear for instance—you will find another kind of humor, a humor more remote (subtle, illusive, not present)—the sort of humor William declares he finds in the Leaves and in me."[31] This "remote" humor, Whitman elsewhere noted, is "humor, in the sense of lubrication."[32] It is a *rhetorical strategy* that is part of a larger argument: "Coarse" humor wants to get a laugh and ends there, but "good humor" may elicit a chuckle on the way to the real point. It is no surprise then that Whitman pointed to an arena outside of literature as a natural home for humor: politics.

In the spring of 1848, Whitman's humor had a clear, political target: promoting a Jacksonian working-class culture of "free soil, free speech, free labor, and free men" and, yes, occasionally mocking its detractors. It was fortunate, then, that Whitman found one of the key figures of his political movement to be a quite accomplished humorist: John Van Buren, the son of the would-be Free-Soil candidate for president, Martin Van Buren. (These political contexts will be discussed in more detail in chapter 8.) Writing as "Manhattan," Whitman in the *Crescent* praises "Prince John" for his "dry and crispy humor" and highlights it as a winning rhetorical strategy:

> His manner [. . .] is serene and smooth: [. . .] a calm complacency more like that of an indifferent, heedless child. He uses very little gesture; when he bends down it is almost a sure thing that he gives one of those sarcastic bits of humor that cut to the very hearts of his victims. And yet all seems done in good humor. There is not a particle of malignance or spite. [. . .]

> Even those at whose expense he launches his jokes may generally laugh with the rest. [. . .] Polished and vulgar, educated and ignorant, alike appreciate John Van Buren[:] his humor, his logic, and his aim. There is a charming abandon about him; you are fully convinced that there are no hidden motives, no finesse, no clap-trap or mean selfishness, behind what he has arrayed before you. [. . .]
>
> Newspaper reports of Mr. Van Buren's addresses, unless they are strictly verbatim, contain but a faint copy of his wit. The latter consists generally in the turn of a sentence, conveying a contrast or an image so irresistibly comic—so Hogarthian—that you cannot for your life help laughing. It is not the broad humor of puns and distortions; it is fine and diffused. It is not farce, but the highest and most intellectual comedy. It is not an idea, one of whose parts is very funny; it is the whole idea, so ludicrous. It is not a dashy stroke of color in the picture, making a novel effect; it is the general color, pervading the whole work.
>
> In England such a man as John Van Buren would command any gift the government had to bestow.[33]

This was the kind of Shakespearean "good humor" that Whitman enjoyed and emulated until old age: It was a humor that was holistic and based in an affirmative, light-hearted outlook. It was more attitude than punchline—a "remote" humor aimed at drawing people in and uniting them around a shared view of the world. In Van Buren Jr.'s rhetoric, according to Whitman, the status quo became a humorous violation of the somewhat more "real" future that Free-Soilers envisioned. As such his humor functioned as a kind of sentimentalism, as its "optimism [was] not organized around unimaginable transformations but around structural adaptations whose justice the [audience] can already affectively pre-experience internally."[34] John Van Buren's "fine and diffused" humor elicited not (just) laughter; it also instilled a "charming abandon" to the political vision it summoned in its audience. One has to wonder if Whitman relied on similar strategies in his own speech endorsing Martin Van Buren later that year, which the local press would praise for its "eloquence."[35]

In Whitman, humor was political, then, but in a manner strikingly different from modern "political comedy." His sense of humor was not, as Richard Chase (who considers Whitman's *Crescent* writings mere "native folk humor") has it, a "radical modification of sentimental comedy"[36] in that it rids itself of the sentimental. Instead, it *built on* the sentimental: it was political by dismissing petty politics (a "dashy stroke of color") for a larger sense of the "the political" ("the general color"). "To enter the world of Whitman is to touch the spirit of American *popular* comedy," Constance Rouke notes in one of the earliest examinations of Whitman's humor.[37] Yet Rouke fails to follow her observation to its logical conclusion.[38] Antebellum American humor had its primary conceptual locus outside of books and newspaper columns. It was a populist humor that required a soapbox—or a theater stage.

It was not just a matter of convenience, then, that John Van Buren's witty speech would take place at the Park Theatre. For its reopening in 1821, Fitz-Greene Halleck (so prominently featured in Whitman's "Ephraim Broadhorn") had composed an ironic dedication that cast the new, pompous Park as the perfect venue for "a public meeting" and for "speech—the modern mode of winning hearts, / And power, and fame, in politics and arts."[39] "Halleck's joke," theater scholar Emily Banta reminds us, "is that a good speech is the making of a great politician, and it is also the making of a great actor." Yet, she goes on, the joke in the poem is also "embracing the slide of performance that draws theater and politics together," cultivating "an ironizing set of social relations within the public space of theater." When Banta argues that "[f]or many theater patrons, a night at the theater could be an exhilarating performance of popular sovereignty,"[40] she could also be describing Whitman's experiences in New Orleans. It is no coincidence that of all the things Whitman would recall late in life about encountering presidential hopeful Zachary Taylor at the St. Charles, he specifically highlighted that the old war hero "in ways and manners, show'd the least of conventional ceremony or etiquette I ever saw; he laugh'd unrestrainedly at everything comical."[41] Taylor, then still reluctant to come out as "Whig" and pretending to stay above the party fray, demonstrated his populism by good humor.

In the antebellum US, bawdy comedy at "the playhouse posed as a mimetic model for democratic governance,"[42] with the push and pull of audience mob and stage performers constituting a "performance of popular sovereignty."[43] Van Buren Jr. eliciting laughs at the Park and Taylor laughing along at the St. Charles were moments of political leaders submitting to this logic. The comic theater, Banta argues, was *the* place for antebellum Americans—perhaps more specifically, young men on the make like Whitman—to experience the contradictions of Jacksonian democracy as pleasurable. The comic theater was then an "*agonistic* exercise of popular sovereignty" that "made the fun of contestation palpable."[44] This attitude toward politics—a republicanism marked by a fundamentally "comic sociality"—echoes not only in Whitman's 1848 writings about what constitutes "subtle" and "good" humor, but also his political rhetoric, which was consistently marked by a tinge of irony.

That Whitman's own works got more and more humorous as his own political dislocation in the Democratic Party intensified was not a sign of cynicism, but an embrace of this notion. When Whitman spoke of the most consequential election of his life up to this date—an election so crucial to him, he would run a party paper and morph into a party organizer—he did so with a humor that is puzzling to modern readers: "Like the man who got drunk in self-defence on the evening of the Fourth of July, our good people would be obliged to kick up in self-defence a revolution about something—though no one can guess about what," he wrote as Europe was engulfed in fire and in the US free soil was on the ballot: "But the election in November saves us. That is one glorious day for over-turning dynasties, and reforming the manifold abuses of bad government, which the patriots out of office can always discover. [. . .] But tame as it is, the misfortune of good government and universal happiness has left us no other, and we must make the best of it."[45] This light tone—this rendering of his own political ambition as drunken rabble rousing by "patriots out of office"—was an attempt to engage in a political rhetoric that left no inkling of narrow party "clap-trap or mean selfishness" but spoke with a subtle Yankee humor, brimming with a good-natured embrace of the wonderful absurdities of popular governance.

In line with John Van Buren's apocryphal "vote early, and vote often," this kind of humor naturally involved an acknowledgement of the mess, the shortcomings and contradictions, of the electoral system. Ever a populist, Whitman ran a short humor piece in the *Crescent* of early April 1848 (and anticipating a similar scene in his 1852 *Jack Engle*), which portrayed the affect of the winners and losers of a recent municipal contest. It was published on the day after a local election that resulted in a confirmation of the Whig status quo and concluded with this telling portrait of a political loser:

> The "sucked in" thought of his yesterday, and the "sucker" of his success. "Cuss me," said the "sucked in," if ever I vote for him again, I wish I may be d—d! Offered to give it to me, and 'taint much, no how; and now election's over, he's jist as proud as a bed-bug that's been feedin' off the hide of a Congressman! Didn't I spend his money liberally? Didn't I cuss his opponents, and swear that he was the only man who deserved to be elected? Didn't I work like a nigger or a tiger, for weeks for him, and when he hadn't no money to do the 'treating,' didn't I use to go borrow it for him? And when the election day came on, who was the man that stood by him? Who was the man who give the "sockdologer" into the face of Jim Brown? Who was it that crossed the names out of some of the tickets, and put 'tother ones in, jist for his benefit? But it "aint no matter, and drinks nothin" but cold water, says, "there's a good time a coming." I'll take an' pocket my difficulties, and say nothin' more about 'em!
>
> So saying, the gentleman who was to have been elected to a party office, with a face that looked any thing but amiable, put his hands in his empty pockets, and with pursed lips endeavored to whistle to the tune of "Begone, dull care!"[46]

Whitman's political humor was no mere propagandistic effort to extol the virtues of the republican process or to dish out jabs purely on behalf of a single political side or persuasion. He knew well that there were always "suckers" and the "sucked in." Yet there was a "charming abandon" in Whitman's winking portrayal of this very kind of politicking. Or to speak with Banta, he embraced a "comic sociality that [. . .] exuberantly celebrate[d the] incongruous and inseparable conjunction" at the core of the American system.[47] At the same time, this kind of satirical writing was a perfect fit for a paper run by radical Democrats that staunchly pretended to be above the political fray.

Richard Chase once argued, somewhat controversially,[48] that "'Song of Myself' is on the whole comic in tone," citing specifically the sheer scale of its "incongruous diversity."[49] Chase's biggest issue is, perhaps, that instead of broadly contextualizing this claim in mid-century humor practices, he isolates it, psychologically, in Whitman and thereby turns him into "a neo-Ovidian poet."[50] Yet, there does seem to be an important insight in Chase: that American antebellum humor *was* an attempt to wrestle with "diversity." To be "large [and] contain multitudes" was, in a way, the program of popular American theater comedy, its "comic sociality" offering a way not to *resolve* diversity but to play with its contradictions. This kind of *underlying humor*—a sort of stage set for the performance of actual jokes—underpinned much of Whitman's writing for the *Crescent*. In news items, "Sidewalks" sketches, and other humorous pieces, the future poet of *Leaves* found and celebrated humor in contradictory experiences that were, nonetheless, typical for cosmopolitan life in the United States: whether being fleeced for one's greed by a "Peter Funk," professionally cleaning and professionally dirtying sheets as a "Grisette," or combining muddy boots with meticulously brushed teeth as a vain dandy.

The intuitive qualms a modern reader develops over this kind of humor also apply to "Song of Myself" as a whole: that in affirming and celebrating contradictions *as they were*—including, famously, "slavery [. . .] and the stern opposition to it"[51]—Whitman practiced a kind of humorous "both-side-ism" that foreclosed a clear path of progress. How could a radical like Whitman forego so much didacticism? The answer, of course, is the grounding of his texts, in the *Crescent* as well as in *Leaves of Grass*. The foundation of his celebration of contradiction is the basis of Jacksonian democracy: the individual workingman.

Indeed, Whitman's "Sidewalks" sketches end on this very note. At the conclusion of the tale of our Kentucky bumpkin, "Broadhorn," bumbling through New Orleans, Whitman advises his readers not to laugh *at* the man, but *with* him. "To see Ephraim as he goes staring and gawking about a city, one would form an unfair estimate not only of the man, but of his class," he cautions. But Ephraim is much more than that. He's the "Western b'hoy"—the future of the country. "To talk about their intelligence, in the sense of learning, as is common with political demagogues, is all stuff; but they possess what answers an excellent purpose in the matter of pure republicanism and which William Pinckney [*sic*], many years ago, avowed to be his main reliance—namely: 'the unsophisticated good sense and noble spirit of the American people.'"[52]

Whitman concludes his humorous series on an expressly political note, quoting (and misspelling) the famous Maryland politician William Pinkney (1764–1822) in his defense of the 1820 Missouri Compromise, a piece of legislation Pinkney helped draft that admitted north-of-the-line Missouri as a slave state but prohibited slavery in other, northern sections of the Louisiana Purchase territory. Whitman, of course, had "accepted" the Compromise, and it formed a basis for his thinking until the prospect of massive Mexican land concessions in 1848 troubled the hitherto significant limitation on slavery expansion the Compromise had implied.[53] Pinkney's plea to respect "the unsophisticated good sense and noble spirit of the American people" made a popular sovereignty argument for slavery—namely that the right to abolish or maintain it should be decided by a state's "body politic or independent political society of men," not by the federal government.[54]

Given the historical trajectory of the United States (and the doctrine's pernicious afterlife), one might then be tempted to charge 1840s Whitman with troubling naivety or with harboring regressive politics (perhaps tailored for his New Orleans audience). But this statement is partnered in the "Sidewalks" sketches with a vision of a workingman's republic: a body politic that, as it grew and expanded, would almost inevitably lead to the kind of progress at the heart of radical politics. Popular sovereignty, to Whitman, was as much a political program as it was a way of life (and, as *Leaves of Grass* would show, a way of art). While the people Whitman encountered on the streets of New Orleans were often hilariously diverse—their "good sense" a source of ample "good humor"—Whitman also noted an overwhelming "Americanness" that united them. This growing "cosmopolitan influence"[55] formed the foundation on which their seemingly "incongruous diversity" played out. It took a trip down South for Whitman to realize that a "nation of nations"[56] could be built on this good-humored premise.

CHAPTER 6

SUDDENLY, out of its state and drowsy air, the air of slaves,
Like lightning Europe le'pt forth,
Sombre, superb and terrible

—WHITMAN, "RESURGEMUS" (1850)

Print Revolutions

WHILE THE WHITMAN BROTHERS busied themselves attending comedy shows, concerts, balls, and parades, a new feeling began to sweep the Crescent City. As March was giving way to April, the population was in uproar and the post-Mardi Gras dull had transformed into an air of eager anticipation and, quite often, outright celebration. The Whitmans' time in New Orleans, of course, fell squarely into one of the most impactful global events of the antebellum period: the European revolutions of 1848. By the time the Whitman brothers stepped off the boat in New Orleans in late February, the continent had caught fire, though it took weeks for news to reach them. As they had left Brooklyn, there had been some fighting in Palermo, which had felt like a provincial squabble to most Americans. Now, revolutionary fervor engulfed France, and King Louis-Philippe had abdicated. Before the publication of the first issue of the *Crescent*, Baden and Bavaria had joined the revolutionary fray, dragging along much of Central, Southern, and Eastern Europe. A brushfire of popular discontent was sweeping through the continent, and its astonishingly swift and decisive early successes promised a quick toppling of the monarchies of old Europe.[1] The language of the French Quarter was once again the mother tongue of revolution—and Whitman and his paper were all ears.

Whitman had already had a taste of this. In his third week in the Crescent City, a French barrister, Pierre Soulé, had been put into the Parish Prison—located at the heart of the French Quarter—for contempt of court by a judge of English stock. To Francophone New Orleanians, this had been an affront. "[T]he French population," Whitman wrote home to New York, "'made a night of it' for him; and, what was worse, they took him out with a band of music and procession the next morning, and marched up in front of the district court, [. . .] and beat the drums and raised the deuce generally."[2] Even four-and-a-half decades after the Louisiana Purchase, significant portions of New Orleans identified as French—and French newspapers, food, fashion, church services, and literature played a major role in public life. Whitman's lifelong fascination with French—and his perpetual regret over his inability to master it—had much to do with immersion in the culture of the French quarter. His poetic celebrations of revolution also disclose a Francophile inflection.

By April, coverage in the *Crescent* was approaching fever pitch. A particularly Whitmanesque piece narrates the strange experience of waiting for news (via steamers, papers, and carriages) that seemed to arrive so much slower than events unraveled in Europe:

> Of France—brave, generous-hearted France! —we all know the late movements. Of the Sicilies, too—of Rome—of Switzerland—we know. Meanwhile the German States are ripe for rebellion. Lethargic Austria seems to be, at least, rubbing its heavy eyes; for Metternich is old, and the people suffer. Prussia has, for years past, had education diffused among its people: is not that enough to make them strive for freedom? Will not Spain and Portugal, too, catch some energy from the vital heat spreading around them?[3]

Europe was ridding itself of the divine right of kings at a pace that seemed hardly believable to American observers: "Three days in 1848 were sufficient to consummate a revolution which sixty years ago required three years," the *Crescent* marveled.[4]

While it took weeks for the news of the revolution to trickle down—by late March the *Crescent* was still doubtful there *was* an actual revolution in France[5]—when it did settle in, it dominated affairs in the city. Between April and their departure in May, the Whitman brothers would have encountered signs of the French and European uprisings everywhere. Tricolored flags popped up in windows, patriotic songs in various languages echoed through the French and American quarters, and the local papers were celebrating Europe on almost every page. "I have never been in Europe," Whitman recalled in *Specimen Days*, but he possessed "a personal and saunterer's knowledge of St. Charles street in New Orleans" (among other "great thoroughfare[s]"),[6] which almost made up for that. The First Municipality around St. Louis Cathedral, with its waterfront markets, oyster peddlers, and Catholic cemeteries had been a favorite destination of the Whitman brothers since their arrival. In less than fifteen minutes' time, it felt like they had travelled to France. Now, more than ever.

The events in Europe were not just foreign news; to Whitman and many of his fellow citizens, they represented a victory of American-style republicanism, popular sovereignty, and liberal self-governance. Toward the end of Whitman's tenure, the local City Council even released a resolution that tendered "heartfelt thanks to the patriotic citizens of Paris, and especially those of the twelfth arrondissement, for the homage paid to the memory of the Father of our Country [George Washington], by selecting the anniversary of his birth-day as the birth-day of their own freedom."[7] Europe, it seemed, was turning American, and the future poet of America was paying attention.

In the first months of the European upheavals, historian Timothy Mason Roberts reminds us, "the revolutionary community that Americans celebrated was a transatlantic one, promising to draw the United States and Europe together in republican partnership."[8] Daily newspapers, then, "performed an important function in helping construct a revolutionary public culture" that soon expressed itself in New Orleans citizens donning red caps, attending mass gatherings for Europe, waving flags, or otherwise expressing themselves as part of "a revolutionary people," welcoming the Old World with open arms.[9] The *Crescent* was aware of its responsibilities and was up to the task. Issue after issue, it decorated its news coverage with celebratory songs and poems dedicated to Ireland, France, Italy, Germany, and the general European struggle against tyrants. Some of these pieces were translated by in-house speakers of Italian (Da Ponte) and French (Larue), some echo the Fenian activism of fellow journalists at the paper (court reporter Reeder). Many would have been, as Larry J. Reynolds speculates, "selected for publication" by "scissors editor" Whitman.[10]

Most notably among these revolutionary pieces is a poem titled "The Old World," which has been misidentified by a leading biographer as likely "from Whitman's pen." Describing it as anticipating Whitman's later poem on the revolutions ("Resurgemus," published 1850),[11] the biographer declares it "difficult to imagine who else on the *Crescent* staff or elsewhere in New Orleans might have composed such a poem" going as far as suggesting "it may have effected [Whitman's] eventual dismissal" from the paper.[12] While newspaper digitization has now made it possible to clearly identify the piece as written more than a decade earlier by English poet-politician John Bowring,[13] its misattribution to Whitman is instructive, as it illustrates a periodical context that appears puzzling to modern readers: a Southern paper that on occasion ran slave ads, nevertheless celebrating self-liberation abroad by comparing the political status quo of the Old World to human bondage and declaring: "The slave must rejoice, the enslaver must weep."[14]

In its first months, the European upheaval—bolstered by revolutionary hegemon France signaling its willingness to defend fellow republics—felt destined for victory. It would not last. In 1850, Whitman would eulogize the short flicker of hope that ended in mass exodus, death, and defeat as "[t]hat brief, tight, glorious grip / Upon the throats of kings."[15] Given Whitman's later embrace of "[t]hose martyrs that hang from the gibbets" of Europe, it is natural to suspect him of being the primary author of the fiery, republican articles that sprinkled the pages of the *Crescent* in spring of 1848. Literary historians like Larry J. Reynolds have done so,[16] turning Whitman into the sole republican voice of the paper—a mistake on occasion echoing through Whitman scholarship.[17] Others, like biographer Jerome Loving, have been more cautious about attributing authorship to Whitman. Casting the poet of *Leaves of Grass* as the sole progressive thinker of the *Crescent*, Loving still points out that celebrations of European revolutions were typical in the American newspaper landscape and that they aligned with the imperialist interests of what he calls the "pro-slavery, anti-Wilmot" newsroom of the *Crescent*.[18] Underlying these assessments by both Loving and Reynolds is a strange ahistorical bent: the idea that Whitman, the revolutionary poet of *Leaves of Grass*, would certainly be more forward-thinking, more internationalist, than anyone else at a local paper from a southern slave state. This idea is based on a misunderstanding of the antebellum political spectrum and, especially, of radical elements within and without the Democratic Party. To make sense of the revolutionary sympathies of the *Crescent*, and Whitman's relationship to it, we must then meet the actual author of most of its revolutionary editorializing: John Cooper Larue (1817–56).[19]

Two years Whitman's senior, the sharp rhetorician Larue was the perfect fit for the kind of detailed, country-by-country analysis of the progress of revolutions that the *Crescent* offered its eager readers. Likely of French descent,[20] Larue spoke French fluently and had already lectured on the (previous) French Revolution across the Crescent City.[21] Editor Whitman later recalled frequently yielding to the expertise of his colleague, resulting in Larue "generally [having] prepared the leading editorials" during his tenure.[22] Larue's friends and admirers lauded him as "a frequent, able and popular orator" as well as a journalist with "a very powerful and caustic pen."[23] Others, though, considered him an "Odd Fellow (in more sense than one)"[24] as well as a "dirty hireling scribbler,"[25] to be counted among the number of "unsuccessful pig-hunters" for political fame.[26] Like many of Whitman's fellow staff members at the *Crescent*, Larue had soldiered in Mexico and had made himself a household name for his wartime letters, having authored correspondence items signed "Our Private" in the *Delta*.[27] After Whitman's tenure, he would run the *Crescent* alongside then-editor William Walker. For now, Walker and Larue served together in leadership roles at the American League for an Undivided Ireland.[28]

Larue, a lawyer-politician and future judge, consistently espoused political convictions that complicate simplistic readings of political identities in the antebellum South. Larue had been born in New Jersey yet was intensely pro-Southern. He was proud of his French background but had been a card-carrying supporter of the xenophobic "Native Americans" (Know Nothings), even editing their local party paper.[29] Additionally, he was a temperance crusader,[30] a French-style communist,[31] a staunch secularist active in the Thomas Paine Association,[32] an outspoken free-trade advocate,[33] and an opponent of slavery extension.[34] Like radical Democrat Whitman, the young Larue admired Andrew Jackson[35] and, by the time he encountered the Brooklyn journalist in

New Orleans, he had already been elected to the Louisiana House of Representatives as a "radical Democrat."[36] The State Government, of course, still resided in New Orleans at that time, allowing Larue to split his days between the *Crescent* and the House, where he served on various tax committees.

A political firebrand, Larue may well have been a template for Whitman's own embrace of radical activism following his return to Brooklyn. Skimming over a proposal for a short-lived paper that Larue ran with an associate a decade prior, called *The Southerner, and People's Friend*, one can hear echoes of what Whitman may have appreciated in Larue, when he recalled him as "a good writer":

> [A]n important epoch has at length arrived in the history of our country, when the agricultural, mechanical, and laboring portions of the community are no longer considered as hewers of wood and drawers of water to the monopolist and speculator; when the simplicity in government, the entire divorce of bank and state, and the securing of equal political rights to every American citizen, begin to be avowed as the only proper means of restoring to the people of the United States, that purity and patriotism which distinguished the patriarchs of the revolution. [. . . It] behooves the friends of civil liberty to sustain, by every honorable means, the rights of the people, menaced as they are by individual cupidity, corporate rapacity, and legislative infidelity.[37]

The *Southerner* under Larue's leadership was later remembered as "advocating extreme Democratic principles and policies" and as "especially vigorous in its assault upon the banking system and in its defense of the financial system of President Van Buren."[38] Worries about monied aristocracies, defenses of "the common people," an embrace of workers and Democratic heroes—Whitman likely encountered Larue as a political ally who shared many of his own deeply held convictions.

In their revolutionary coverage, then, Larue supplied the dry facts to Whitman's "vital heat";[39] in tandem they wrote to encourage, maintain, and entertain "a revolutionary public culture"[40] via the daily press. In their sense of self and their mission, they behaved like the "bohemians" that historian Mark Lause has traced in 1850s New York: class-conscious print creatives responding to economic pressures and the increasing impossibility of social rising with a propensity to pursue a startling number of reformist causes, activist outlets, and literary-philosophical pursuits.[41]

Rhetorically, however, Larue expresses his form of cultural alienation from the political mainstream quite differently from fellow Free-Soiler Whitman. Knowing that any news from Europe was outdated as soon as it arrived at the *Crescent* office, the paper decided to present its readers with the kind of in-depth sociohistorical examinations into the various revolutionary movements that only an erudite lecturer like Larue could offer. Calling his essays "statistical exposition[s],"[42] Larue examined Russia, France, England, Ireland, and Germany in order to provide historical and demographic background to revolutionary developments. He argued that "many of the leading newspapers on our side of the Atlantic" were implicitly biased because of their monolingualism, forcing them to provide commentary "founded principally upon the notions and speculations of the *British* aristocratic press,"[43] which hoped to slander and suppress the true revolutionary potential of the moment. This was not just a quest against monarchy and for representative government but a far-reaching revolution that aimed to change the fundamental economic conditions of the working classes. Consequently, Larue argued:

> *Communism* is the mighty bugbear which they have invested with every thing horrible in appearance and dreadful in intent, and with which they labor to frighten all the grown up children who shall have the bad taste or temerity to look favorably upon the progress of liberal principles. It is something, in their apprehension, particularly dreadful—it proposes to give food, clothing, education, and comfort to the whole people; even to the poor and the laboring man. [. . .] Socialism, St. Simonism, Fourierism, Communism, "Liberty, Equality, and Fraternity," may all be erroneous in theory, may all be inapplicable to the real wants of man and to the improvement of society—they may all be impracticable, whether put in operation by the consent of a portion of the people, or by the political power of the country, but to intimate that any or all of them are systems of robbery, plunder, or outrage upon the rights of any person or class of persons, is grossly to

slander the best meaning men who ever lived, for the mere purpose of checking inquiry into existing abuses.[44]

Larue's work was a materialist examination of the root causes (and revolutionary potential) of the European revolts by a political activist. In this argument, he went much further than Whitman had ever done (or would do), even toying with that "mighty bugbear" of pre-Marxian Communism. "Relief" for the masses, Larue wrote in a different piece, "can only be hoped for from a reconstruction of the whole social system" that includes abolishing "inequality of condition," not just establishing adequate representation for the poor.[45] And, of course, many of the societal ills that fermented revolutionary unrest Larue found echoed his personal convictions: restrictions on free trade (especially in the case of Germany), insufficient or nonexistent secularization, and a strong centralization of the state. For work like this, he would later be remembered in town as a leading "Democrat of the school then known as subterranean, which inclined toward socialism and communism."[46]

Notably, the very specter of slavery so perplexingly invoked in the republication of "The Old World" poem was present across Larue's editorials. He, too, decried European nations debased by the "most degraded state of predial slavery"[47] and described Russian serfdom as a "state of absolute slavery."[48] He even went a step further, commenting a few days after Whitman's departure from New Orleans about a censorship law in England, that "it seems a little singular that the same individuals who turn up their eyes in such pious horror at a statute of Louisiana, which makes it penal to teach our slaves to read and write, should applaud themselves on the passage of such a law, intended to keep some millions of white slaves from a knowledge of their rights, and of the means to obtain them."[49] Of course, the racial regime of the South made it quite possible to conceptualize a categorical difference between Black and white slavery—for Larue and Whitman. And within a week of this article, the *Crescent* was back to its old (though somewhat infrequent) practice of advertising slave auctions.[50] But Whitman was not the only Wilmot man able and willing to point out potential convergences between liberation abroad and bondage at home—and to brave the cognitive dissonance it brought about. Ultimately, there was no need to sneak such arguments into print via a poem that Whitman did not write (and that did not get him fired). Instead, they were endorsed by the editorial columns of the *Crescent* and espoused by one of its future co-editors.

Grounded in classical liberal theory and often over three thousand words long, Larue's articles marshal a host of sources, historical contexts, and demographic data in a way that Whitman always admired (and to which he at times aspired)[51] but could never successfully muster himself. Stylistically, these pieces are also at odds with the slang-heavy, highly emotional (often jovial) work that Whitman contributed to the paper elsewhere. Instead of reading Whitman as in radical opposition to his own paper (as some scholars would have it), we find that he appears more and more like an enthusiastic follower of the true radical in the office: Larue.

Indeed, the most Whitmanian voice in the *Crescent* is to be found in editorials focused on what we might call revolutionary affect: those tears of joy, loud exclamations, and jubilations that are strikingly absent from Larue's writings. For Larue, the European uprisings of 1848 primarily promised a potential for radical, economic reform. For Whitman, they suggested, most viscerally, the spread of a Jacksonian way-of-being abroad and a reaffirmation of its tenants at home. As in his later poetry, that core identity was the lodestar guiding all other concerns (tariffs, free soil, direct democracy) that are its logical consequence. This attitude was mirrored in Whitman's actual writings on the conflicts—all of which center on men's emotional responses to and affective participation in revolution.

In cities across the United States, enthusiasm over developments in Europe was not confined to newspaper columns, of course, but frequently expressed itself through parades, political receptions, and speechifying. New Orleans was no exception. On April 17, for instance, German residents "assembled *en masse* in the St. Louis Exchange [. . .] to make a public expression of their approval of the recent revolutionary movements in France." Afterward, they paraded through the city singing "La Marseillaise."[52] A week later, it was the Italians' turn.[53] Naturally, emblems of Irish Nationalism dominated St. Patrick's Day, which Whitman attended with his brother,[54] and on April 11, of course, French citizens had held a "Great Meeting at the St. Louis," at which

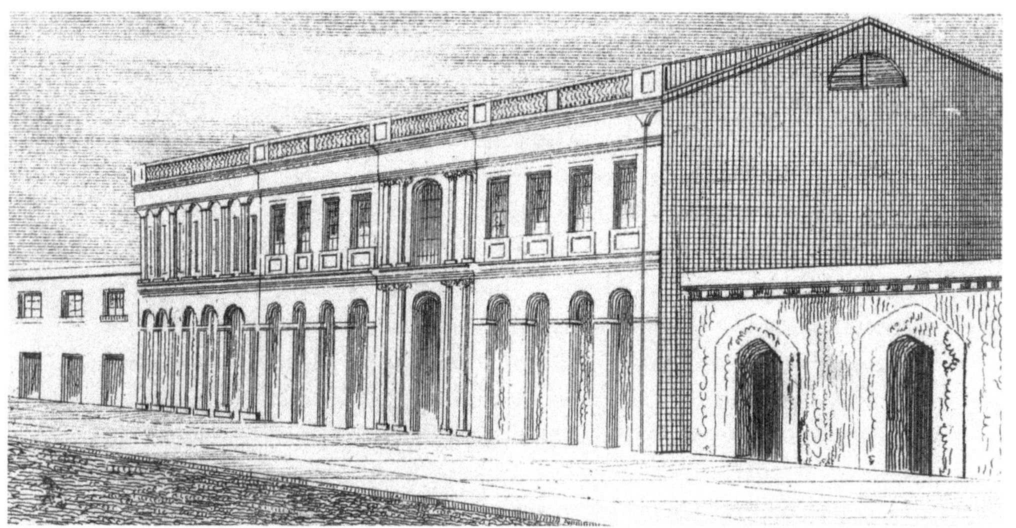

FIGURE 17. Orleans Theatre, from *Gibson's Guide and Directory of the State of Louisiana* (New Orleans, LA: J. Gibson, 1838), 312, courtesy of Beinecke Rare Book and Manuscript Library, Yale University.

Larue acted as one of the principal orators (and which Whitman may have covered in their paper). "The immense rotunda was crowded to excess," the *Crescent* noted the following day, "and the enthusiasm and unanimity which prevailed, proved that the feelings of 'the people' are interested in the subject."[55]

A week later, a "Grand Banquet in Honor of the French Revolution" was held at the Orleans Ball Room, which resolved somewhat less magnificently. Whitman is our likely reporter for the *Crescent*, covering the tumultuous evening.[56] The event took place just a block north of St. Louis Cathedral in one of New Orleans's oldest establishments: the Orleans Theatre, a "lower story Roman Doric," which connected to an impressive grand ballroom (built in 1817) that "when brilliantly lighted, [offered] a *coup d'œil* not to be surpassed for effect in America."[57] It was one of the centers of Creole culture, hosting the French Opera (which Whitman likely attended)[58] and annual quadroon balls. A *fête* at the New Orleans always promised to be a raucous affair. "In this ball room, the resort of the demi-monde, the fiercest human passions have run riot, and here have been laid the foundations for future tragedies, fatal duels, or bloody rencontres," a nineteenth-century guide to the city waxed poetic.[59]

The night in question was one of pomp and circumstance. The "Governor, Secretary of State, Treasurer, Attorney General, and most of [New Orleans's] Federal, State and City dignitaries" crowded into the room. They were joined by a Consul representing the French Provisional Government. All sat at a long table "loaded with luxuries and elegancies," a "splendidly illuminated" banner behind them proclaiming "liberté, égalité, fraternité." Around them, the room was filled to the brim with spectators, many of whom were dressed in revolutionary regalia. The Governor then toasted to "*The Will of the People*—the only foundation of all Government,"[60] followed by salutations to America, Louisiana, and revolutionary France. A brass band played songs to "awake all the Gallic enthusiasm of these fiery sons of France."[61] Afterward, "three lovely, dark-eyed Creole girls, who personated Liberty, Charity and Pity" collected funds intended to aid wounded French revolutionaries.[62] Whitman, in his account of the evening, was particularly taken by the "Goddess of Liberty," writing that he had "no doubt that the bewitching influence of her beautiful countenance contributed essentially to elicit the generosity of the company."[63] The notoriously broke poet-journalist appears to have chipped in some funds himself: "We know [her beauty] had that effect upon us," he explained, "and we are not *very* susceptible."

Then a final toast was offered, and the room gasped. It came from a renegade in the audience, proposing a salute to honor the leader of a failed 1835 assassination attempt on the French king. This suggestion "produced a perfect storm of excitement," Whitman recorded. After some shouting, however, the "practical Jacobins" in the audience triumphed "over the dreamy, theoretic Girondins," resulting in the leading men of Louisiana loudly exclaiming a paradoxical "*vive*" to an executed would-be assassin. After that, the meeting slowly descended into drunken chaos: "Every gentleman seemed perfectly willing that every one else should speak, so that he was permitted to exercise his oratorical faculties at the same time. In view of this state of affairs, [. . .] and having gratified our appetite and our republican enthusiasm, we concluded to leave, which we accordingly did, before the ceremonies were ended."[64] Here, we get a conclusion most reminiscent of Whitman's typical style of reportage: a thrilling, humorous "peep" into an exotic locale, ending in our premature retreat alongside the reporter, who serves as his audience's eyes and ears. Articles like these, as Jason Stacy has noted, served as "a means of echolocation, a consumable good that helped readers situate themselves within a community beyond their immediate ken."[65] It created a mode of belonging for urban floaters like Whitman. Not everyone might have been there with the *Crescent* "peeper," but through his sonorous body, the "republican enthusiasm" of the moment can leap from the paper's columns into a readers' reality and form a bond around a shared-though-mediated experience.

In tandem with event coverage like this, the *Crescent*'s adoration for one French figure, in particular, bares Whitman's mark. In the spring of 1848, during the period of Whitman's tenure, the *Crescent* was full of celebrations of the poet-statesman Alphonse de Lamartine (1790–1869), who was then heralded as the ideal next candidate for the leadership of revolutionary France. Lamartine represented a more moderate wing of the Revolution and aroused less fear of Jacobin terror in Americans. Consequently, US newspapers *loved* Lamartine. Larry S. Reynolds reminds us that, "[d]uring the spring of 1848, Lamartine became one of the most celebrated figures of the world, and his idealism, courage and eloquence received much praise in America."[66] In New Orleans, "Lamartine hats" would soon become a popular fashion trend before the Whitmans' departure.[67] While *Crescent* editorials post-Whitman still fully endorsed the "wise, statesmanlike" politician,[68] Whitman appears to have contributed the more hagiographic coverage of the man (a tone which ceased after Whitman's departure). In the columns of the *Crescent*, Whitman turned Lamartine into a representative Great Man: "It is beautiful to see such a man! [. . .] Lamartine has a wondrous union of physical and moral courage," one such piece gushed,[69] while another turned Lamartine's *History of the Girondists* (which had become a bestseller once more) into an ethnographic lesson: there, one discovers "*the Frenchman* himself—full blown, excited by all the most powerful passions that can actuate the soul—warriors, demagogues, men and women—the rabbles, the nobles, the learned—poets, ruffians, the king and queen!"[70] Somewhat similar to Whitman's scene of a crying Washington in *Leaves of Grass*,[71] readers of the *Crescent* were also treated to a sentimental account titled "The Man of His Country and of the Age!" that depicted a crying, embracing populace listening to a speech by Lamartine in defense of the tricolor flag.[72] "Does he not resemble our own Washington?" another editorial asked.[73]

Pieces like these, which broke with the "succinct and logical style of reasoning"[74] typical of Larue's revolutionary coverage to instead indulge in em-dashes, exclamations, humor, and generalizations, were somewhat rare in the revolutionary coverage of the *Crescent*—though they did exist. Some were even published at times when Larue was out of the office. On March 16, for instance, a piece titled "Happy Are We" appeared in the editorial columns of the paper. Larue, as we learn in the very next column, spent much of the previous night at the late-evening session of the Democratic State Convention.[75] Consequently, we get a short filler piece on the next day, sounding quite a bit different from Larue's typical fare. It was written by an author who positioned his own identity in contrast to a "travelled European" and did not comment on specific developments on the continent but synthesized what readers had learned in the past days to contrast revolutionary Europe with the United States. Together with the untitled piece cited at the beginning of this chapter (which congratulates "brave, generous-hearted France!"), it is perhaps the most Whitmanesque article on the revolutions. It skipped the usual framing of Whitman's commentary in the *Crescent* (as "pen and scissors" reworking of news received on the exchange) and replaced it with a more familiar Whitmanian setup—a street encounter:

> We heard an intelligent and travelled European, a few days since, utter some thinly concealed sarcasms on the difference between the "tone" of the richer classes here and the tone abroad. He would have shown more wisdom, now, by considering the difference between the condition of *the people* here and in the Old World. Nor is it amiss for Americans themselves, now and then, to reflect on "the blessings we enjoy"—or rather, we should say, the political curses and cramps we are free from.
>
> The United States have the only real representative Government in the world. In order to prove this, it needs merely the statement of the following facts: In France, only one person in 137 has a vote for his legislators; in Great Britain and Ireland, one in 42, and half of these are coerced by lordly influence; in the United States, *one in seven*—or, in other words, every man who is a citizen. [. . .]

While the condition of certain fractions of society may possibly be not as favorable here (though we confess we see no earthly reason why) as in Europe, the condition of the forty-nine fiftieths is better beyond all comparison, both as to rational freedom and physical comforts.[76]

Especially the last paragraph echoed Whitman's political stance at the time. Larue's editorials on the issue never quite broached into such broad celebrations of America, but they were typical of Whitman in 1848. In a letter to the *Crescent* later that year, for instance, Whitman—then the editor of the Brooklyn *Freeman*—advised, "At danger of being somewhat trite, I cannot help calling the attention of your readers to the superiority of American institutions over those of all other governments on earth, as exhibited in the operations of an election for the Presidency. What in France would cause collisions certainly, and perhaps massacres, will here cause but a collision of opinion, and all will peacefully submit to the decision of the majority."[77] Even as Whitman was actively participating in the splintering of the Democratic Party, his sense of the superiority and resilience of democratic institutions remained unscathed, the revolutions abroad only serving to reinforce, not trouble, his belief in the American system.

This reading carried over into Whitman's most direct encounter with the revolution. In October 1848, after his return home, Whitman wrote to his old paper in the South to inform its readers of the arrival of a revolutionary star from Europe: exiled Badensian radical Friedrich Hecker (1811–81). Hecker's bombastic reception by the Democratic Party of New York allowed Whitman to praise revolutionary politics abroad while celebrating the American system as a natural antidote to revolution:

Something that troubled Presidents Washington and Adams fifty years ago—an article called "Red Republicanism" now-a-days—has been paraded at Tammany Hall lately. I mean, of course, the meeting last Saturday night, to compliment Mr. Hecker, and listen to a speech from him and other ultra radicals. All day long the great folds of the flag of "gold, red and black," had been flaunting from the staff at the top of old Tammany, joined with our own "Star-Spangled;" and at night, the immense room was an absolute

> jam of human beings. The Socialists, National Reformers, and Free Soilers, gathered in great force; Old Hunkerism, and all sorts of Conservativism, looked on with a sour face, and retreated from the scene. It was a gala time for all the highest and most enthusiastic doctrines of "Liberty, Equality, Fraternity!" I, too, caught the enthusiasm, and though I understand German about as much as Choctaw, found myself cheering the Herr as loudly as the rest. Ah! there is something in the breast that bursts all control, in responding on such occasions to high and lofty dreams of political perfection—the wish to stab all sorts of tyranny that have for so many ages enchained the physical and mental powers of the "lower orders" of human kind! The popular feeling in New York would, even now, receive such men as Rollin and Blanc with joy. We do not so much wish their doctrines tried here in America, for we are doing well enough; and every successive ten years shows an opening still wider of radicalism—about as fast and as far as the people can stand it. But there is a deadly hatred toward the oppression and misery which the continent of Europe has received as its black legacy from the past. Devastation and blood seem horrible enough, but folks think they are not much worse than the wretchedness of stagnation, poverty, and death, for the millions of the old world.[78]

Revolution, Whitman told his *Crescent* readers, was made unnecessary by democratic governance and any slowing of progress was an act of popular wisdom that slows things down to keep a republic from stretching itself too far and risking dissolution. "For Whitman, as for Marx, the movement of history is revolutionary, progressive, and the triumph of freedom and the masses is *inevitable*," literary scholar Betsy Erkkila has argued.[79] Yet for Whitman, as we see here, the American republic was instead inherently *evolutionary*, moving steadily but slowly toward progress and thereby keeping actual popular revolution at bay. Whitman was a gradualist.[80] It was a conviction he held until his final years. In reply to a question about how he positioned himself against socialists trying to court him for an endorsement, the aged poet would famously exclaim: "I am with them in the result—that's about all I can say."[81] Their method—revolution—Whitman did not endorse.

The clearest, early expression of this idea comes in a late-April *Crescent* editorial titled "The Presidential Campaign," which, ostensibly, embraced this same view of democratic politics as self-regulatory and naturally opposed to dissolution:

> In this age of revolutions, it is well that the people of the United States can find some relief from the unpoetical quiet of confirmed republicanism, in the temporary excitement and sport of a presidential election. [. . .] Like the man who got drunk in self-defence on the evening of the Fourth of July, our good people would be obliged to kick up in self-defence a revolution about something—though no one can guess about what. But the election in November saves us. That is one glorious day for overturning dynasties, and reforming the manifold abuses of bad government, which the patriots out of office can always discover. [. . . W]e use the ballot box instead of the barricade as bloodless substitutes for balls. [. . .] This is our revolution. Rather a tame affair to be sure, when our ears are daily assailed with the hurrahs of enfranchised millions, and when our eyes are greeted on every side with the sight of falling diadems and shattered thrones. But tame as it is, the misfortune of good government and universal happiness has left us no other, and we must make the best of it.[82]

Here, the American Republic figured as a potentially revolutionary process, slowed into permanence by institutions governed by popular will. Or as Whitman put it in a letter of late 1848: "What in other countries, would be thrown off by a revolution, or an attempt at one, exhausts itself here in politics."[83] This, Whitman made sure to underscore, was a testament to the *strength* of the American system. "It is the fashion of a certain set to assume to despise 'politics' and the 'corruption of parties,' and the unmanageableness of the masses," Whitman had already noted a year prior. "But to our view, the spectacle is always a grand one—full of the most august and sublime attributes."[84] To Whitman, revolutionary affect united European stormers of barricades with Americans in line at the ballot box.

Betsy Erkkila has argued that Whitman may have "found a more revolutionary version of democratic history in Europe [in 1848] than in the United States, where the working people did not rise up in defense of their rights," and that Europe's "uprising renewed Whitman's faith in the ultimate triumph of liberty." Yet this reading seems to misrepresent Whitman's evolutionary politics as well as the conclusion of his poetic statement on 1848. "Resurgemus," Whitman's 1850 free verse poem on Europe's brief flirtation with freedom, famously ended not with a reproach of the timidity of American workers, but with a celebration of America as a beacon of freedom and homeland for defeated Republicans in Europe:

> Not a grave of those slaughtered ones,
> But is growing its seed of freedom,
> In its turn to bear seed,
> Which the winds shall carry afar and resow,
> And the rain nourish.

In "Herr Hecker" and his fellow political refugees, Whitman saw the tragic defeat of the revolutions in Europe as nourishing the republican blood of the United States. Shortly after his return to New York, Whitman would therefore inform his readers in the Crescent City about these new immigrants arriving in the United States:

> Immigration pours in without the least abatement. Hardly a day passes that hundreds of poor wayfarers from Europe do not land upon our wharves; some no doubt, to sink amid disease or poverty, but most, I am happy to say, to take a start which brings them amid better times and far more comfort. What is most astonishing to me, is the fact that with such prevalent poverty as characterises the masses of the immigrants, there is so little criminality. [. . .] Moreover, this city is the great receiving point of European emigration.[85]

"Let them come and welcome—the more the better," he wrote in another letter, adding, "[l]et them, however, not remain in cities, but post westward forthwith, and vote themselves farms."[86] He may as well have been describing the life of Hecker, who would settle in Illinois, set his sights on abolition, and even become a potential state elector for Free-Soil Frémont, alongside Abraham Lincoln, no less.[87] "Vote yourself a farm," of course, had by then been incorporated into the Free-Soil Party platform (among issues such as harbor and river reforms as well as reduced postal rates—also core issues in Whitman's *Crescent* editorializing).[88]

Whitman, in line with his previous writings for the *Eagle*,[89] was subscribing to a melting pot idea of the United States—or rather, Walter Grünzweig reminds us, to the idea of a "nation of nations." In his reading of Whitman's 1855 preface to *Leaves* as theorizing a "world literature," Grünzweig concludes:

> If a nation "contains" most other nations of the world, it is not a superior, but a *diverse* nation. The multiethnic composition of American society changes, and in fact relativizes, the concept of the nation itself just a few years after it was invented [. . .] . As a "teeming" nation, it is the opposite of a melting pot, which *homogenizes* a nation; the procreative metaphor rather brings forth—or at least supports—the multi-nationality of the United States.[90]

While it was Larue, then, not Whitman, who was discussing, and defending Socialism, Fourierism, and Communism in the pages of the *Crescent*,[91] there remained a radical bent to Whitman's arguably less "revolutionary" writings in 1848.

On the rare occasion that the story of Whitman and the revolutions of 1848 has been told, it has been told as one of radicalization and self-censorship: that Whitman held revolutionary attitudes that he largely repressed at the *Crescent*; that this sentiment only burst forth in his 1850 "Resurgemus" and, later, his revolutionary 1855 volume of poems; that Whitman's papers were too timid, too conservative to print these sentiments. None of this is strictly true. Instead, Whitman's encounter with the revolutions—in the columns of his paper, via the voices of his colleagues, the mass events in town—served to confirm attitudes the populist Democrat had held for a while: that Jacksonian mass enfranchisement led to progress, that political change was often necessarily slow and came with setbacks, and that representative republics were a natural antidote to violent revolution. With these attitudes,

Whitman lagged behind fellow *Crescent* writers like communist Larue and was certainly no proto-Marxist in disguise.

Of course, Whitman's celebrations of republicanism in the context of the European upheavals take on a quite different shade in another contemporary context: the ongoing peace negotiations with Mexico. While Mexico had been militarily defeated prior to Whitman's arrival, it wasn't until his departure that an actual treaty had been settled. This treaty would strip large areas of land from Mexico and inaugurate a conflict over the extension of slavery that would lead to the Free-Soil election in 1848—as well as the long genesis of the Republican party in the 1850s and the subsequent Civil War its president ended.[92] During the contentious debate over the peace treaty we get Whitman's increasingly draconian vision of utter Mexican defeat—much of it couched in a similar Americanophile rhetoric to his coverage of Europe. Whitman's internationalist "multi-nationality of the United States" here sounded more like a jingoistic "United States of North America."

While Whitman would come to regret his stance on Mexico and his inability (or unwillingness) to learn more about the Spanish-speaking population in New Orleans at the time, his Southern sojourn only served to radicalize Whitman *for* Polk's imperialist project. While Walt had pushed for a swift end of the war in the spring of 1847 and had cautioned against full annexation in the winter of that same year, his time in New Orleans did not mellow his attitudes toward the southern neighbor. Instead, it pushed him further into expansionism. In a piece that may have been too extreme, initially, for the *Crescent*—and was hence framed as a noneditorial contribution by "W."—Whitman expressly argued against a peace with Mexico. The peace plan was nicknamed the "Trist Treaty" after the US diplomat, Nicholas Trist (1800–1874), who negotiated what would ultimately be the Treaty of Guadalupe Hidalgo that ended the war. It not only contained concessions of what is now the American Southwest, but also financial support to Mexico and a settlement of debts, aimed to ensure a permanent peace and a stable southern border. Indeed, Trist was so convinced of the importance of these measures, he negotiated them against the express wishes of the President—even after being officially recalled by Polk. Hence, Trist became a controversial figure in the US and a target of Whitman, who morphed into one of Trist's most ardent critics in the South.

"Americans and Mexicans will find themselves face to face with a fact which they cannot conceal, and whose consequences they cannot avert," Whitman argued in the first week of the *Crescent*'s run: "They will see that a peace between the United States and Mexico is impossible; and it needs no great learning or wise reflection to perceive, that when such a relation exists between States, the weaker must yield to and become incorporated with the stronger." Whitman's answer to Trist was "might makes right"—and he shifted the blame for farther expansion on Mexico. Mexico, he claimed, had been too thoroughly defeated, and had never been politically stable enough, for there to be any way for the country to accept or permanently honor peace. As he continued:

> Mexico has been weighed in the balances, and found wanting. For twenty-five years, she has been trying to maintain a place among the nations of the earth. For twenty-five years, other nations have borne with her wrong-doings and short-comings. During this period, she has been left almost entirely to herself; and if revolutionary experience could teach wisdom, she ought to have learned it. Statesman after statesman—General after General—Congress after Congress, has been placed at the head of Mexican affairs: and the country has groaned successively under the rule of them all. Her sufferings have taught her nothing; or, if they have inculcated lessons of government, they have taken away the strength necessary for putting them in practice. Now she lies prostrate and helpless at the feet of a neighboring nation, better skilled than herself in the science of government. Is there but one way by which the unfortunate people of Mexico can be reclaimed from anarchy and semi-barbarism? The only conclusion we can see, is in the words of the prophet, Peres: "Thy kingdom is divided, and given to the Medes and Persians."[93]

As swift, initially successful European revolutions indicated to Whitman a bright future of popular self-governance, he glanced back at two decades of changing governments in the Mexican state (where a conservative, centralized Republic had replaced a liberal federal

Republic—only to be replaced, yet again, by a federal system after the beginning of the American invasion) and a history of strong-man rulers. In Whitman's eyes, the Mexican Republic resembled monarchic Europe and needed to be overcome. Indeed, Whitman picked up the word *pronunciamento*—official decrees by the Mexican president—from this line of anti-Mexican rhetoric and would use it ironically until his final years in Camden.[94] Invasion and annexation, hence, would be the only necessary antidote to bring Mexico into proper republican governance. Whitman's previous plan for Mexico already envisioned a peaceful incorporation of the remaining Mexican lands once it had fully developed republican systems on its own. Now, it seemed to Whitman, this process would have to be sped up.

In a series of scathing, mocking attacks on Mexico and "Trist-Megistus,"[95] Whitman argued for a position that had likely played a role in the *Crescent* proprietors' departure from the *Delta*: excessive territorial expansion that challenged the 1820 compromise line. Indeed, the revolutions in Europe, Whitman wrote in a news column, "renders it certain that Mexico cannot receive any assistance from England or any of them, by word or deed. She would then be entirely at our mercy—or rather our sense of justice—were it not for this wretched Trist treaty."[96] Whitman's *Crescent* even went as far as reprinting fake news items that claimed the treaty was actually hand-written by a British diplomat.[97] Whitman had previously preached this same gospel to the readers of his *Eagle*:

> Why, at this moment [Great Britain] is intriguing with all her might, against us in Mexico, upon no doubt the base pretext to other powers, that she wished to prevent the complete subjugation of Mexico by her annexation to the United States—a thing she does not believe, and has no reason to dread if it were so, as the only evil that could flow from it, would be to establish a peaceable liberal government, where the most horrible despotism now exists, and to induce a horde of mountain robbers to become quiet and orderly citizens and peaceable cultivators of the earth. That having once enjoyed the blessings of a free government, they might never after be willing to change it, is highly probable; and here is the rub, they never could be

> induced to consent to a monarchy. As a matter of course, then, the time to intrigue with them, is while they are in a state of semibarbarism.[98]

Conspiracy-minded Whitman had long envisioned an autocratic Mexican state as part of the old world, nipping at the heels of the American republic. The treaty now proposed to end the war read to Whitman as an invitation to let monarchism flourish just beyond the southern border.

When the United States ratified the peace treaty on March 10, 1848 (months before Mexico would), Whitman responded with a typically Whitmanian diatribe: "Mr. Trist has humbugged the President, the President has humbugged the Senate, and the Senate has humbugged the people. [. . . T]his is a *triste* affair and deserves to be considered in a more serious tone than its many laughable features will, perhaps, permit us to regard it."[99] Afterward, all hope of Whitman's editorials focused on the prospect that Mexico would refuse to ratify and supply a pretext to further war and annexation. All of these editorials, like Whitman's celebrations of Europe, were fundamentally affect-driven rhetoric. In both scenarios Whitman post-hoc rationalized sentiment into argument, his persuasive, colorful prose manufacturing consent for continued hostilities with defeated Mexico.

Whitman framed expansion not merely through the lens of powerful self-interest of a victorious force, but as an act of liberation: "[T]he great Yucatanese nation is ready to deliver herself up, body and soul, to whatever power will take upon itself the onerous task of regulating her affairs and delivering her from the *Barbaros*," one *Crescent* piece claimed.[100] This item is, of course, nonsense. The propagandistic logic of this reasoning followed the blueprint of Texan independence and subsequent statehood—as well as of various filibustering endeavors in its wake.

It may, then, not be entirely coincidental that Whitman's tenure at the *Crescent* ends around the time that local papers learn that Mexico had ratified what was then the Treaty of Guadalupe Hidalgo and all negotiation was over. In place of Whitman's fiery articles, the *Crescent* in May starts to resemble a very different paper: correspondence increased, harsh anti-treaty rhetoric was toned down. In contrast to its previous stance against the possibility of *any* peace, this was the grumbling acknowledgement of it, after the fact—and after bellicose Whitman had left:

"The Treaty is a tolerable cover under which to back out from our position and abandon some rather costly and troublesome acquisitions. [. . .] No administration would have been safe in proposing the annexation of the whole of Mexico, nor in advocating a Proconsular Government over it as a conquered dependency."[101] Gone were the punning, fiery editorials of Whitman, and one has to wonder if his over-the-top agitation against peace—and the paper's return to its more subdued brand of reporting on the issue post-Whitman—may have had something to do with his swift departure just days after the ratification of the treaty.

This, of course, does not mean Whitman himself gave up on the hope of annexing more of Mexico. Indeed, while running the Free-Soil *Freeman* out of Brooklyn, he would inquire via letters about the "Buffalo Hunt" in the Mexican state of Tamaupilas. Led by factions who claimed to miss "the abundance which was experienced during the American occupation" and hence yearned for a "true Republican form of government," the plan was to establish a "Republic of Sierra Madre"[102]—which would, subsequent to independence from Mexico, join the United States. In reality, as a New York paper put it, the project was "The Next Slavery Foray,"[103] led by American Anglos under the leadership of Col. Henry Kinney (1814–62)—a soldier in Mexico who would become a Nicaraguan filibuster and who founded the city of Corpus Christi—and John Peoples, *Crescent* correspondent "Chaparral," whom Whitman until late in life would recall as a great newspaper asset.[104] Kinney and Peoples had a small amateur army waiting in the dunes of St. John's island for a signal to cross the Mexican border disguised as a hunting party. But the plan faltered when Kinney finally got cold feet. Whitman had egged on the project from afar, writing that in New York "there are ten thousand dare-devils [. . .] in want of adventure and excitement, who would like to join such an expedition."[105]

Perhaps Whitman was thinking himself a bit of a "Daggerdraw Bowieknife" (his *Crescent* caricature of a Texian filibuster), when writing of the *Crescent* in a subsequent letter:

> We don't hear any thing more of that "Buffalo Hunt on the Rio Grande." Is it given up? A thousand adventurous spirits here hope not. The President, it is true, per the Washington Union, talks dignifiedly about observing our "obligations of treaties

> toward Mexico." Well, let him—as far as concerns him. But if there be a real disposition, in earnest, to go on this hunt, and three thousand tough fellows could be got together for the purpose, with American officers, I should say, "go it;" and it seems difficult to imagine how Mr. Polk could stop 'em. However, there may be something about the move, which you in New Orleans understand better than we do here. One thing there can be no mistake about; that the timid, malignant, idle and shiftless Mexican population south of us, must give way, sooner or later, to Anglo-Saxon energy and selfishness—for we have about as much of the last as the first.[106]

This is Walt Whitman, editor and delegate of Free Soil, explicitly endorsing a filibustering excursion that aimed to turn parts of free, independent Mexico (which had outlawed slavery for decades) into an Anglo slave state that would replace local Latinx populations with a Southern planter class. Perhaps no clearer illustration of the difference between abolitionists—who decried the venture—and Free-Soilers may be made. Whitman was quite typical in this regard, with many fellow Free-Soilers having been outspoken expansionists, who envisioned a white, workingman's republic stretching to the Pacific. Not only the presence of slaves but other non-white populations had the potential to spoil this vision.[107]

When he heard news of the venture's failure, Whitman was disappointed but remained optimistic about an expansionist future for the United States: "Sorry are 'some folks' here to see a telegraphic announcement from your city that that 'Buffalo Hunt' has been nipped in the bud. What and how is it? That miserable Mexico must crumble from her present organization, and gradually merge in the United States, there is no doubt. But all in good time."[108] The US, the future poet of America here mused, would annex Mexico yet.

In the year of revolutions (and, perhaps, throughout his writerly life), Whitman's internationalism was delineated by an affect-based thinking in *ethnic types*. From thrifty and boozy Dutchmen, to unvarnished German music troupes bursting with Goethean feeling, to French Oyster peddlers with pretentions to aristocracy, Whitman's writings frequently relied on racial or ethnic heuristics to prop up a joke, promote an event, or make sense of an encounter on the streets. This kind of thinking held true for Whitman's engagements with European revolutions. Lamartine thus became a version of "*the Frenchman* himself" and in cheering "Herr Hecker" Whitman was overcome with foreign enthusiasm. By yelling in German, he became a German Romantic: "Ah! there is something in the breast that bursts all control[!]"[109] Whitman's politics was always a politics of the body—and the cultural and ethnic makeup of this body was often its most salient feature in its encounter with the future poet of *Leaves of Grass*. Notably, in 1848, Whitman's body politic did not include Mexicans (yet) and all empathy in the North with the defeated country only triggered derision and charges of Whiggery from Whitman.

The spring of 1848 was a profound moment for Whitman. It bolstered his messianic view of America as a beacon of republicanism. This put Whitman in touch with Europe and, by extension, the world, in a way he had not experienced before. The kind of radical thinking that Grünzweig sees in Whitman's theorizing of the United States as a "nation of nations" echoed in the image in "Resurgemus" of "seed[s] of freedom" carried afar and blooming on new shores. It rendered mass immigration not only a potentially useful but, indeed, a *necessary* requirement for the "teeming" nation that Whitman would celebrate in *Leaves of Grass*. Yet it also clearly embraced the notion of America as a colonial player on the global stage—one that might trample you and earn Whitman's praise for it. In 1848, Southern filibusters and European revolutionaries looked like two sides of the same coin to Whitman.

In thinking in national types, Whitman was also beginning to wonder what "types" of Americans there were. He was, for instance, fascinated by the prudence and plainspokenness of "Western" types he encountered. He found humor in Kentuckian country bumpkins, Texian desperados, Northeastern businessmen. Whitman discovered in New Orleans a "citizen-of-the-world disposition"[110]—a cosmopolitan urbanism that, on occasion, could transcend the kind of othering typologies that structure his writing and thinking. While seeing Hecker or reading about Lamartine were moments of encountering embodiments of Germany and France—they also constituted an act of identification. Lamartine was France's Washington, Whitman argued. And Whitman could *feel* what the Germans of New York felt, when they saluted the Badensian revolutionary in their mother tongue. These types, notably, were still all white men: neither Mexicans nor slaves were included in Whitman's civic imaginary in 1848.

In the end, it was not an erudite analysis of the material conditions for revolution in France, Austria, or the various German states that pushed Whitman into "radical" thinking on global issues. What drove Whitman was *revolutionary affect*. It was Whitman noting that though he understood "German about as much as Choctaw," he "found [him]self cheering the Herr as loudly as the rest"[111] and dipping deep into his pockets to donate some of his scarce funds to wounded revolutionaries in France because he was moved to his core by impassioned oration, free-flowing liquor, and skimpy costumes. It was the kind of affect that Whitman celebrated so frequently, for instance in "Calamus," where he exclaimed that he "can look over and behold [men like him] in Germany, Italy, France, Spain—Or far, far away, in China, or in Russia or India—talking other dialects."[112] While many of Whitman's immediate political concerns in the 1840s were intensely national, often nationalistic, his encounters with European republicans in 1848—be it "Herr Hecker" in New York, the French Consul at the Orleans Theatre, or his Italian, French, and Fenian coworkers—suggested a continuum between his political beliefs (Jacksonian, Free-Soil, workingmen's rights, etc.) and the revolutionary fervor gripping the continent. Or to put it in the words of an 1849 caricature of Whitman in the *Brooklyn Daily Advertiser* (a puff piece, likely written by himself): "From the South he brings the French motto 'Liberty, equality, fraternity,' and he stands before us a 'Freeman.'" Breathing the air of revolution, had made Whitman one of the "hot-headed ultras" of the world.[113]

Encountering the European revolutions in the Francophone metropolis of the South added a crucial, internationalist bent to the democratic affect that would form the core of *Leaves of Grass*. Toasting, boasting, and hanging out with revolutionaries and their local proxies, Whitman imagined himself storming barricades, breaking shackles, and guillotining kings. Likewise, he celebrated with returning soldiers and future southern filibusters and imagined himself violently stripping the Mexican Republic for parts. To Whitman and many fellow Free-Soilers, both constituted an expression of "popular sovereignty."[114] The populace in question for Whitman were modern working (white) men who embodied Jacksonian America—those "quiet and orderly citizens and peaceable cultivators of the earth"—not the semibarbarous "horde[s] of mountain robbers," easily swayed by despots and monarchs.[115] Whitman's revolutionary pronunciamentos were at times indistinguishable from other forms of jingoistic rhetoric. It took Whitman decades, and a Civil War, to reconsider his expansionist stance. "Mexico," he reflected when discussing the southern neighbor's support for the Union, was "the only [nation] to whom we have ever really done wrong." This change of heart came late, was never loudly proclaimed, and, in 1848, could not have been further from Whitman's mind.[116]

"It may indeed be said that we live in exciting times," Whitman would write back to his former paper in August 1848. "Political matters connected with our own country, involving questions as profound and far-extending as any [. . .]—the problem of French Republicanism [. . .]—the revolt in Ireland, and the deep-seated wish in the American heart, for its success— [. . .] not forgetting the important one in Germany and Italy—all these form indeed subjects for the most engrossing interest."[117] No longer could these interests, in Whitman's eyes, be neatly divided. The world, the journalist from rural Long Island realized on his first big trip across the country, was intimately connected. New Orleans allowed him to *experience* this connectivity. His celebration of this insight in *Leaves of Grass* is key to Whitman's enduring, and controversial, global impact.[118]

CHAPTER 7

H. and M'C, after a while, exhibited a singular sort of coldness,
toward me, and the latter an irritability toward Jef., [. . .]
I thought it would be better to dissolve the connection.
They agreed to my plan (after some objections on the part of me);
and I determined to leave on the succeeding Saturday.

—WHITMAN IN AN UNDATED NOTE LATER ADDENDED TO A MARCH 5, 1848, NOTE

I enjoy'd my journey and Louisiana life much. Returning to Brooklyn a year or two afterward I started the "Freeman."

—WHITMAN IN THE *Camden Courier* (REPRINTED IN *Specimen Days*), 1882

Jeff was with me, and he grew very homesick; but the climate
of the place, and especially the water, seriously disagreed with him.
From this and other reasons (although I was quite happily fixed)
I made no very long stay in the South.

—WHITMAN IN THE *New Orleans Daily Picayune*, MAY 1887

Northern Birds, Departing

MANY TALES HAVE BEEN SPUN AROUND Whitman's departure from New Orleans. Ed Folsom and Kenneth M. Price, for instance, speculate that abolitionist attitudes precipitated the end of the Southern sojourn: "The *Crescent* owners probably feared that this northern editor would embarrass them because of his unorthodox ideas, especially about slavery."[1] Biographer Jerome Loving, on the other hand, attributes the move more to Whitman, who, he contends, realized that the temporary nature of his *Crescent* appointment meant "he was fast wearing out his options in journalism."[2] Earlier scholars, too, point to the editorial relationship between Whitman and Hayes/McClure as a primary culprit, beginning with Emory Holloway, who suggests that possibly the poet's "slovenly writing" was at issue, or "perhaps he was [. . .] hard to get along with."[3] That reading is only marginally less believable than Holloway's more outrageous, and similarly unsubstantiated, claim that "the owners of the *Crescent* had heard [. . .] that Whitman had taken up with [. . .] an octoroon."[4] Overall, though, such a multitude of assessments makes sense, since Whitman's own story about his departure morphs across the decades—all colored by shifting projects of self-promotion and nostalgia that attended their various retellings.

What does appear to be true is that in early May, Whitmanian contributions to the *Crescent* slowly decreased and were replaced by lengthy, rather matter-of-fact coverage of the settling of peace arrangements, largely via Mexican correspondence. In a short piece welcoming the month of May, the paper described itself as now fully matured: "The seasons [. . .] are but emblematical of the phases of life," it philosophized, suggesting that clearly the *Crescent* had long passed its "youth" of early spring and the "coy April" of its adolescence.[5] Whitman, hired as we have argued, to serve as the paper's professional wetnurse for "but a season" appeared to have been eying the exit. Like the business trips of other northerners, Walt's stay was never supposed to last into New Orleans's scorching summer, when life ground to a halt, theatres closed their doors, and trade slowed. Indeed, in a languorous, weary-sounding letter, penned on May 12 to New York's *Sunday Times*, Whitman anticipated his departure two weeks later: "The warm weather is down upon us now in earnest, and 'northern birds' are fast winging their way toward their native hills. Business is gradually decreasing, and everything indicates that the city of New Orleans is getting 'too hot to hold us' much longer."[6] Spring was giving way to summer, the Mexican war had finally concluded with a much-maligned peace treaty—and the radicals of New York were planning a June 22 meeting in Utica, New York, that would finalize the formation of the Free-Soil Party (and give a raison d'être to the dormant-but-nascent *Freeman* paper). And, of course, the seasonal horrors of yellow fever, cholera, and omnipresent mosquitodom could be felt fast approaching—especially when Jeff had already experienced bouts of dysentery, which Walt always opined was worse than either of those more feared maladies of the Southern Necropolis.[7] Plus, as biographer Loving speculates, a fire near their lodgings, shortly before their departure, may have felt like an additional bad omen.[8] In any case, there was a variable push and pull of motives: New Orleans was getting dull and swampy, New York promised exciting political prospects. It was time to go.

In a Whitman manuscript that begins "1848 New Orleans" and which combined contemporaneous notes from 1848 with late-life reflections, Whitman was most direct about the machinations of their departure. Whitman's decision to remove some of the manuscript's details from its later published version—one aimed at self-mythologization in old age—may lend some credence to the details omitted. In these manuscript notes, Whitman recalled an increasingly unpleasant working atmosphere at the *Crescent*. In this version of the story, the beginning of the end was a mysterious workplace disagreement: "Through some unaccountable means," Whitman wrote, "both H[ayes] and M'C[lure], after a while, exhibited a singular sort of coldness, toward me, and the latter an irritability toward Jef., who had, at times, much harder work than I was willing he should do."[9] This atmosphere culminated in the in-office announcement of the brothers' departure almost two weeks after Walt first disclosed an eagerness to leave to his friends at the *Sunday Times*. Perhaps prompted by this very letter now arriving back in the *Crescent*'s office in its printed form via the newspaper exchange, Whitman on May 24, 1848, finally broke the news to his editors:

> I had been accustomed to having frequent conferences, in my former situations with the proprietors of newspapers, on the subject of management, etc. But when the coldness above alluded to broke out, H. seemed to be studiously silent upon all these matters. My own pride was touched—and I met their conduct with equal haughtiness on my part. On Wednesday May 24th I sent down a note requesting a small sum of money. M'C returned me a bill of what money I had already drawn, and stated that they could not make "advances." I answered by reminding them of certain points which appeared to have been forgotten, making me not their debtor, and told them in my reply I thought it would be better to dissolve the connection. They agreed to my

plan (after some objections on the part of me); and I determined to leave on the succeeding Saturday. Accordingly on Friday I packed up my traps [. . .].

We know from McClure's later business dealings (surrounding his own departure from the *Crescent*) that the newspaper was dealing in "promissory notes"—i.e., private paper currency that functioned similarly to modern checks during the so-called "Free Banking" era (1837–62). Jacksonian Whitman had bristled against such measures but clearly had to accept paper currency as the only practical way of financing his Southern sojourn.

The $200 up-front payment in February 1848 would then have to have been intended to cover more than just the travel to New Orleans. It was a lot of money: Jeff, we know from his letters, made five dollars per week. An average compositor in New York would make around a dollar and a half per day, and a press operator up to two dollars.[10] *If* the trip down had cost them about seventy dollars,[11] and *if* Jeff's reporting of his sizable wage is correct, this would leave Walt with just a payment of seventy dollars for his total labors, or a little over a dollar per day (six days per week). This seems quite unlikely. If, on the other hand, the $200 were supposed to cover the trip to *and* fro—which, when including hotel costs, seems much more plausible—perhaps Whitman had been dipping into these funds while in New Orleans and now found his coffers empty. Why else would he be asking for more money from McClure in the context of his much-anticipated return to New York?

As in all paper currency, Whitman would have had to make withdrawals from the two one-hundred-dollar bills (similar to modern checks) that had been handed to him at the old Broadway Theatre on that fateful evening in February 1848. He would then have had to convert these promissory notes into hard currency (in dollars or British pounds) or use them at establishments that honored bills from the private bank used by McClure. It appears that Whitman had made ample use of the full funds by May 24. After all, New Orleans, his brother had bemoaned, was an expensive city; as he wrote in a letter, "every thing is so much here that you hardly know whether you get a good bargain or not."[12] In any case, it is worth pointing out that the ensuing pay negotiations, albeit unpleasant, did not suggest the outright hostile departure that some scholars, like Folsom and Price, have made it out to be: there was clearly a negotiation and a "plan" being hatched that made McClure and Hayes supply more funds for the two Whitmans to return to New York.

Walt needed the money; he could certainly not rely on support from his parents, who would that month become delinquent on municipal improvement fees, struggling for over a year to pay off the $5.50 the city had assessed them.[13] As in his previous arrangement with McClure, this new "plan" would see Walt work off the promissory note—and he would do so by supplying the *Crescent* with additional installments of his successful "Sidewalks" sketches series as well as agreeing to serve as the paper's New York correspondent. He would do so, as we have noted, until McClure resigned from the *Crescent* in January 1849.

While Whitman in his self-mythologizing tended to emphasize radical shifts—firings, fallouts, other renegade behavior—and many biographies have fallen into his trap, we can say with certainty that Whitman's departure from New Orleans was not as abrupt as it has been made out to be. Indeed, Walt may have met his replacement as "editor-in-chief" before the two brothers found themselves, that Saturday morning, aboard the steamship *Pride of the West*.[14] On May 13, the *John-Donkey* announced that journalist, one-time blackface singer, and hopeful filibuster "George Washington Dixon has accepted the post of editor-in-chief of the 'New Orleans Daily Crescent.'"[15] If this bit of gossip trickled up from New Orleans, it would have departed town at least a month before Whitman left, significantly predating his "northern bird" letter. It is unknown whether Dixon, in the end, acted as editor for the *Crescent* for any amount of time, but he did relocate to the city during this period: on May 24, 1848, he was sending letters from New Orleans to the Yucatan, threatening invasion *en amateur*.[16] Perhaps these activities kept him busy enough; yet when Dixon entered the New Orleans Charity Hospital in 1861, only weeks from his death, he *would* list his occupation as "Editor."[17] All in all, it seems reasonable to believe that by early May 1848, Hayes and McClure had already tapped Dixon, or someone like him, to be Whitman's replacement. At the very least Whitman's soon-to-be-empty seat was becoming a talking point well before his departure. (The *Crescent* ultimately landed on a different filibuster: William Walker, who officially joined the paper in March 1849.) Meanwhile, Whitman and Jeff, two "northern birds," were likely making their preparations even then to "wing their way towards their native hills." And once he and his brother stepped aboard the *Pride of the West*, on the afternoon of May 27, 1848, Whitman's tenure was officially over, and his time at the *Crescent*, and in the Crescent City, came to an end. Whereas their arrival in the midnight gloom had felt ominous, their departure was accompanied by a similarly sour note: Jeff was sick until the next morning.

On their trip home, Whitman continued to do what he had done on the voyage down, jotting down a number of the sights, people, and experiences of the journey northward—notes that he would later mine for his 1887 reminiscence in the *Picayune*. Among those experiences, Whitman recorded one last view of Southern Black life, in a small manuscript now known, for its first words, as "wooding at night." In it, sandwiched between descriptions of the bad food, "raw strong coffee," and the "excessive flatness of the country," comes this moment: "Long monotonous stretch of the Mississippi—Planter's dwellings surrounded with their hamlets of negro huts—groves of negro men women and children in the fields, hoeing the young cotton."[18]

No further comment was made. While Whitman did not explicitly note that these were enslaved people, the detail that "[p]lanter's dwellings [are] surrounded with their hamlets of negro huts" suggests that he was viewing, and recording, Southern slave plantations, where plantation houses could be contrasted with the more ramshackle cabins allowed to slaves. Similar imagery would eventually filter its way into Whitman's poetry, as in "Our Old Feuillage," first published in 1860 as part four of the "Chants Democratic" cluster in *Leaves of Grass*. When thinking of the "feuillage" (foliage) that covers the United States, Whitman begins not with that of Long Island or of Brooklyn, but that of the South: "Always our old feuillage! / Always Florida's green peninsula—always the priceless delta of Louisiana—always the cotton-fields of Alabama and Texas." Later in the poem, Whitman's long catalog of places and greenery gives way to people and daily work, including those whom he depicts as "[d]own in Texas the cotton-field, the negro-cabins, drivers driving mules or oxen before rude carts, cotton bales piled on banks and wharves."[19] Similar imagery will appear in his depictions of the American South for the rest of his life, as in his 1887 memories of New Orleans for the *Picayune*: "The diagonally wedg'd-in boats, the stevedores, the piles of cotton and other merchandise, the carts, mules, negroes, etc., afforded never-ending studies and sights to me."[20]

Here, as in the poet's "wooding at night" manuscript, Black slaves were emplaced within a geographic and economic network that connects them, in tableau, to cotton, a cash crop that drove the Southern marketplace, undergirded Southern slaveholding apologists' claims of the necessity of forced labor, and yielded literally what Whitman would later call figuratively "the vast fabric of our social system."[21] Homeward bound now, with the Crescent City at his back and the Mississippi River stretched out before him, Whitman may have thought about the slave auctions he had seen in New Orleans, the hardworking Freedpeople he had encountered on the streets, or the Creole New Orleanians of all types he had recorded in his editorials for the *Daily Crescent*. But here, as the slaves of Louisiana slip past his steamboat and sink behind him, Whitman recorded the sight with emotional distance, even romanticizing what he saw: the clutches of slave cabins were bucolic "hamlets" to him, as if they contained contented medieval serfs—and as for the "negro men women and children in the fields, hoeing the young cotton," he saw their groups as "groves," as if they merge with the crop they were forced to pick and become little more than a crop, a commodity, themselves. It is clear that, as he headed back to New York from the South's most prominent shipping port and slave market, Whitman had not yet adopted the more radical poetic attitude that would create the speaker of *Leaves of Grass*, the speaker who would proclaim that through him are channeled "many long dumb voices, / Voices of the interminable generations of slaves." The "runaway slave," the "hounded slave," seen and cared for so up close, centered so prominently in what would become "Song of Myself"—for now, for Whitman, they were still primarily "feuillage," seen only from afar.[22]

That *something* would need to be done with these impressions, he was almost certain. And indeed, "wooding at night" reads like a fiction draft, replete with colorful characters, enticing Western slang—and direct editorial instructions to himself. "Describe this old gentleman['s] manner on the boat[,] his kid gloves," he instructs himself in one place; "describe his appearance, his silver mounted cane etc.," he notes about another character. Around these characters, we get the outlines of an exciting story here: a steamboat race. Indeed, the eponymous "wooding" describes the practice of a flatboat refueling a steamer by running alongside it, allowing the vessel to skip unnecessary stops. "Our competition, or race, with the 'Grand Turk,'" he wrote, "continued from day to day," and there may have been some "[d]eceptiveness of the steamboat officers" about how pleasantly this high-speed journey would unfold (see Figure 18).

Steamboat races were, indeed, quite common and a good way for a clever captain—like the *Pride*'s Captain James J. Warman (1811–80), a stoic Tennessean[23]—to get his "new, elegant, and fast-running passenger steamboat" in the news. He couldn't have picked a better opponent: At the helm of the *Grand Turk* stood Newman Robirds (1816–68), who had long made a name for himself as a daring racer of steamboats.[24] Not only was there often prize money involved in these unofficial races—but one's prestige was on the line. Newspapers would frequently cover these events, especially when many racing steamboats inevitably blew up or caught fire. We get a hint of this, when Whitman notes:

> wooding at night—the 20 deck hands at work briskly as bees—in going up the river the flat-boat loaded with wood was attached to the side of our steamer and taken along with us, until the wood was transferred—
>
> Spectacle of the men lying around in groups in the forward part of the lower deck at night—some asleep some conversing—glare of the fire upon them—Some emigrants on their way "up country"—young fellow and his stout young German wife.—Gruffness of the mate to the boat hands—(Life, lot, appearance, characteristics, pay, recklessness, premature deaths, etc etc of the western boat-hands.)[25]
>
> Expressions of the mate.—"Step-along, my bullies!" Come, bullies, hop, now! hop now!"

Whereas the trip down the Mississippi had been one of opulence and recalled to Walt and Jeff the nation's best hotels—their return had them sleeping on deck and contemplating "premature deat[h]" as the flames of the racing stern-wheeler's engine illuminated the night. It would be

FIGURE 18. *Giant Steamboats at Sugar Levee, New Orleans* (1853; detail), by Hippolyte Victor Valentin Sebron, courtesy of the Collection of the Newcomb Art Museum of Tulane University. The steamer on the center left is the *Grand Turk*.

nearly a week at this breakneck pace ere both ships reached St. Louis. In the end, all of the stress of "wooding" had been for naught—the *Grand Turk* topped the port arrival announcements for that day.[26]

Yet while Whitman was more attentive to the "Northern birds" crowding the steamer, and consequently reduced Black life to background color, it was nonetheless a "political" prose draft. Notably, several of the passengers he focused on in his notes were Whig delegates en route to the National Convention that would nominate the man he had encountered at the St. Charles: Zachary Taylor. After a long period of Taylor skirting questions about his Whiggery and vowing to stay above party politics, the general had finally declared himself "a whig but not an ultra whig" in late April.[27] Yet Whitman, who would soon agitate for Van Buren, still found himself attracted to the populist appeal of the "Old Hero": "[I]n case of the old General's election, the Republic would not have a *party* President—and that's more than can be said of several late ones," he would write to the *Crescent* in late July.[28] Indeed, Whitman's steamer notes with its host of strange characters—rheumatic doctors, gruff Germans, manly deckhands, etc.—almost evoke, in embryo, the nation-as-steamboat metaphor of Melville's *Confidence Man*.

What colored these and subsequent writings about the trip was their apparent confirmation of Whitman's initial speculations that "manners and ways of the West" might be the antidote for what ails northerly Yankeedom. Once the brothers left behind the *Pride of the West* at St. Louis on June 3, 1848—where Walt "rambled with [his] brother over a large portion of the town, search'd after a refectory, and, after much trouble, succeeded in getting some dinner"—they boarded another packet ship to head north on the Illinois River. They also found it "excessively crowded with passengers, and had withal so much freight that we could hardly turn around." Even though Walt "slept on the floor, and the night was uncomfortable enough," he was quite taken by the Western panorama stretching into the horizon beyond the helm: "The Illinois River is spotted with little villages with big names, Marseilles, Naples, etc.; its banks are low, and the vegetation excessively rank. Peoria, some distance up, is a pleasant town; I went over the place; the country back is all rich land, for sale cheap. Three or four miles from P., land of the first quality can be bought for $3 or $4 an acre."[29] After switching boats at La Salle, Whitman added, "Illinois is the most splendid agricultural country I ever saw; the land is of surpassing richness; the place par excellence for farmers. We stopt at various points along the canal, some of them pretty villages."[30] Something about what we now consider the Midwest stuck with Walt. It wasn't its scenic nature (there was little of that) or just the affordability of it all. The "West" to Walt smelled of Jeffersonian renewal—a lived echo of his political project.

He must have been musing on this issue. In his travelogue, which appears to have been based on detailed contemporaneous notes (some extant), we only get a glimpse of mighty Chicago, where the two Whitmans arrive on the morning of June 7. They were "looking around" and enjoyed their lodgings at Brown and Tuttle's "American Temperance House" at Lake Street and Wabash Avenue—that's about all Whitman jotted down.[31] Yet once the brothers boarded the steamer *G. P. Griffith* to cross Lake Michigan to Lake Hudson, Whitman again interjected musings about the West and marveled that "[t]he towns have a remarkable appearance of good living, without any penury or want." He added that the "country is so good naturally and labor is in such demand," even leaving himself a parenthetical reminder: "It seems to me that if we should ever remove from Long Island, Wisconsin would be the proper place to come to."[32]

Not everyone on board seems to have been in the same utopian state of mind, however. Some days later, on June 8, Whitman recorded that

> About 5 o'clock one afternoon I heard the cry of "a woman overboard." It proved to be a crazy lady, who had become so from the loss of her son a couple of weeks before. The small boat put off, and succeeded in picking her up, though she had been in the water 15 minutes. She was dead. Her husband was on board. They went off at the next stopping place. While she lay in the water she probably recover'd her reason, as she toss'd up her arms and lifted her face toward the boat.[33]

The woman's name was Jane Augusta Hinckley (1804–48) of Racine, Wisconsin, whom the papers described as having been "for some time past partially deranged" and who jumped to her death off South Point, within view of the Milwaukee harbor.[34] She had been "on her way to an insane asylum," some papers later claimed.[35] We are left to wonder about the impact of watching this woman drown in the cold waters of Lake Michigan. Whitman, in his recollections, certainly sounded nonchalant. Yet perhaps we can hear faint traces of Mrs. Hinckley in the "half-caught voice sent up from the eddies" that, in late life, speak to Whitman of

> Some suicide's despairing cry, *Away to the boundless waste, and*
> *never again return.*
> On to oblivion then!
> On, on, and do your part, ye burying, ebbing tide!
> On for your time, ye furious debouché![36]

More unpleasant incidents delayed some of the remaining voyage aboard *Griffith*, as when, on June 11, the boat got stuck in shallow flats while crossing through the narrow gap at Mackinaw City between Lake Michigan and Lake Huron. Perhaps because they had nowhere to go, Whitman's notes from the day briefly became diaristic, noting things as they happen: "The day is beautiful and the water clear and calm [. . .]. The tug has fasten'd lines to us, but some have been snapt and the others have no effect. We seem to be firmly imbedded in the sand [. . .]. Later.—We are off again—expect to reach Detroit before dinner."[37] They would not stop at Detroit, in fact, but steamed right past, likely to make up for lost time. Whitman could only admire the city from afar, while also "especially lik[ing] the looks of the Canadian shore opposite."[38] The steamer would finally stop in Cleveland, where Whitman, as was his habit, "took the opportunity of rambling about the place" at night, admiring the buildings, the wide streets, and block after block of planted parklands.[39]

From Cleveland, the final legs of the Whitman brothers' journey took them across Lake Erie by steamer to Buffalo, New York, where they once again explored the city. They also did as many do and "went to Niagara; went under the falls—saw the whirlpool and all the other sights." It was an impression Whitman would not forget; when describing the sublime majesty of the American continent in his first edition of *Leaves of Grass*, he mentions having been "[u]nder Niagara, the cataract falling like a veil over my countenance."[40] But he clearly yearned for home: The last passages from his notes on the return journey are brief and clipped, primarily noting that he and Jeff traveled all night long from Buffalo toward Albany, presumably by train. Along the way, "the country all seem'd very rich and well cultivated," but Whitman's interest in the localities themselves seems to wane, probably with the discomfort of having been traveling for several weeks straight. All he can muster is: "Every few miles were large towns or villages." Finally, having reached Albany in the evening, Walt and Jeff boarded the *Alida* the next morning, headed down the Hudson River, and "arriv'd safely in New York that evening."[41]

There is one more telling detail in his last notes from the trip home. While in Albany, the state's capital, the brothers "[s]pent the evening in exploring," as they had in the other major cities along the way. Whitman took the time to note one bit of the city that he made sure to avoid, however: "There was a political meeting (Hunker) at the capitol," he wrote, "but I pass'd it by."[42] Naturally, Whitman would not have relished the idea of visiting among the state's establishment Democrats: as the more conservative faction of the Democratic party, the self-styled

"Hunkers" had hunkered down over the position that slavery and its (non)extension was a political issue best avoided, rather than confronted. Whitman felt differently. As we demonstrate in the next chapter, his commitment to Free-Soil values was not only undiminished, but strengthened, by his sojourn in New Orleans and by his experiences at the *Crescent*. Now, having returned home safely to New York, his long-laid plans finally came to a head: Within a month of his arrival, plans for a new paper were being finalized, and a subscriber's list was drawn up at a Free-Soil meeting to finance the paper.[43] It would be a fiery Free-Soil organ called the *Brooklyn Freeman*, supported by a start-up budget of $1,000. Immediately following the meeting that inaugurated Whitman as the editor of this new paper, he would morph into yet another role: the Free-Soil correspondent for the *Daily Crescent*, under the moniker "Manhattan."[44]

CHAPTER 8

Yet who can hold the balance, and weigh what is to be? One year ago, who thought that in two months the then newly elected President would be shrouded in his coffin . . .? . . . Who thought it possible that the whig party, having full swing in every branch of the government, would refrain from chartering a national bank? Still these marvellous things have come to pass. And in that mighty volume wherein are recorded the events and changes of the future years, haply there may be wonders greater, and occurrences more unimagined, than any we have now spoken of.

—WALT WHITMAN, *New York Aurora,* MARCH 28, 1842

"Barnburner" and "Hunker,"—Taylor, Cass, and Van Buren—"What are Taylor's principles?"—"Is there no way to compromise?"

—"MANAHATTA" LETTER, *Daily Crescent,* PUBLISHED JULY 24, 1848

Back on Free Soil

WHITMAN'S NEW GIG after the *Crescent*, the weekly *Brooklyn Freeman* (which would later expand into a daily)[1] is often heralded as a return to free speech for Whitman, following a "muzzled" period in New Orleans. It is lauded for containing Whitman's "most passionate antislavery" writing to date,[2] and, on its surface, could not be a bigger contrast to the *Crescent*—even throwing around terms like "emancipation" and "abolition." The *Crescent,* in differentiating itself from the Hunker-Democratic *Delta,* had embraced a faux-neutral stance and downplayed heavy-handed political editorializing, though it had clearly signaled, as we have traced in this book, the complicated allegiances of its editorial staff to a number of "radical" Democratic concerns. The *Freeman,* on the other hand, would be blatantly party political—and proud of it.

Of course, this posits the question: What, if any, evidence is there for scholars to find in the *Freeman* a more unfiltered, "unmuzzled" Whitman than appeared in the *Crescent*? Does the *Freeman* really disclose more of his "deep concern over the issues" than Whitman's other newspaper work—or is this largely wishful thinking by biographers?[3] Of course, as at the *Crescent*, Whitman was only a hired gun at the *Freeman*. His new paper was bankrolled by Samuel E. Johnson,[4] who had finally been adjudicated county judge by the New York Supreme Court in October, after months of legal headache. This victory had seemingly also alleviated Johnson's previous financial troubles, which had postponed plans for the new paper and given Whitman leeway to pursue the *Crescent* gig. Johnson was a disgruntled Democrat who, like Whitman, had broken with the party after the disastrous state election of 1847 (which had nearly cost him his judgeship). He was also the son of antislavery preacher Evan Malbone Johnson (1791–1865),[5] who at the time of the *Freeman*'s founding still gave fiery, controversial sermons in Brooklyn that urged that "the Church, as a Church, should enter upon a crusade against slavery, and [. . .] denounce all those [. . .] who are owners of slaves"[6] and worked to desegregate the Anglican church in Walt's conservative hometown.[7] The son seems to have inherited his father's fiery liberation theology, even associating himself by name (and office) with the American and Foreign Anti-Slavery Society, organized by local Underground Railroad icon William H. Harned (1796–1854).[8] Consequently, Johnson initially wanted his paper to be called *The Banner of Freedom*,[9] a title which sounds a lot more like abolitionist papers such as *The National Anti-Slavery Standard*, the *Signal of Liberty*, or *The Anti-Slavery Bugle*. Whitman, apparently, pushed back against the name.[10] When literary historian Jason Stacy rightly observes that the term *abolition* was only "used loosely in the *Freeman* [and] as a means of maintaining the dignity of white labor,"[11] he points us to the obviously conflicted nature of Whitman's employ there. In the *Crescent*, Whitman had bent his working-class radicalism to fit the self-proclaimed nonpolitical program of that Southern paper; in the *Freeman*, he dressed it in the verbiage favored by its owner: Northern abolitionism.

The staff of the *Freeman*, it seems, consisted solely of owner Johnson, editor Whitman, and Whitman's assistant, the young would-be lawyer Daniel M. Tredwell (1826–1921), who split his time between the news and his legal studies, the latter supported by a weekly salary of ten dollars. Tredwell apparently rarely set foot in the office and mostly made copy. As the son of a proud Whig family, he would later claim to have known little about the paper's politics, though he had been intimately involved with its founding from the get-go. The young lawyer was a complicated man, who bemoaned how the *Freeman*'s meagre salary kept him from marrying a woman and settling down, all the while drafting a lengthy manuscript on the symbol of the phallus in ancient cultures.[12] (Tredwell would also go on to produce numerous works on the Native history of Long Island and likely deserves closer attention by Whitman scholars.) As for Whitman himself, Tredwell remembered him, with quite a bit of vehemence, as a scandalous figure of ill repute.[13]

Most issues of the *Freeman* are now lost, but in the few surviving articles we can witness the energy that propelled the scrappy little paper. In its programmatic opener, Whitman described its mission thus:

> Hardly any one who takes the trouble to look two minutes at our paper will need being told, at any length, what objects we have in view. That our doctrine is the doctrine laid down in the Buffalo Convention, and expounded in the letters of Van Buren and [VP candidate] Adams—that we shall do what we can to help the election of those candidates—that we shall oppose, under all circumstances, the addition to the Union, in future, of a single inch of *slave land*, whether in the form of state or territory—those are our first objects. Whatever can be done by the *Freeman* for this purpose, will be done heartily.[14]

Through the *Freeman*, Whitman would once again enter the arena of explicitly political print, in which many newspapers commonly declared themselves for—indeed, were sometimes founded solely to support—major political parties and their respective candidates. He had had experience doing as much for several Democrat and Whig dailies, the latest being the *Brooklyn Daily Eagle*. Now he would do it again, this time at the service of a third-party platform.

Before the small office could settle into a rhythm, disaster struck. The very night after its first issue, September 10, 1848, a fire broke out in a furniture store near the *Freeman*'s subterranean editorial office at 110 Orange Street, Brooklyn. Spreading swiftly among the tightly-packed

BROOKLYN FREEMAN.

BY WALTER WHITMAN. BROOKLYN, SATURDAY, SEPTEMBER 9, 1848. Vol. 1.—No. 1.—Price Two Cents.

THE FREEMAN,

Brooklyn, Saturday, Sept. 9.

FOR PRESIDENT,
MARTIN VAN BUREN,
FOR VICE-PRESIDENT,
CHARLES F. ADAMS.

"The Brooklyn Freeman."

"The Daily Freeman."

Jefferson on the Non-Extension of Slavery.

How things have been managed in Kings County.

Van Buren's last best Letter.

One Enmity to the South.

FIGURE 19. Front page of the first issue of the *Brooklyn Freeman* (1848), courtesy of the Library of Congress (Charles E. Feinberg Collection).

wooden buildings, the blaze grew into a massive conflagration, burning eight square blocks of Brooklyn to cinders, including the *Freeman*'s newly rented editorial office. News of the fire travelled far and was reported not only in East Coast newspapers but also in the *Crescent* itself.[15]

In the end, the fire destroyed over two hundred wooden structures. As reported in the *Crescent*, the blaze, possibly started by a burst camphine lamp, ultimately grew so large that Brooklyn and New York firefighting teams, who could not pump enough river water to stanch the flames,[16] had to resort to blowing up structures with gunpowder to prevent the fire's further spread.[17] Yet a biographer like Gay Wilson Allen still prefers to imagine Whitman's "office was burned by a mob,"[18] attempting to play up his abolitionist credentials. In any case, Whitman's and Johnson's *Freeman* office was obliterated, likely destroying their printing press, type cases, and printers' materials.

Whitman's bad luck in losing his paper to a fire during such crucial political times has also been to his biographers' detriment, considering that the few scant issues of the paper still extant were long believed to be the future poet's only surviving statements from the latter half of 1848. Yet, as we have demonstrated,[19] Whitman always kept busy: While he had been ginning up his new Free-Soil paper, he was also already discretely writing letters back to the editors of the New Orleans *Crescent*, apprising his late public of events in New York City and Brooklyn, describing scenes on the street, and keeping readers abreast of the latest political developments in the region. It was a practice he himself had encouraged while editor of the *Crescent*: Its very first issue prominently featured a letter from a Whitman associate (signed "Sunshine") proclaiming the inevitable victory of Free-Soilism over Democratic politics on the *Crescent*'s front page,[20] its genre (correspondence) shielding the *Crescent* from any fallout such statements might bring. For us it means, though the fire nearly wiped out the *Freeman* at the start, there is continuity in Whitman's biographical print record.

For Whitman, this period marked an attempt to join and influence the newsprint-led debate over the roiling political evolution underway in American presidential politics—an evolution that would soon culminate in the birth of the Republican Party.[21] His writings in the *Freeman*, the few still extant, make it clear that the Free-Soil movement was energizing young political participants like Whitman not only by offering the possibility of optimism and change, but also by shaking up the very notion of what might be accomplished in a presidential contest. The *Crescent* itself would admit as much, in an editorial published shortly after Whitman's return to Brooklyn. Speaking of the upcoming convention at Buffalo that would lead to the formation of this new "free soil and free labor" party, Whitman's old paper explained that "if a popular man is taken up" as the Free-Soil presidential candidate, "it may put an entirely new aspect on the face of the canvass [. . .]. Such a move would throw all parties into a beautiful state of excitement and dubiety, and would make the chances of election of any named man less certain than the winner of a sweepstakes in a field of twenty horses."[22] Though the readers of this piece could not have known it then, such would more or less end up being the case. Presidential politics in 1848 ultimately became a moment in which the antebellum multiparty system of the US underwent a radical evolution, leading to rather stunning party changes that nevertheless avoided major destabilization.[23]

As a newly self-appointed advocate for Free-Soilism, Whitman went at his work with vigor. In the *Freeman*'s first issue, Whitman complained volubly about Brooklyn Hunkerism's lack of concern with the spread of slavery:

> Probably no part of the state is so poisoned with Hunkerism as Kings county. Are the masses of our citizens, then, indoctrinated with its sentiments? Probably they are not to any great extent—certainly not enough to form a majority. But the "leaders"—those who have been thrust, or have thrust themselves, forward into prominent positions—those who have either been sent to Congress or the Legislature by the Democratic party, or who have had the "regular nominations" for those high places, without getting elected—these, it must be confessed, are very many of them Hunkers, or Conservatives; or, if it pleases them better, Cass and Butler men. Political action, here, by these people, has been literally *reduced* to a mere game of cunning, of fishing through caucusses for nominations, and then fishing through any means for votes.[24]

Whitman's opposition to the politics of "cunning" would become more and more evident as he transitioned to his radical brand of democratic poetics in the 1850s, in which he valued the earthy "unrhymed poetry" of American presidential politics, including "the terrible significance of [the American people's] elections" and "the President's taking off his hat to them not they to him."[25] But his specific opposition to Hunker politics, which he here described as conservative vote-fishing, was immediately evident in his *Freeman* writings. By 1848, Whitman's partisanship had become so fiery, not only in support of Van Buren but also against conservative Hunkers, that the entirety of his editorship of the *Freeman* was bookended by it: Days before the first issue appeared, the *Brooklyn Evening Star*—edited by Whitman's friend Edwin Spooner—noted that "Mr. Walter Whitman, formerly editor of the Brooklyn Eagle, contemplates issuing the first number of a Barnburner paper [. . .]. Among the Loco Focos of Kings County, the 'Old Hunkers' have had almost undisputed sway. We shall now see how the 'young Democracie' get along."[26] Though a Whig newspaper (the page mentioning Whitman was topped by a large banner reading "For President / Gen. ZACHARY TAYLOR / of Louisiana"), the *Star* typically treated Whitman as a rising political voice. Other partisan papers were less charitable regarding his anti-Hunkerism. Even in his very last act at the *Freeman*, Whitman would thumb his nose at a former employer-turned-antagonist, by publishing a note, which was reprinted in the *Brooklyn Daily Eagle*:

> After the present date, I withdraw entirely from the BROOKLYN DAILY FREEMAN. To those who have been my friends, I take occasion to proffer the warmest thanks of a grateful heart. My enemies—and old hunkers generally—I disdain and defy the same as ever.
>
> WALTER WHITMAN.[27]

The *Eagle*'s editorial comment following this letter was far from kind, possibly because of the political differences that may have contributed to Whitman's decision to leave the Hunker-Democratic *Eagle* and head to Louisiana in the first place: "Although Mr. Whitman has some talents, yet the tone of his mind and morals is too low to sustain a respectable journal. He lacks, besides, the industry and tact so necessary to the conduct of a political paper; and is more gifted in alienating friends than in making them."[28] Clearly, Whitman's *Freeman* had been both a political opponent and a business rival in Brooklyn.

Yet in agitating against his old party, fueled by years of misgivings,

Whitman was not just a malcontent. His writings in the *Freeman* illustrate that he believed in the party platform strongly enough to throw his full support behind it.[29] Whitman's advocacy for the Free-Soil movement, as an editor as well as a party organizer, underscore that he still felt he had a direct political contribution to make for his state and, more broadly, his nation—something more than a mere gut feeling or matter of style. His political participation of that period was, however, more complex than has been previously thought, and does not constitute a straightforward catalyst to his radical poetry of 1855. Indeed, much of it serves to unsettle truisms about America's poet and how multitudinous the representative, democratic "I" of *Leaves of Grass* might really be. In 1848, we meet two very different Whitmans: Walter Whitman, a quasi-abolitionist firebrand editing the *Freeman,* and "Manhattan," the *Crescent* readers' working-class confidant, giving his Southern friends an inside scoop of New York politics and pitching them Free-Soilism. At the center of this Venn diagram of performativity stood the historical Whitman, who may be approached through the differences and overlap between the two.

On July 24, 1848, not long after Whitman returned from New Orleans to Brooklyn and a month before the Buffalo convention, a letter signed "Manahatta" appeared in the New Orleans *Crescent*, addressed to its editors but clearly written for a larger audience. The editors eagerly shared it with their readers: " ☞ For a clash of New York life, read our correspondent 'Manahatta's' letter," they recommended.[30] It is a pen name that would soon be closely associated with Whitman, a budding poet who (like his *Freeman* colleague Tredwell) had always had a fondness for the "aboriginal name[s]" associated with New York and Long Island,[31] such as "Paumanok" (the Algonquin name for Long Island) and "Mannahatta" (eventually with two *n*'s for the central island of New York City). However Whitman chose to spell it, it is clear that "Mannahatta" captured for him the living personality and bustling multiplicity of Manhattan.[32] Correspondence like Whitman's was, as we have discussed in a previous chapter, crucial to smaller and regional papers, increasingly left out of the professionalizing news networks (based on rapidly expanding telegraph lines). In places where news was always already belated, the specific local color provided by correspondence added immense value for readers.[33] Even as a correspondent Whitman was a real "get" for his old paper—he excelled at what was required from the position. His personality and multiplicity were on full display from the very beginning of the first "Manahatta" letter, whose opening words left no doubt that its author was unafraid to speak directly about the politics of race, reform, and western expansion:

> *Eds. Crescent*—"Barnburner" and "Hunker,"—Taylor, Cass, and Van Buren—"What are Taylor's principles?"—"Is there no way to compromise?"—Tammany Hall in a Pandemoniac state—the Tribune corner a focus for all sorts of loud words and excitement—a huge crowd around the Globe bulletin-board—dust flying in the Park—men whose names are known from one corner of the land to the other walking unnoticed along the walk, and across from the great gates, to the Nassau street side-walk—the cracked tones of the man with "leg of mutton candy," now and then piercing through the din—a mighty and never-ceasing tide of humanity rolling along from day-dawn till midnight, a majority of whose members would not stop two minutes to look at Queen Victoria, or even a street assassination;—there you have, in disjointed sentecnes [*sic*], and some words that are heard in every part of the neighborhood every five minutes, a picture of current "life" as developed in that part of New York where Nassau street pokes its nose out to the Park, at the south end of City Hall.[34]

So began a series of more than thirty letters from "Manahatta"—soon to be "Manhattan," the pseudonym to which the letter-writer shifts in the fifth installment.[35] These letters appeared with regularity in the *Crescent* until the last installment on January 19, 1849, a few months into the post-fire publication of the *Brooklyn Freeman* (and when editor McClure resigned from the *Crescent*). From these "Manhattan" letters, readers could see from the outset that the pseudonymous speaker was a theater fan and urban rhapsodist from New York, who had recently lived in New Orleans and was heavily invested in the Free-Soil movement. In a highly personable style, "Manhattan" shared his city with the readers of the *Crescent*, relating impressions of walks through the city, sharing news about goings on in town, and soapboxing about politics.

Indeed, politics was one of the primary subjects of these letters, especially presidential politics, since "Manhattan" discussed in detail the lead-up to and aftermath of the Buffalo Convention of 1848, the convention at which the Free-Soil party formed in earnest, and which Whitman attended as a delegate. Considering that Whitman would run the paper's party organ in Brooklyn, it is tempting to describe him—as has previously been done—solely through the political arguments put forth by the leadership of his new party and broadly supported by the *Freeman*. Whitman, of course, was always a "deep-dyed heretic" in his politics,[36] and he maintained his independent streak in the new party.

US political parties were undergoing a major shift when Whitman returned from New Orleans in 1848. But this was nothing unusual. Political parties in nineteenth-century America existed in a very different state than they do today, and it is worth emphasizing what historians Rachel A. Shelden and Erik B. Alexander have dubbed the "party fluidity" that characterized US politics prior to the twentieth century. "Rather than conforming to rigid two-party competition with intraparty squabbles and occasional realignments," they write, "the first one hundred years of U.S. politics were instead marked by a constantly shifting partisan landscape."[37] This is evident from the countless political newspapers printed during Whitman's lifetime, as well as the endless variety of party names that came and went, particularly at the state and local levels: the Liberal Party, the People's Party, the Know Nothing Party, the Anti-Division Party, the Anti-Monopolists, the Anti-Rent Party, the Anti-Restrictionists, and many, many more. State legislative elections scholar Michael J. Dubin has actually counted more than one hundred party names in state elections prior to 1900.[38] As all these "Anti-" party names make clear, one of the primary dynamics that drove party formation in the nineteenth-century US was the coalition of otherwise diverse voters around a single salient political or economic stance, on issues like slavery, the gold standard, free trade, and the like. As one might imagine, party platforms could therefore shift as issues of significance to various constituencies rose and fell over time. Voters, in turn, found themselves shifting their allegiances to parties—and those parties would consequently swell or collapse regularly—much more often than is common in twenty-first century American politics. As one might expect, the US was effectively a multiparty system (though often with two leading parties) until the beginning of the twentieth century, when the now-familiar dynamic of the two-party system hardened around the leading parties at the time.

This fluidity was not so much a sign of political instability (indeed, the 1840s in the US were a relatively stable political period) as an indicator of the noncentrality of political parties to American individual identity prior to the twentieth century. Unlike today, when many Americans often identify *as Democrat* or *as Republican* (the two major national parties since the US Civil War), voters like Whitman in 1848 more often identified *as voters for* a given party. Whitman says as much in a later editorial on "Party Allegiance," published in the *Brooklyn Daily Times* in 1857 (a Republican paper). "The primary object of voters, in forming themselves into parties," he would therein argue,

> is supposed to be, the election of those men, and the adoption of those principles, by which they think the public affairs can be best administered. In order to join any party, a citizen must be convinced that its general principles are correct, and that its selection of candidates is generally discreet. But in isolated cases of local elections, he may surely disapprove of a nomination made by the local branch of his party, and vote against the nominee, without forfeiting his standing as a member of the national party, to whose principles and policy he still firmly adheres.[39]

In other words, party allegiance for nineteenth-century Americans was much less important than it is for those of the twenty-first century, for the simple fact that many political parties came to be at the state or local level, shifted constantly based on salient political issues, and dissolved frequently. Advocacy for a "third party," like Whitman's, was less of a fool's errand in the antebellum United States than it is in today's ossified two-party system. Naturally, then, the personal identity of a voter often had less to do with party allegiance than did his adherence to a "general principle" of some kind, around which a party or parties might continually form, grow, split, and collapse.

These general principles were often not the broad philosophical categories one might expect today, like "progressive" and "conservative," so much as they were specific governmental or policy issues, like federal government size, national banking, the gold standard, tax minimization, and the like. Such issues were not determined by intraparty mechanisms, but instead often derived directly from voters. Hence, if a certain coalition of voters within a party or among multiple parties agreed upon, say, the nonextension of slavery into new US territories—as members of both the Democratic and Whig parties did in 1846, after the failure of the Wilmot Proviso—those coalitions might form into a new political party solely over that issue.

And indeed, they did. On May 26, 1848 (the day before Whitman and his brother Jeff left New Orleans), the Democratic National Convention, after three inconclusive ballots in the prior days, finally nominated Lewis Cass as their presidential candidate. The senator from Michigan shared military credentials with Zachary Taylor (who was being courted by Whigs): Cass had fought in the War of 1812 and later, as Andrew Jackson's Secretary of War, oversaw the forced removal of Native Americans. Cass downplayed the importance of the slavery issue, pointing to the very same principle that Whitman saw his old party abandoning: popular sovereignty (here translating to "leaving it up to the states"). Cass's nomination upended the Democratic party. At the National Convention, held in Baltimore, fellow competitor Martin Van Buren realized, correctly, that too many of his fellow Democrats were "Hunkers"—supporters of federal governance and minimizers of the issue of slavery—for him to earn the nomination. Having anticipated this outcome, Van Buren performatively walked out of the convention, taking with him most of the party's "Barnburners," its radical, working-class, anti-establishment faction. The party had officially split. The Democrats who were left would run the establishment candidate Lewis Cass for president, while the Whigs—following their own convention held in June in Philadelphia (whose delegates the Whitmans met aboard their steamboat)—finally chose Taylor for their ticket. Taylor, though a slaveholder himself, was a declared agnostic on the subject of slavery. Who, then, would represent the many Wilmot-supporting Northern Democrats who had just left the party and who seemed inclined to join with antislavery Whigs to form a new coalition? In August, with Whitman himself attending as a delegate, the Free-Soil Party would hold its own convention to decide, ultimately choosing former president and Wilmot-supporter Martin Van Buren as their candidate.[40]

"Manhattan" recorded the convention as it happened. It "seems to be formed in utter defiance of all precedents and 'party usages,'" he wrote to the editors of the *Crescent*. "Much of it is on a charming voluntary principle—I mean that of a man making himself a delegate, because so it seems good in his own sight. Any body, therefore, who wanted to go to Buffalo, (for $13 and 50 cents, which takes one all the way from New York, and back too), has had his wish gratified, or else it was his own fault."[41] Whitman was one of fourteen delegates who traveled from Kings County to the convention, which opened in Buffalo on August 9. He had been chosen just the prior Saturday at a Free-Soil meeting in Brooklyn. For the *Freeman*, he had framed the event as "Democracy of Kings aroused," to which the local Democratic paper, the *Eagle*, sneered that this was *not* a Democratic meeting but a "meeting of soreheads, from all parties."[42] Delegate selection took place at Washington Hall, where illustrious men like Lafayette had once dined, but which by 1848 was mostly known as an event space and oyster hall. About "one hundred men and boys" showed up,[43] consisting of a variety of party backgrounds. The *Eagle* provided this helpful, mocking summary of the delegates:

> Gilbert A. Grant, dem.
> F. C. Tredwell, locofoco[44]
> Hiram Barney, whig-abolitionist[45]
> Sam E. Johnson, dem.
> Marcus Spring, whig.
> A. R. Turner, whig.
> Wm. E. Whiting, whig-abolitionist.
> Seth B. Hunt, independent.
> Amos P. Staunton. do.
> John S. Noble, whig spouter and office holder.
> Alden J. Spooner, an old whig, lately converted.
> H. B. Claflin, whig.
> Walter Whitman, not much of anything.
> Francis Pares, radical democrat.[46]

A number of these men, including Whitman, then rose to speak and a joint resolution was passed, outlining the group's grievances with either party, and adding that they "disclaim and abhor a party or sectional spirit—that [they] have no ill-will against our fellow-citizens of the south—that [they] love the Union and Constitution of these States." This love for union, the resolution continued, translated into their opposition to slavery extension, which threatened it. There was some bickering over whether delegates would be bound for Van Buren or not (with Whitman apparently supporting the former), and a compromise was reached: The delegation would be bound to the Buffalo-selected candidate.[47]

Within a week, this colorful group—including Whitman's current boss, Judge Johnson, and Alden J. Spooner, the son of a former boss—set out from Brooklyn to Buffalo. The atmosphere upon their arrival seems to have been particularly charged. Attendance numbers as high as fifty thousand people were thrown around in the press, and news from the telegraph wires suggested that "two acres of grounds were completely covered with committees, delegations, &c, and that meetings were holden, besides, in almost every public room in the city."[48] In a later meeting, *Freeman* boss Johnson would marvel that "saving the mass meeting in the Park [of July 18, 1848], New-York, he had never witnessed any similar assemblage."[49]

Excitement was in the air, and Whitman believed the political establishment was scared. "Manhattan" proudly records the remarks of the Whig General Committee chair of New York, who had estimated that among six thousand Henry-Clay-Whigs present, "they are, almost to a man, going for Van Buren."[50] Similar intensity emanated from the Barnburners at the Convention, the contingent of radical Democratic activists (like Whitman) so named for their willingness to endorse drastic measures to get the party back to its Jacksonian roots on issues like debt-spending, paper money and banks, monopolies, and government meddling with the free market.[51] "The principle beauty of our 'Barnburner' friends," wrote Whitman to the *Crescent*, "consists in their delightful, youthful, aspect of *defiance*—quite picturesque and refreshing to one's tired consciousness of party obedience and 'harmony.'"[52] Their pugnacity was notable, even among many disputatious factions:

> Nothing will please [the Barnburners]—these don't-care-a-damnative young men. They reject advice, and insult even the senators and venerable editors who give it. They seem to glory in kicking up the most precious of rows—in rebelling against all the political etiquette of the last thirty years. Then the ease and complacency of the rascals—with what cool vanity they dare their elders and superiors in station, to do battle with them—either in argument or any other way.[53]

Writing as much to a New Orleans reading public, particularly *Crescent* readers who probably leaned largely Democratic, these letters can sound as much like political theater as they can authentic self-disclosure. After all, despite "Manhattan's" suggestion that the New York Free-Soil convention was "formed in utter defiance of all precedents and 'party usages,'" it was in fact held according to the relatively standard norms of party nomination and candidate selection of the period. What Whitman was talking about here, then, was not an upheaval of procedural norms, but the kind of revolutionary affect he had fallen in love with in New Orleans: a body politic constituted by young, Jacksonian men. It also suggests that Whitman had not entirely abandoned Democratic politicking with his de facto exit from the party, and in framing his Free-Soilers as the *proper* "Democracy of Kings" county suggested the movement always also constituted a power play aimed at the leadership of a party that had abandoned its roots. Whitman, it appears, still identified as a Democrat even while joining a third party.

He may not have been alone in this perspective. The nascent party consisted of a somewhat haphazard mishmash of reform movements, single-issue complaints, and former parties: There were Barnburners, antislavery Whigs, western homesteaders, internal reformers, abolitionists with a realpolitik bent, and members of the unsuccessful Liberty Party (the only major abolitionist party of the election)—all of which joined elements that were still nominally within the Democratic tent to fuse themselves into a new political entity. It is important, at this point, to look at the constituent population through which Whitman joined the party: Barnburners. Especially in Whitman scholarship, the term has become a synonym for proto-Free-Soilers,[54] but there were distinct differences that were deeply meaningful to Whitman's life in the 1840s.

Indeed, Whitman was a Barnburner long before Wilmot catalyzed their split with his Proviso.[55]

Barnburnerism was a Jacksonian inner-Democratic reform movement first spawned during a contentious debate around debt spending in New York State in 1842–43.[56] Establishment Democrats around the governor (according to dissenters) had figured out that infrastructure funding was a good way to win over votes in a state with significant working-class populations who depended on rivers and coastlines for their trade. Yet big government spending, for such projects as an enlarged Erie Canal, was a thorn to the Jacksonian principles the party espoused. Up stepped Michael Hoffman (1787–1848), who accused the current Democratic status quo of "open profligacy" and, like Luther to the Catholic Church, began a reformation. He would help create a small-government, antimonopoly, and pro-worker reform movement in this nominally anti-federalist party. Buying votes through internal improvements constituted brazen Whiggery, after all. "The slavery question," an 1850s article reminds us, "was not prominent at the outset" of the Barnburner movement.[57] Indeed, Whitman at the time sounded *most* like a Hoffmanian Barnburner when he decried the immense "money [. . .] that has been spent" upon harbor improvements at Cairo, Illinois, as driven by "speculating interest" and a waste of funds[58]—not when he would write "I Sing the Body Electric."

Hoffman himself died in 1848 and was eulogized in the "Manhattan" letters. Whitman conveyed news of the Barnburner's death as follows, using the same word ("radical") to describe Hoffman that he used for himself:

> Michael Hoffman, Naval officer,[59] for this city; he was aged sixty years, and died last night at his residence in Pacific street, Brooklyn. Mr. Hoffman was a well-known politician of the Radical stamp, and had filled offices in the Legislature and other positions. He was much beloved by the Silas Wright democracy,[60] who were in daily expectation of hearing of his removal by the National Executive, at Washington. The removal, however, has been by a more solemn power, and more potent mandate. He is to be taken this afternoon to Herkimer county, his former residence, for burial.[61]

Rural Herkimer, of course, had been the seat for the Barnburners' convention (pre-Buffalo) in preparation for the split from the Hunkers—as well as a purposeful site that played to their constituents: establishment Democrats met in capitals and trade hubs; the radicals met in the country, where the "real people" were. Subsequently, "Manhattan" wrote of customs houses closing in honor of Hoffman and officials in similar positions being removed for Free-Soil sympathies.

A discourse around popular sovereignty was key to the politics of Hoffman's Barnburners. Besides retrenchment on new government spending and debt limits, Hoffman, in his theses nailed to the proverbial gate of Tammany Hall, called for protection of the common school, restrictions on paper money, the election of *all* officer holders (to curb the spoils system), limits to the salaries and power of government officers, an end to the appointing power for the legislative and executive branches, and a popular vote on the state constitution every twenty years.[62] Popular government, Hoffman had insisted, had been taken over by careerists and monopolists—and a reformation was needed to turn the ship around. The whole Whitman clan agreed; in this, they were somewhat typical, as the Barnburners drew their popularity from small farmers and working-class families.

Indeed, Whitman was at his most fiery in 1848 when he discussed larger, more philosophical concerns about the future direction of America: Would it be Whiggish federalism or a people's government? We find evidence of this in a striking document: a never-printed note on John Quincy Adams, written after his death in February 1848. It was intended to run in one of the first issues of the *Crescent* but was pulled after the proofing state, perhaps for political reasons, perhaps because the timing was off.[63] It is a piece that Whitman later recalled, in a jotted note, had been "one of my articles in [the] paper" while he was "an editor in the Daily Crescent newspaper office."[64] In it, Whitman briefly commented that the Whig statesman-turned-abolitionist was certainly "a virtuous man," before spending most of the editorial attacking him as "not a man of the People. Never," Whitman wrote, "did he heartily espouse the side of any of those hot struggles for the rights of men, as opposed to wealth and conservatism, which the last years of the last century, and all the hitherto years of the present one, show so many of."[65] Whitman rejoiced that the grave closed on men like Adams, and he ends with what might be his political program for 1848:

> Even if temporary circumstances [. . .] lead the masses for a moment to frown on those who really befriend them, there is always a chosen circle, a body-guard, who faithfully make head-way for the truth and its dauntless leaders. [. . .] [Adams] was "a gentleman of the old school," no doubt; but the old school, with all its polish and grace, had its sources too near monarchy and nobility to be entirely free from their influences. Only master minds, *radical* minds that went to the roots of things, and scored mere precedent, leaped over such influences. [. . .]
>
> Some spirits there were, of that age, towering not only above it, but above the ages yet to come. They need no *elogium*. For those of another class, whose names have mention in our records, there is another grateful remembrance in the American heart—a remembrance fresh and loving for many a future year.

Whitman's referent for the "master mind" that did not need mention is clear: Andrew Jackson—who had won the popular vote in 1824, but lost to Adams through the electoral college.

Whitman's radicalism was, then, one that went "to the roots of" the American system and that he saw embodied by Jefferson and Jackson[66]—not coincidentally the names of two of his brothers. "The disputes at the commencement of the present century between the Jeffersonians and the Federalists, were milk and honey to the present," he wrote in one letter to the *Crescent*. Whitman was by no means exceptional here, of course, as the numerous off-shoot parties spawned by the Tammany machine in previous decades illustrate. Jackson and Jefferson embodied "popular sovereignty" to many Democrats in these years—and as it did for many fellow radicals, it became the rallying cry of Whitman's political identity and personal style. It was also still, of course, nominally party doctrine of the Democrats and would famously be evoked by their candidate Cass to justify fence-sitting on slavery extension (by making it not a federal issue). To Whitman, though, the concept went deeper than anti-Whig politicking. To him, it was a fundamental reorientation of politics toward a long-abandoned and never fully realized principle that underwrote the American Revolution: common-sense self-rule by the body politic, i.e., white workingmen. It was time to get back to those roots, and he hoped his new party would be up for the task. At Buffalo, elements like Whitman had to find common ground

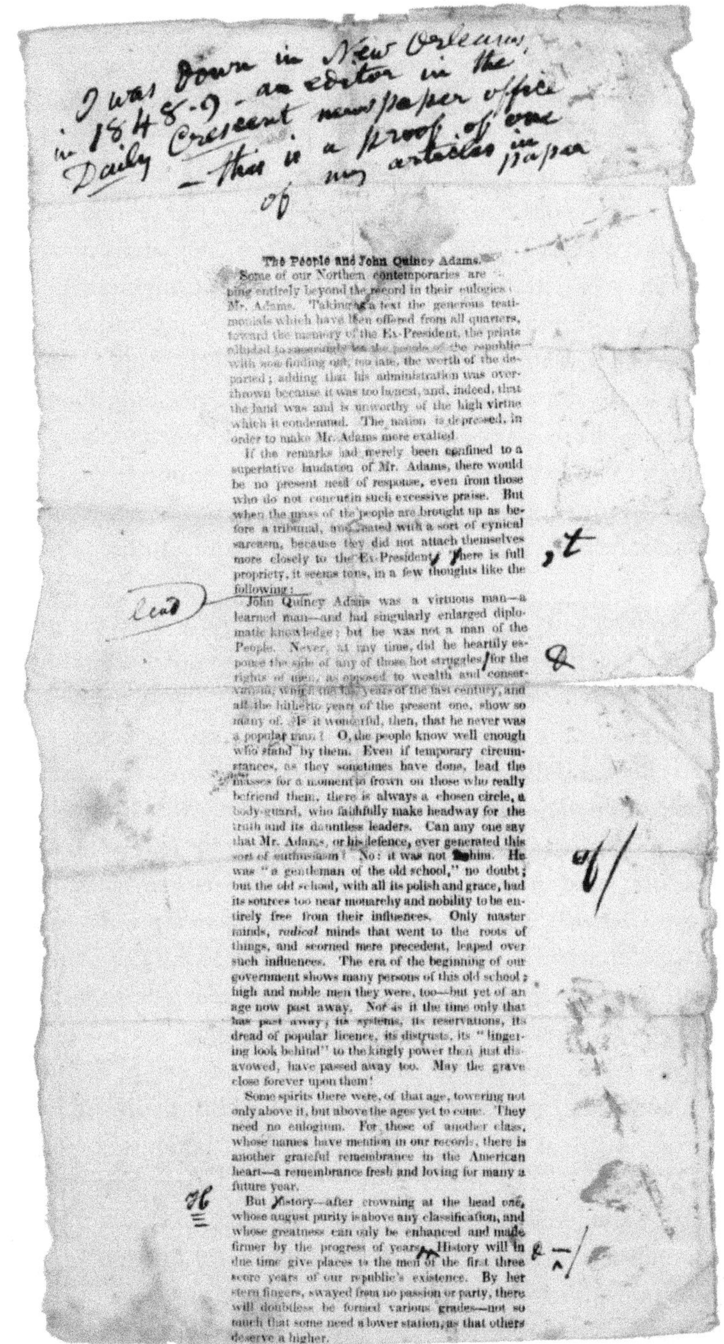

I was down in New Orleans, in 1848-9 – an editor in the Daily Crescent newspaper office – this is a proof of one of my articles in paper

The People and John Quincy Adams.

Some of our Northern contemporaries are [illegible]ping entirely beyond the record in their eulogies [illegible] Mr. Adams. Taking as a text the generous testimonials which have been offered from all quarters, toward the memory of the Ex-President, the prints alluded to [illegible] the people of the republic with now finding out, too late, the worth of the departed; adding that his administration was overthrown because it was too honest, and, indeed, that the land was and is unworthy of the high virtue which it condemned. The nation is depressed, in order to make Mr. Adams more exalted.

If the remarks had merely been confined to a superlative laudation of Mr. Adams, there would be no present need of response, even from those who do not concur in such excessive praise. But when the mass of the people are brought up as before a tribunal, and [illegible] with a sort of cynical sarcasm, because they did not attach themselves more closely to the Ex-President. There is full propriety, it seems to us, in a few thoughts like the following:

John Quincy Adams was a virtuous man—a learned man—and had singularly enlarged diplomatic knowledge; but he was not a man of the People. Never, at any time, did he heartily espouse the side of any of those hot struggles for the rights of men, as opposed to wealth and conservatism, which the last years of the last century, and all the hitherto years of the present one, show so many of. Is it wonderful, then, that he never was a popular man? O, the people know well enough who stand by them. Even if temporary circumstances, as they sometimes have done, lead the masses for a moment to frown on those who really befriend them, there is always a chosen circle, a body-guard, who faithfully make headway for the truth and its dauntless leaders. Can any one say that Mr. Adams, or his defence, ever generated this sort of enthusiasm? No: it was not [illegible] him. He was "a gentleman of the old school," no doubt; but the old school, with all its polish and grace, had its sources too near monarchy and nobility to be entirely free from their influences. Only master minds, *radical* minds that went to the roots of things, and scorned mere precedent, leaped over such influences. The era of the beginning of our government shows many persons of this old school; high and noble men they were, too—but yet of an age now past away. Nor is it the time only that has past away; its systems, its reservations, its dread of popular licence, its distrusts, its "lingering look behind" to the kingly power then just disavowed, have passed away too. May the grave close forever upon them!

Some spirits there were, of that age, towering not only above it, but above the ages yet to come. They need no eulogium. For those of another class, whose names have mention in our records, there is another grateful remembrance in the American heart—a remembrance fresh and loving for many a future year.

But History—after crowning at the head one, whose august purity is above any classification, and whose greatness can only be enhanced and made firmer by the progress of years, History will in due time give places to the men of the first three score years of our republic's existence. By her stern fingers, swayed from no passion or party, there will doubtless be formed various grades—not so much that some need a lower station, as that others deserve a higher.

FIGURE 20. "The People and John Quincy Adams," proof sheet with corrections and notations, courtesy of the Library of Congress (Charles E. Feinberg Collection).

with principled crusaders against slavery, bitter former Clay supporters, anti-Cass voters, Western land activists, and even a few Freedpeople.

The larger diversity of opinion at Buffalo was, of course, echoed in the *Freeman* as well, with a Whiggish young copyist, an abolitionist owner, and a Barnburner editor like Whitman. While it is, of course, apt to call Whitman a "Free-Soiler"—he was a political actor in the party, after all—this should not sweep the diversity of his own opinions under the rug. What drove Whitman to the Free-Soilers, as we have discussed in this book, was not a moral objection to the stain of slavery (as an abolitionist or anti-slavery Whig might say) but an outgrowth of what Sean Wilentz has termed the Democratic Party's "Jacksonian Contradictions"[67]—its identity in perpetual crisis between prolabor, radical rhetoric and an establishment politics of power.

Van Buren, of course, had a direct connection to Jackson (he was his vice president), which made him look good enough to Whitman, but there is some indication he was *not* his first choice. In the lead-up to the convention, the *Freeman* editor signaled as much by supporting a compromise measure that would ultimately have been beneficial to the slaveholding South—but was rhetorically grounded in popular sovereignty. Writing to the *Crescent* on July 19, 1848, Whitman expressed his support for the so-called Clayton Compromise, an ultimately failed predecessor to the Compromise of 1850, which provided "for the establishment of territorial governments in Oregon, New Mexico, and California [and which left the] question of whether to establish slavery in any new state to the territorial convention that would draw up a constitution preparatory to the territory's admission to the Union."[68] Whitman celebrated it thus:

> The great beauty of the "laissez faire" doctrine is exemplified here—the gem above all price for our country—contains more vital and preservative power for the Union, than all the schemes of all the modern politicians combined.
>
> How are you receiving this report in the south-west? Do you not like it? Is it not perfectly consistent with the rights of all parties; and, above all, with the rights of the inhabitants (whom, by-the-bye, nobody seems to think any thing about,) of the territories themselves? The probability appears to be, almost beyond

a doubt, that the plan reported by the committee of eight will satisfy the body of the "Free Soilers" of the north and west.

On a matter that split both establishment parties into pro- and antislavery forces, as the ultimately unsuccessful Clayton bill did, Whitman, writing to the *Crescent*, here favored the legislation supported by slavery forces. He did so because it emphasized Whitman's core belief: a politics centered on self-determination of the population of a given territory or state. The measure was decried as "an insidious device for establishing slavery judicially" and found support from John C. Calhoun and Jefferson Davis[69]—and Walt Whitman. Ideological abolitionism to Whitman in 1848 was either Whiggery or anti-unionism. Compromises like Clayton's made the issue one for the people of a given state. Whitman, above all, was an ur-Jacksonian populist.

Whitman, then, took on the position of a Free-Soil freethinker, bemoaning that even though, to his reading, this proposal lined up with core tenants of Free-Soil populism, the party convention would "*however* [. . .] in less than three weeks [. . .] 'pile up' their endorsement of Van Buren for the Presidency" anyway.[70] It is notable that even in the Free-Soil Party, Whitman saw a disconnect between leadership—wealthy, respectable statesman Van Buren—and interests of "*the body* of the 'Free Soilers.'" "Even the New York Tribune, you see, endorses Van Buren," he had previously written to the *Crescent*—tacitly associating Van Buren with Whiggery yet also marveling at the political turning of tides such favor might imply: "These are wonderful days, when such things come to pass!" he joked.[71]

If Whitman had his suspicions that Van Buren was the mainstream, establishment candidate, his worries were confirmed when the VP pick was settled: Charles Francis Adams, the son of the very elder Whig statesman whose shuffling-off into the dustbin of American history Walt had wanted to celebrate in the opening issue of the *Crescent*. Now his party of "the People" had picked Adams's son to fill the second slot of their populist ticket. His letter to the *Crescent* sounded disgruntled:

> Much astonishment is felt, however, at the nomination for the Vice Presidency. Very few people had hitherto heard of Charles Francis Adams—except, perhaps, in the demesnes of Boston,

> where he has occupied, for years past, a position among the editorial corps. What the reasons of bringing him forward are, do not as yet appear upon the surface. The managing men at Buffalo, however, had some good reasons in their own minds, no doubt. McLean or Hale had been generally fixed upon for the station.[72]

Whitman's "body" versus "leaders" suspicions were alive and well, casting the results from Buffalo, which delegate Whitman had participated in, as the meddling of "managing men." John Van Buren, however, the candidate's son, as we have shown in a previous chapter, managed to capture Whitman's enthusiasm. In the younger Van Buren, Whitman had finally found his "don't-care-a-damnative young m[a]n" to embody the youthful verve of a party whose leadership was dominated by geezers of previous political generations.

Yet Whitman's infra-party squabbles were inflected, geographically, in a quite telling way: the body of the party was "of the north *and west*." The geographical addendum to his populist outrage is telling and, as previous chapters have shown, grounded in his new-found love for the American West. And Whitman's attitudes here did seem to echo the sentiments of western Free-Soilers, who tended to downplay nonextension (or even abolition) in their own publications to focus on core Jacksonian concerns. One might look at how the Free-Soil platform was communicated by a party paper in Indiana, to its Western readers:

> *Free Soil Platform.*
> No more Slave Territory.
> No interference with Slavery in States where it now exists.
> Cheap Postage for the people.
> Retrenchment of the expenses of Government.
> Abolition of all unnecessary offices and Salaries.
> The election of all Civil Officers of the Government, so far as practicable, by the people.
> Provision by the Government for all such River and Harber improvements as are required for the safety and convenience of Commerce, with Foreign Nations or among the several States.
> Free grant, to actual settlers, of the Public Lands, in limited quantities.

Revenue Tariff sufficient to defray the expenses of Government, and pay annual installments, together with the interest on the National debt.[73]

The argument here echoed Whitman's: since slavery is not mentioned in the constitution, it may not be established or prohibited by federal decree (and, of course, "territory" was administered federally). It was a point conceded by many voices in the South. What we see here instead is an emphasis on older Barnburner programs of small government, direct elections, and popular rule. To Whitman and many working-class Free-Soilers, especially outside of New England, these were the bread-and-butter issues that affected them. Instead of a marginal footnote to a party catalyzed by the Wilmot Proviso, these were often at the heart of the party's appeal. While they might vote alongside antislavery Whigs who had joined their coalition party, these Barnburners had a distinct vision for America.

This snippet then also illustrates the variety of issues that attracted men to the party who would never have joined a Liberty Party or, heavens forbid, become antislavery Whigs. These were all workingmen's issues—and Whitman had espoused many of them in the *Crescent*: from incessant complaints about the inadequacies of the postal system, to articles celebrating river infrastructure while preaching fiscal prudence (like "Naval Officer" Hoffman), to his plea (as "Manhattan") to have revolutionary immigrants flooding into the West to "vote themselves farms."[74] Indeed, as we've shown in the previous chapter, Whitman himself was on occasion picturing a life for himself as a Wisconsin homesteader. Encountering the men of the West had reinvigorated a Jeffersonian spark in Walt, who could now imagine himself a proper yeoman republican, overlooking the banks of the Illinois River or the coast of Lake Michigan. "Manhattan," then, was thrilled to see hundreds of delegates from Ohio at Buffalo.[75] He appears to have been serious about turning his back to the big city and moving to the country: later that same year, he would be running classified ads, looking to purchase "15 acres of land" ("with a little woodland, if possible") near the eastern shores of rural Long Island.[76] For now, however, his observations suggested one thing: If the men of the new territories of the South-West self-governed like these rugged men of the West, the end of slavery was a foregone conclusion and the future of the Union looked bright.

New Orleans, to put it plainly, did not turn Whitman into an abolitionist. Instead, living among radical fellow-travelers in New Orleans and agitating for the cause in Brooklyn seems to have underscored for him abolition as a political obstacle. For instance, we see "Manhattan," in a letter to the editors of the *Daily Crescent* just a few months later, addressing rumors of Black delegates visiting the Free-Soil convention at Buffalo alongside delegate Whitman. "Those stories of negroes going to the Buffalo Convention," wrote "Manhattan," "are nonsense. If any have gone, they were sent by the enemies of the Convention. Every effort is determinedly made by these 'Free Soilers' to steer clear of the Abolitionists proper—a faction who have no respectable power, on their own platform, here."[77]

In reality, Black attendance at the convention was not, in fact, "nonsense." Nobody less than Frederick Douglass himself was present, though his reception was a cold one: "The most politically awkward presence was a small group of black abolitionist leaders, including [. . .] Douglass," historian Wilentz summarizes: "Simply by showing up, Douglass and the other black leaders caused consternation—a sign of important racial divisions" at the heart of the convention.[78] Democratic papers like the *Eagle* exploited this apparent discord, mocking the proceedings.[79] The salient question is: Did Whitman express such "consternation" too? Or was his letter to the *Crescent* all public performance for a Southern paper? The odd phrase "abolitionists proper" certainly suggests that Whitman, post–New Orleans, had come to see himself as a bit of an "improper" abolitionist, an activist who (as he would later say about socialism) was "with them in the end" but disagreed about the method.

"Manhattan" was particularly reassured that, regardless of youthful fervor, the Buffalo Convention's results could only lead to good, since voters and party delegates were far less wedded to party identities then than they would be today: "Amid all the wrangles of the politicians," "Manhattan" noted, "a man may safely wrap himself up and take comfort in the fact, that the great self-interest of the people of the Republic never *can* let any imminent danger happen to our land. Besides, I am confident that more than a third of the Americans are not much interested in *party* politics—but always hold the balance, and only turn it when the times demand."[80] The balance, such as it was, seems to have held. Without either imploding or deadlocking, the delegates of the Free-Soil Convention, bolstered by a surprising number of delegates from northern rural-agricultural districts, settled on a ticket.

Yet despite Van Buren's relative popularity, he faced an uphill battle, running against two similarly viable candidates on an issue that was highly divisive. How could Van Buren defeat *both* Cass and Taylor, each widely perceived as, respectively, a hero of the War of 1812 and of the US-Mexico conflict? It would take more than force of personality. Besides having nominated a candidate seen as a strong force for the nonextension of slavery—and Van Buren was increasingly antislavery, even publishing a manifesto on the issue in 1848—Free-Soilers would need to generate a groundswell in favor of their brand-new party. Such a swell would require constant and widespread publicity. Hence the need for what was then a common tool for presidential campaigns: partisan local newspapers, like Whitman's *Brooklyn Freeman*.

As Shelden and Alexander explain, the formation of new political parties in the nineteenth century not only required a state-level "network of political allies and operatives; strong ties to constituent groups; [. . .] financial backing; and friendly local and state election laws." It was not enough that, as they argue, these elements were generally "in such wide supply that a coalition of men with a particular political concern could organize quickly." In order to not "disband just as quickly," the new party would need exposure to the electorate, since, without "access to a printing press and a willing newspaper editor," news of a party's platform, its candidate nominations, even its voters' access to voting tickets, could dissolve quickly.[81] That exposure primarily came through the vehicle of the partisan paper; until practically the close of the nineteenth century, these political newspapers were a vital element of the constantly shifting political party landscape. We can see the overlap between party organizing and party press in Whitman himself: he not only edited the *Freeman* but served as convention delegate *and* organizer for Brooklyn's Seventh Ward (in today's Park Slope neighborhood, around Washington Park).[82]

Yet Whitman did not focus his partisanship exclusively on Brooklyn or wider New York City. As the *Crescent*'s "Manhattan" letters reveal, he was also advocating for Free-Soilism in the South—a region that he knew, from recent experience, was not at all a solid proslavery bloc but was, on occasion, open to radical proposals. "[T]he slave owners and breeders of their states," he wrote in the first issue of the *Freeman*, "are not 'the South,' and [. . .] we of the free states know it. We know that at this moment a very large majority of the aggregate white citizens of Virginia, Kentucky, Missouri, Maryland, and Delaware, entertain anti-slavery and emancipation doctrines."[83] For that reason, "Manhattan" repeatedly advocated for Free-Soilism or, to put the matter in an earlier formulation, "states' rights." Whitman's (previously discussed) humorous "Ephraim Broadhorn" sketch for the *Crescent* suggested the merits of letting such Westerners decide the (non)slaveholding status of new states, since "they possess what answers an excellent purpose in the matter of pure republicanism."[84] Whitman had quoted Maryland senator William Pinkney on this matter of popular sovereignty, from an 1820 speech on the Missouri Compromise in which Pinkney emphasized "the unsophisticated good sense and noble spirit of the American people."[85] The message was clear: It was not politicians but common people who would determine whether or not their state's soil would be free.

If many *Crescent* readers would have felt compelled by this Jacksonian appeal in the Free-Soil Party is unclear. Yet "Manhattan" also made an implicit argument for its natural growth. In a clever hedging of bets, Whitman positioned the spread of free soil not only as a preferable party position, but also as a natural consequence of the recent national party realignments: "The separate nominations for State officers by the whigs, hunkers and barnburners have exercised considerable influence toward re-marking distinct lines between the parties. [. . .] Probably, however, as much mischief has already been done as could be done, on this point. Those among the masses who have been carried over from the whigs to 'free soil' cannot easily be recaptured."[86] Whitman here reassured Southern readers that the change in the wind was natural and unlikely to upend their lives—while nevertheless implying that the political developments of 1848, once done, could not be undone.

Much of this, he noted in a separate letter, was likely due to dissatisfaction with party sluggishness, which until the recent realignment may have kept the primary parties from addressing American presidential politics' elephant in the room: the (non)extension of slavery. Such dissatisfaction did not have to be visible in public as violence or instability; "Manhattan" argued that, to the contrary, many average voters silently seethed, with the result that their defections—over to the Free-Soil party, for example—might end up being more numerous than currently predicted:

> Nor will disaffection burn less intensely because it makes no open show. The flames may be smothered, but they are there still. Party organs (on both sides) are not reliable, now, as to their statements; because, never before were the old landmarks so utterly broken up. You can tell where disaffection exists, but you can't tell where the disaffected will "go," or, indeed, whether they will vote for any body at all. This is a pretty state of things, isn't it?[87]

That said, in courting Southern voters, Whitman was careful to distinguish between the Free-Soil Party being against the extension of slavery (which it was) and being fully abolitionist (which it was not). Speaking a "word of justice to the New York Free Soilers," "Manhattan" insisted to *Crescent* readers not only that "[n]ot a breath, not a thought, of unfriendliness, exists in the Van Buren party of New York, toward the South, or Southern men," but also that the party had no intention of eliminating the institution of chattel slavery where it currently stood:

> Certain persons, either in error themselves or from the worst of motives, are in the habit of painting the Van Buren party of the North as identical with the "Abolitionists." A greater or grosser untruth was never written. Nearly every document emanating from the Free Soilers, recognizes the well understood constitutional guaranty, that over all subjects not expressly reserved to the General Government, States, whether they be North or South, have sovereign jurisdiction within their own limits. Of the remainder of the points at issue, I pressure you do not desire any labored disquisition. Common justice, however, demands that no one in the South should charge the Radicals of New York with enmity toward their Southern fellow countrymen, as

> no one will make that charge who *knows* New York. As to any danger, from this at present warmly conducted dispute, to our Republican Union, we laugh the idea to scorn! The acorn has not yet germinated, whose product oak shall be ruffled by winds that howl the tidings of her dissolution.[88]

Indeed, there were two articles in the first (and only fully surviving) issue of the *Freeman*, aimed at making Free-Soilism palpable to Southern readers: one defending Van Buren's vote for a postage matter that has been described as anti-Southern, and the quoted piece titled "Our Enmity to the South"—which hoped to defuse such a notion. Free-Soilism, Whitman argued, was a shared front against aristocratic tendencies in North and South (what George Lippard called the "cotton Lord and the factory Prince").[89] It was a unified people's reform movement against a cabal of monied interests.

Here is where Whitman's partisan advocacy for the Free-Soil movement reached its political limits. Whitman's insistence that Northern Free-Soilers had no designs against Southern slavery, was partially due, no doubt, to the "Manhattan" letters' primary audience being citizens of a major slavery hub in the South. Whitman, here, was in line with the platform of Free-Soilism itself, which had coalesced around the "moderate" position of a Wilmot-Proviso-supporting, live-and-let-live nonextension of slavery. It was an attempt at appeasing the South specifically echoed in the delegate resolution that had sent him to Buffalo. And with the election so close at hand—little more than two weeks away—Whitman and other Free-Soil advocates seem not to have wanted to scare away undecided whites concerned about "abolitionism." Within that constraint, however, Whitman exerted all his efforts toward maximizing Free-Soil turnout in the 1848 election.

Indeed, having spent several months reviving the *Freeman* following the September 10 fire, Whitman got it back into print on November 1, just in time to deliver his final word on the election to be held the following week. While it now had new offices, Whitman ran the paper largely out of 106 Myrtle Avenue, in a house that he built with his father and shared with his family and that featured a small print shop on the ground floor.[90] The resurrected *Freeman* was welcomed by puffs from papers like the *Evening Post*, the *Tribune*, and even the *Long-Islander*, who congratulated its old friend for "emerg[ing] from his late misfortune, with a spirit no wise daunted."[91] On the same day, "Manhattan" wrote a letter to the editors of the *Daily Crescent*, exclaiming more than once that "we are in the midst of exciting times!"—describing how "[e]very vacant wall [. . .] is covered with huge posters," every newspaper chock full of political chatter, every ball and tavern "'teem[ing]' with political gatherings."[92]

In Louisiana, Van Buren never made it on the ballot. But would the readers of the *Crescent* have voted for Van Buren, had he been on the ballot? Possibly, though Whitman worried about "a remarkable apathy and lukewarmness" in populations outside of New York. Within the state, however, there was to be no contest: Voters in New York, he wrote, were almost certainly going to deliver the state to him, and victory to Free-Soilism:

> For me—I stick to my prediction of a month ago, that, as the most probable event, Van Buren will get this State. If he does, it will be one of the most remarkable triumphs ever achieved on the ground of an abstract principle, in our Republic! The Administration, using without scruple its immense scope of power against the ex-President—openly putting itself in the field against him; both of the old phalanxes united in an enmity toward him; no chance of his carrying any other State than this—and thus not the remotest probability of his being President; hardly a prominent, well-known leader, except a few of the faithful old Van Buren guard, coming out for him; and yet, I tell you again, Martin Van Buren is going to get the thirty-six electoral votes of New York. It is rather hazardous to say so—but I venture to say it.[93]

Ironically, by the time this "Manhattan" letter appeared in the *Crescent*, on November 13, the election had already occurred, and ongoing vote tallies—which appeared on the same page as the letter—were grim for Free-Soilers. Van Buren had *not* carried New York; Louisiana planter Taylor had. In fact, by the time all votes had been counted, it became clear that Van Buren, despite the advocacy of Free-Soil editors like Whitman, had been dealt a crushing loss. All told, Van Buren received just 10 percent of the popular vote; worse yet, he did not receive a single

FIGURE 21. Whitman's former home at 106 Myrtle Ave (*The Gathering of the Forces*, vol. 2, ed. Cleveland Rodgers [New York, NY: G. P. Putnam, 1920], 242f.). The photo was taken in 1919 for a commemorative issue of the *Brooklyn Daily Eagle*, which celebrated the centennial of Whitman's birth.

electoral vote. Meanwhile, Cass would earn 127 and Taylor 163, a majority of electoral votes that delivered the latter the presidency.[94] (In Louisiana as in much of the South, of course, Van Buren had not even been on the ballot; in New Orleans he nonetheless received a single vote.)[95]

It would not be the end of the Free-Soil movement, nor of Whitman's Free-Soil newspaper. Having missed the presidency, the party nevertheless placed twelve of its members in Congress and many more in various state legislatures.[96] Whitman not only accepted the result with a surprisingly light heart but he also, apparently, identified a reason for it: the Free-Soil Party had felt like a Northern abolitionist party to other sections of the country. The populist appeal of Taylor—this rugged soldier who proclaimed to stand above politicking—had embodied some of the working-class gusto Barnburners believed to be their own. The future of the party would be found in emulating this appeal. So, in the Summer of 1849, Whitman proposed a new name for the future of the Free-Soil Party and nominated Thomas Hart Benton (1782–1858) for the presidency. It was not a controversial pick, though Whitman would later brag he was the first to make it.[97] Of course, Benton had been floated in 1848, and in 1849 was ultimately supported by Van Buren himself. In any case, Whitman's endorsement is telling: It suggests that his politics had shifted from a New-York-centric Barnburnerism to a national Free-Soil politics that had to court the sentiments of the majority of Southern and Western citizens who had cast their vote for the Louisiana planter Taylor. For the party to ever gain national traction, it ought to no longer preemptively give up on the South, as it had done in 1848.

In some ways, Benton made as much sense as Van Buren: He, too, had served under and for Jackson, during both his military and his political campaigns. He also had a certain rugged appeal—he was a "great imperious, animal man" Whitman recollected, fondly, in 1858[98]—yet another factor likely made him a good candidate in Whitman's eyes: He was the senator of a slaveholding state from "the West"—Missouri. Indeed, this preacher of Manifest Destiny also fully embodied the westward expansionism that Whitman had celebrated in the *Eagle* and the *Crescent*.[99] Additionally, the Free-Soil sympathizer Benton had been instrumental in the Compromise of 1820, which Whitman had positively referenced (indirectly) in his Broadhorn Sketch. While Benton had been lukewarm, even dismissive, of the Proviso, he was now beginning to espouse antislavery sentiments. Somewhat akin to Whitman, this slave owner had undergone a "shift from states' rights agrarian to Free Soil Democrat."[100] The longer the association lasted, the more like an abolitionist both men sounded. In any case, Benton's westward appeal allowed Whitman to dream of a prosperous Free-Soil future: With Benton as president, Whitman quipped in his new paper, the "Freeman will then be one of the most profitable newspaper establishments in the land—which will enable us to sell out for enough to buy us a good farm, to retire to."[101] With some luck, Whitman might have turned "Western b'hoy,"[102] after all.

All the while, the continued existence of the Free-Soil Party assured (at least for now) that Whitman's *Freeman* likewise soldiered on (by then a daily paper). But his disappointment with the election was evident, both in the "Manhattan" letters and in what *Freeman* reprints survive. The former lamented the lack of principle of the other, more successful parties. "Well, election times are over," wrote "Manhattan," and "[w]e have recovered from the heat and burden of the battle, and most folks breathe freer. Taylor is President, the republic is comparatively quiet for about three years—quiet at least on one great subject—and the Universal Yankee Nation is 'saved.'"[103] While he did not sound especially pleased with Southern voters in his following remarks, he at least added that "I confess I did not vote for the old General, but I am willing to see all the good developments of the election, nevertheless. To me it is a beautiful thought, that the 'fraternity' which forms the third ingredient in what Monsieur Crapean is after, already exists—with 'liberty' and an elsewhere unequalled amount of 'equality'—in this Republic."[104]

Such recourse to the language of the French Revolution made sense, as we have demonstrated in chapter 6. Whitman, who believed republican government negated the need for revolution, was a staunch adherent of popular rule—even if it blew up in his face.

Whitman would end his association with the *Freeman* in September 1849. One of his last acts in the office was removing the large Barnburner flag that had hung outside its business office and carrying it home with him. This act was to be a programmatic one: The new editor of the paper, Whig Samuel F. Cogswell (c. 1827–58),[105] soon declared that it would stay true to its rebellious spirit, albeit not its party affiliation. As many former Barnburner dissidents were returning to the Democratic tent in 1849, the new *Freeman* would be "an independent liberal thinking man," willing to speak to "both parties, Democratic as well as Whig."[106] Whitman, in the meantime, stuck with his third party.

By 1852 the Free-Soil Party would still be large enough to nominate a candidate for the presidency: New Hampshire Senator John P. Hale, to whom Whitman would even write a letter in that year eloquently asking him to join the newly renamed "Free Democrats" party. That party would then still function as a political home and Jacksonian vanguard for Whitman. "At this moment, New York is the most radical city in America," Whitman insisted, adding that, likewise, "[i]t would be the most anti-slavery city, if that cause hadn't been made ridiculous by the freaks of the local leaders here."[107] That said, further Free-Soil successes were not to be. Following the incendiary passage of the Fugitive Slave Act of 1850, most Free-Soilers had either rejoined the Democrats or gone back to the Whigs as anti-slavery Conscience Whigs. Though they left the Free-Soil Party depopulated and once again unable to win any electoral votes (this time garnering only about 5 percent of the popular vote), these factions would ultimately join the coalition that gave birth to the Republican Party in 1854.[108] It is notable that Whitman would stick with the Free-Soilers—even when they move to outright abolitionism in the Pittsburgh Platform of 1852 (which even included the recognition of Haiti).[109] This is the Whitman many biographers have tried to find emerging in New Orleans—the 1850 Whitman who had cast aside any remaining political moderation and who would call Southern slaveholders "Crawlers, Lice of Humanity [. . .] Muck-worms, creeping flat to the ground" and compare those who returned fugitive slaves to "Judas, [who] sold the Divine youth"—the Whitman who rages at the hypocrisy of anti-abolitionist Southerners and complicit Northerners alike. If Whitman had become a Free-Soiler through the push of Wilmot, he would become an abolitionist via James M. Mason—and the Fugitive Slave Law of 1850 that the Southern statesman had authored. Said law would violate not only Whitman's sense of popular sovereignty, but—*finally,* it seems—his morality.

While Whitman's association with increasingly minor splinter movements may have furthered his transition from Barnburner to abolitionist, the experiences of 1848 had a different lesson in store for him: that the interests of Northern and Southern workingmen were aligned, and the North needed to court the South—as Whitman did in the *Freeman* and as "Manhattan" in the *Crescent*—to fulfill the country's Jeffersonian/Jacksonian promise. Following New Orleans, the region of American slavery was still his "magnet-south / O glistening perfumed South! my South! / O quick mettle, rich blood, impulse and love! good and evil! / O all dear to me!"[110] Betsy Erkkila's claim, in her groundbreaking *Whitman the Political Poet*, that Whitman's pre-*Leaves* period was characterized by a "refusal to compromise on the issue of slavery extension" and that the Southern sojourn only "deepened his opposition" to it is incorrect.[111] If anything, the Crescent City suggested the South to Whitman as a partner in his vision for an American nation built on popular sovereignty.

Seeing the city of New Orleans and, at a distance, plantation slavery along the Mississippi did not unsettle Whitman into sectarian conflict and outrage but presented him with a complex political reality that he believed could, and *should*, be addressed through national compromise as well as through respect for regional differences and the popular will of citizens. In this approach, Whitman was not significantly less enlightened than most of his contemporaries—though certainly less than *some*, including the poet he would become. Yet this strange negotiation between seemingly irreconcilable beliefs—that humans should live self-determined lives, and that this determination can include a decision *for* slavery—still reverberates in the grand poetical expression that is the first edition of *Leaves of Grass*. There, Whitman would celebrate the conflicted status quo of the antebellum US in its perhaps most eloquent form, pledging to sing of "the southern plantation life—the character of the northeast and of the northwest and southwest—slavery and the tremulous spreading of hands to protect it, and the stern opposition to it which shall never cease till it ceases or the speaking of tongues and the moving of lips cease."[112]

New Orleans, not at all attractive in itself—not what would be called beautiful by an artistic eye—is yet a pure necessity: America, traffic—traffic even before the railroad; none the less since—ordained that a city was needed at just that precise point—a distributing center—a depot—and so this city grew, and so is likely to last for some time yet—last while the need lasts.

—WALT WHITMAN, IN *With Walt Whitman in Camden* (1889)

[Walt] asked: "Is there anything in it which you think ought to be changed?—I should like to hear. I have a sort of remembrance that at the time it first went into type, you felt so. I don't know that there's any point at which it can be attacked, except perhaps this—about the New Orleans trip—passing over Lake Huron"—he quoted the line. "Strictly speaking, that is not true—I see now that I did not at that time cross Huron—at least, I do not think I did. Now, what is your opinion? Should I change it?"—I said—"I suppose the man after origins, would insist upon the change." W. then: "That's so—I can understand."

—WALT WHITMAN, IN *With Walt Whitman in Camden* (1889)

Conclusion

A Journey and Louisiana Life

FOR SCHOLARS WHO ARE "AFTER ORIGINS," as Whitman's scribe Horace Traubel put it in the epigraph above, the facts about Whitman's Southern sojourn have, until recently, been rather maddeningly few and contradictory. In this book, we have sought to remedy this dearth of information, if not the information's sometimes-contradictory nature. It is worth remembering that many of the events and personages depicted in this volume have never received serious scrutiny or, in some cases, any extended discussion at all. Added to that, prior biographers of Whitman have had to rely almost exclusively on the nexus of his signed New Orleans–era writings and the manuscripts of his notoriously fanciful late-life reminiscences. What scholarship resulted from this was often either itself fanciful or fairly drawn but thin on detail, usually narrativized in a way that leads too cleanly to Whitman's later career as a poet. In this short book, we have endeavored to avoid both traps as much as possible.

The Whitman who went down to New Orleans was not a budding national poet—though he also produced poetry—but a newspaper writer. In the history of journalism, antebellum newspapers, especially local papers, remain largely understudied and conceptually neglected. Measured against the benchmark of professional, fact-based journalism of the twentieth century, the multitudes of textual voices, attitudes, and arguments put forth by a professional newspaperman like Whitman barely hold up as "journalism" from today's vantage point, after all. The teleological narrative at the core of much of journalism's professional history-making mirrors that of Whitman scholars: In contrast to a later standard—*professional* journalism for one, *Leaves of Grass* for the other—preceding newspaper work is often branded as either deficient or adolescent. In any case, it represented standards and results to be overcome. No matter how one might value what came after, we still believe this is an unwise approach, and we hope to have demonstrated in this book the value of taking antebellum journalism seriously in its own right: both for Whitman and for his culture at large. More people read Whitman's work in a New Orleans daily than ever touched his first edition of *Leaves* during his lifetime.

In the Crescent City, Whitman excelled at what he did: He entertained, amused, informed, agitated, and persuaded. He tried to manufacture consent about hot-button issues like the Mexican peace treaty by slandering, spreading falsehoods, and grandstanding. He made impassioned pleas for the dignity of urban men and presented nascent Free-Soilism to the South not through political didacticism but as common-sense attitude, street smarts, and Jacksonian gusto. He connected readers of the *Crescent* with the rest of the country by selecting and framing the news as it slowly trickled in from the North, bringing with him professional networks of exchange and widening them across the South. He took his readers by their hands and, through him, led them to encounter their bustling metropolis anew. Antebellum newspapers offered a broad-appeal entertainment medium, after all, and Whitman was the kind of journalist who excelled at the various genres that that medium spawned: be it scathing editorials, sentimental poetry, lurid prose, correspondence, news and miscellanea clippings, or early forms of reportage ("peeps"). None of these elements were mere fillers—they were the meat and bones of the daily press. The Whitman of the 1840s, then, is not only worth studying in his own right but as an exemplar of the newspapermen of his day as they plied their trade in local papers. He is certainly more representative than the famed editor-proprietors that dominate many scholarly accounts of this period (the Horace Greeleys and James Gordon Bennetts of the day).

For a professional wrangler of fact and fiction, Whitman's late-life recollections of the period often moved uneasily back and forth between mythmaking, anecdote, and factual recollection. As we have emphasized throughout this volume, the primary chronicler of Whitman's sojourn in New Orleans was Whitman himself. Because of the resulting reliance upon his writings during his time there and his remembrances much later, we have tried to be up-front about the need to take his depictions of himself and his brother in the Crescent City with a grain of salt, and we have tried to corroborate them in their historical print contexts whenever possible. After all, Whitman's own versions of events became so muddled in later life that, to a knowledgeable reader, they can look more like hallucination than merely dimmed memory. Take a slip of manuscript that Traubel came across in the summer of 1891, less than a year before Whitman's death. "Among 'the odds and ends that get nowhere,' as W. put it, is this, autobiographical" page, wrote Traubel, noting that the poet suspects it was "probably intended for something when I wrote it, but the purpose now lost." The one-page slips begins:

> Walt Whitman was born May 31, 1819, in Huntington, New York. He moved early to Brooklyn and grew up and worked here and in New York fifteen years. Went off west and south about 1847, lived in New Orleans and Texas; went thence to St. Louis and other cities. Working a while and then moving on, he practically

explored every state and city south and west. Was healthy, temperate and industrious; he worked as printer and reporter.[1]

Beginning with the second sentence, the manuscript is so riddled with errors that it may as well be fiction—though Traubel, who must have had some awareness of this, said nothing. Whitman did not travel "west and south about 1847" (it was 1848), nor did he ever even visit Texas, much less live there. His closest encounter with a Texan was likely the fanciful sketch he wrote for the *Crescent* about encountering one such specimen. And, of course, the political issues inaugurated by Texan statehood—slavery extension, aggression against Mexico, the era of filibustering—featured prominently in his thinking of 1848. Whitman certainly "went thence to St. Louis and other cities" but only briefly at that time, via steamships on his return to New York in summer of 1848. (He would not truly visit St. Louis until 1879, when he stayed with his brother and New Orleans companion, Jeff, who had by then lived there for more than a decade.) And, as is plainly clear, it is not remotely true that "he practically explored every state and city south and west" after "[w]orking a while and then moving on" from New Orleans. Far from it. Whitman's travels to and from New Orleans certainly took him far across Appalachia, the Great Plains, the Midwest (then "West"), and down the Mississippi. He did not at any point, however, visit Texas, New Mexico, Alabama, or any of the Deep South states. All of this is to remind the reader that Whitman, though a dedicated chronicler of himself, had few scruples about contradicting the basic facts of his pre-*Leaves* life, when to do so served the purpose of building up his self-created persona of the well-traveled loafer-poet.

That said, his contradictions often contain kernels of truth. (Little wonder he could be so at ease, later, when writing, "Do I contradict myself? / Very well then . . . . I contradict myself."[2]) A prime example is his later-life note stating that "I was down in New Orleans, in 1848–9—an editor in the Daily Crescent newspaper office."[3] The untruth of the literal statement (Whitman did *not* live in New Orleans for the better part of two years) concealed what we believe to be a subliminal slip on Whitman's part: an accidental recognition that he spent 1848 and 1849 not just *editing* the *Crescent* but, rather, also contributing to it as the letter writer "Manhattan" in the early weeks of 1849. It is from such slips, of which Whitman made several regarding his New Orleans days, that we have been able to refine a new, more complex picture of Whitman's relationship to New Orleans, the polestar of the American South, a place undergoing remarkable growth in Whitman's lifetime, a bustling site of concentrated American activity and contradiction, a city that Whitman would later call "a pure necessity," one that "is likely to last for some time yet—last while the need lasts."[4] In this way, we have endeavored to expand the zone of truth—and when necessary, of educated guess—regarding Whitman's time spent in New Orleans.

Such an endeavor is aided by a quirk of Whitman's memory: while his commitment to reliably recording dates and places was notoriously poor, his attention to the aesthetic experience of a place could be stunningly accurate, even decades later. What results—unsurprisingly, considering his later calling as a poet—are recollections that record with exactitude the *beauties* of place. This is why Whitman could remember in such stunning detail the people on the streets of New Orleans, the sailors and coffee sellers and longshoremen, long after he'd begun mixing up the dates of his sojourn. The vitality of New Orleans and its mighty river delta lay not just (as we have argued) in the racial and economic and political, but also in the purely aesthetic. This is why, more than four decades later, Whitman could still speak passionately "of Mississippi floods—of his own experiences in New Orleans—'the wonder and delight of the levee there: a place of places, picked out of the offerings of the world. [. . . T]he levee at New Orleans—its own type—curious among river fronts—certainly in America.' The whole Mississippi valley subject to floods—'the country low—yet with a lordly look, too.'"[5] In all its multitudinousness, New Orleans stuck with Whitman because, no matter what else it was, it was beautiful.

Beauty and simplicity are not always the same, however, and we have tried to ensure that our narrative of Whitman in the Crescent City accounts for the complicated nature of the place itself and for the evolving attitudes of the man who visited it. Those attitudes—rolling onward with experience toward a more and more egalitarian bent—are nevertheless sometimes repugnant. As a young professional man, traversing a fundamentally racially diverse city for the first time, Whitman could note the complex personhood of the non-white citizens around him (the coffee seller at the market, for example, or the *grisettes* on the street), while also extolling the appeal of a white slaveholder like "good true, simple [General] Zach Taylor," of whom Whitman would much later recall: "I hobnobbed much with him in New Orleans. He was a man accustomed to contact with assistants, hired men, slaves—accustomed to command, armies, placemen—yet wholly unspoiled—a wonderful tribute to the essential soundness of American life."[6] The same tableau, of a benevolent Taylor surrounded by slaves in New Orleans, seems to have imprinted itself on the journalist's memory, since he would soon recall more or less the same scene again:

> There were many of the old fellows—thoroughly democratic—approachable. There was old Zach Taylor—General Taylor—afterwards the President. In New Orleans—forty years ago—about the close of the Mexican War—I came to know him there. A plain man—without the first sign of airishness—yet a man with his entourage of slaves—a man used to being served—military—a disciplinarian, yet a jolly man—fond of a good story—living well—realizing life.[7]

Our goal in preparing this book has not been to paper over such moments. Quite the opposite; it was our intent to leave Whitman's faults out in the open: to counter hagiography and teleology and to present, to the best ability afforded by our sources, a truthful picture of a successful mid-century journalist's foray into the Deep South.

The picture painted here, we cannot but briefly state in closing, has often been a troubling one. Scholarly work is never done in a historical vacuum, and our work on this book has coincided with a forceful wave of anti-intellectual, right-wing populism sweeping the United States, Europe, and much of the rest of the world. It has been eye-opening for us to see Whitman employ many talking points that are still politically potent in 2026: distrust of office-holders and career bureaucrats; aversion to government spending and debt; the valorization of the Jacksonian white, working-class male as the "real American"; the virulent jingoism targeted against our southern neighbor; and an attendant vision of a "United States of North America." Sean Wilentz has described such talking points as resulting from "Jacksonian contradictions" encoded into the fabric of the Democratic party. Whitman, certainly, embodies them. At times, these contradictions fuel a liberatory, quasi-revolutionary program for a radically democratic society; sometimes they appear in calls to Americanize the "semi-barbarous" Mexican "hordes" by force. Whitman, as the future "poet of America," embodied America's Jacksonian contradictions—which remain unresolved.

The Whitman who visited New Orleans in 1848 was, then, a reflection of the wider United States: its delight in expansionism; its interest in revolutionary Europe; its humorous send-ups of itself; its turning of a terrible blind eye to the plight of Black Americans; its experimentation with new artistic genres; its fervor; its growth; its optimism. To depict all these and be true to their contradictions and ragged edges, we have had to likewise give a truer, less romanticized account of Whitman's Southern sojourn. What resulted was not a cleanly rounded-off portrait of Whitman's "long foreground" as a poet, but rather a messy and revealing look into the growth of the character and identity of that writer, via a formative year shared between New Orleans and New York. The connection between the two locales was one that Whitman himself couldn't help but acknowledge. "My belief," he wrote as "Manhattan," "is that New York and New Orleans have more identity of character and interest than any other two cities in America."[8] Thus, we contend that the former city, long the central character in Whitman's life story, may only properly be seen in concert with the latter: the Crescent City.

The journalism is, in many ways, the final set of Whitman's writings that is still largely unread, undiscovered, and uncontextualized. It is also the largest set of texts Whitman ever produced and, perhaps, Whitman's most consistent writerly outlet. We have, at times, spoken of Whitman as a "poet-journalist" in this book. Conceptualizing Whitman as a writer who consistently moved back and forth between these two modes, each influencing the other, does not, of course, minimize the fact that, at least until 1855, both of these creative outlets and professional endeavors took place in the columns of a newspaper. Yet we think it is a worthwhile framework for rethinking Whitmanian style, politics, sense of audience, and personal-yet-public oratory. And, of course, the term attests to the fact that Whitman never stopped being a journalist. His famous *Specimen Days* passage about New Orleans that introduced this volume, for instance, did not originally appear in (and was neither, perhaps, composed for) that book. Instead, it was published months earlier as a signed contribution to the pages of the *Camden Courier*, framed there as "impromptu yarns."[9] Even after his final substantially expanded edition of *Leaves of Grass* was already published, Whitman was still on occasion writing the kind of journalism he produced for the *Crescent* (in this case, correspondence). What would it mean, then, to think of Whitman not as merely a poet who got his start in journalism, but as a life-long journalist who also wrote poetry? Looking over the dense columns of nineteenth-century newsprint, we believe there is much more Whitman to be found, understood, and wrestled with—but the same is true of many more antebellum writers, popular then and/or popular now, who maneuvered the newspaper sphere in much the same way. We hope that this case study—of one writer's work during one crucial year—will also serve as an example of the kind of granular, historicist inquiry into the local press that has the potential to further illuminate key aspects of antebellum literary production.

Acknowledgments

WITHOUT THE UNTIRING EFFORTS of scholars to edit and publish Whitman's journalism, his fiction, his art criticism, his manuscripts, and his health pamphlets, this first book-length account of Whitman's time in New Orleans could not exist. The foundation for this inquiry is, in many ways, the Walt Whitman Archive, an editorial achievement three decades in the making and still growing rapidly, shifting, enriching, and clarifying our understanding of the life and work of America's poet. Having contributed to the project in various positions over the years, we would be remiss not to highlight the incredible work of scholars working for, or in the orbit of, the *Archive*: Caterina Bernardini, Matt Cohen, Ed Folsom, Nicole H. Gray, Kenneth M. Price, Brett Barney, Karin Dalziel, the late Douglas A. Noverr, Stephanie M. Blalock, Kevin McMullen, and Jason Stacy. The journalist Whitman you meet in this book is not our brainchild alone; we rediscovered him in conversation with our colleagues of the Whitman Archive journalism team (Blalock, McMullen, and Stacy) in long Zoom meetings, Whitman Camp sessions in Iowa City, Iowa, and Lincoln, Nebraska, and messy, seemingly never-ending email threads. Whatever achievement is contained in these pages is theirs, too.

Once it became manuscript, our book benefited greatly from incisive, thoughtful, and exceedingly generous input of a number of early readers, particularly Kevin McMullen, Stephanie M. Blalock, and, above all, Jason Stacy. Without the generosity and care of each, this book would not exist. Likewise, we must thank the editors of and anonymous reviewers for the *Walt Whitman Quarterly Review*, in which our "Manhattan" findings, described in detail in this book, first appeared. Their belief in this project gave us the confidence to begin, just as the unwavering support of our spouses and families gave us the determination to see it to the end.

We should note that the Library of Congress's Chronicling America project, as well as its proprietary competitor, Ancestry's Newspapers.com, have allowed us access to many of the newspaper contents that form the spine of our inquiry and method. Digital archives and databases that provide public access to cultural history rely on public funding, and we as researchers, likewise, have relied on such funding. Thus, we would like to acknowledge the National Endowment for the Humanities as well as the National Historical Publications and Records Commission, who have generously supported the editorial work that allowed us to research and write this book, including by underwriting grant projects that directly and indirectly left their imprint on *Whitman's Southern Sojourn*. Additionally, we would like to extend our appreciation to our universities, which have unstintingly supported our research.

Finally, we extend our gratitude to Allison Carey (Marshall University), Karen Copp (University of Iowa Press), James W. Long (Louisiana State University Press), Natalie Fritz and her volunteers (Clark County Historical Society), Walter Grünzweig (Technische Universität Dortmund), Tara MacDonald (University of Idaho), Jim McCoy (University of Iowa Press), William D. Moore (Boston University), Susan Hill Newton (University of Iowa Press), Robert A. Rabe (Marshall University), David Mindel (University of Wisconsin–La Crosse) and Nori Muster (Steamboats.com), Jim Blanchard and Kevin Kelly (Houmas House Estate and Gardens), Denise B. Bethel, Tyler Hoffman (Rutgers University), Leo Blake (Walt Whitman House), Glen C. Cangelosi, Cassandra Simms and Margaret Elizabeth Bean (both Texas A&M University–Central Texas), Allen H. Redmon (Texas A&M University–Central Texas), Abby Seow (tirelessly traveling promoter of Whitman's New Orleans), and Steve Brunwasser (who braved the Whitman tour). Special thanks are due to Meredith Wadkins-Stabel and her entire team at University of Iowa Press. This book would never have come to be without her encouragement, suggestions, and good humor. Nor would it read half so well without the incredibly acute attentions of copyeditor Susan Boulanger, to whom we owe a debt of gratitude; any errors or typos, should they somehow have evaded her keen eye, are ours. Finally, and most especially, we would like to thank our spouses and families, who supported us, loved us, and learned more about Whitman and New Orleans than they ever hoped to.

Short sections of this book have previously appeared in an article for the *Walt Whitman Quarterly Review* and an (even shorter) section in the introduction to the illustrated reader's edition of Whitman's writings about New Orleans, published by LSU Press (*Walt Whitman in New Orleans*, 2022). We are grateful to these publications and the editorial teams that supported them.

All authors' proceeds from the sale of this book will be sent to the Walt Whitman Archive. We have had the wonderful opportunity of being a part of the Whitman Archive journalism team, which, by the time this book was finalized, had spent sixteen months identifying, annotating, and editing Whitman's nearly two hundred journalistic contributions to the *Crescent*. Unfortunately, in early 2025 this work was abruptly terminated "in furtherance of the President's agenda." As a result, this invaluable trove of Whitman writings will remain unpublished for now. We hope a revival of public grant funding for the humanities will allow us to make Whitman's New Orleans journalism freely available on the Walt Whitman Archive in the future.

ABBREVIATIONS

BDE	*Brooklyn Daily Eagle.*
DC	New Orleans *Daily Crescent.*
DD	New Orleans *Daily Delta.*
DP	*The Daily Picayune.*
ENCYC	Donald D. Cummings and J. R. LeMaster, eds., *Walt Whitman: An Encyclopedia* (New York: Garland Publishing, 1998).*
JOURN	Herbert Bergman, Douglas A. Noverr, and Edward J. Recchia, eds., *The Journalism* (New York: Peter Lang, 1998–2003), 2 vols. Vol. 1: 1834–1846 (1998); Vol. 2: 1846–1848 (2003).
LG (1855)	*Leaves of Grass* (Brooklyn: 1855).*
LG (1860–61)	*Leaves of Grass* (Boston: Thayer and Eldridge, 1860–61).*
LG (1891–92)	*Leaves of Grass* (Philadelphia: David McKay, 1891–92).*
MHTN	Letters by Walt Whitman, signed "Manhattan" (or "Mannahatta" for the first five installments), published in the New Orleans *Daily Crescent* under the recurring header "Northern Correspondence" (or variants thereof) between July 1848 and January 1849; the dates provided are publication dates, not mail dates.*
PW	Floyd Stovall, ed., *Prose Works 1892* (New York: New York University Press, 1963–64), 2 vols.
WWA	Matt Cohen, Ed Folsom, and Kenneth M. Price, eds., Walt Whitman Archive (whitmanarchive.org, 1995–); citations to documents exclusive to *WWA* include unique ID numbers for ease of finding.
WWQR	*Walt Whitman Quarterly Review* (Iowa City: University of Iowa, 1983–).
WWWC	Horace Traubel, *With Walt Whitman in Camden* (various publishers, 1906–96), 9 vols.*

*Available on the Walt Whitman Archive.

Notes

CHRONOLOGY

1. While the *St. Cloud* cannot be traced in newspapers from Cincinnati, other lines can, and these take less than twenty-four hours. See, for instance, mail steamer *Pike No. 9*, which left Cincinnati on February 18 at 4 p.m. ("Transportation," *Cincinnati Enquirer*, February 18, 1848, 3) and arrived in Louisville the next day with enough time to depart again at 4 p.m. for Cincinnati ("Ports of Louisville," *Courier-Journal*, February 21, 1848, 3). Steamboats travelled around five to eight miles per hour, and the distance between the two cities via the Ohio river is 133 miles (Carrie Blackmore Smith, "You don't see this every day," *Cincinnati Enquirer*, June 6, 2018). The record time in 1849 for the trip from Louisville to New Orleans was 5.5 days, performed by a ship about one year newer than the *St. Cloud*, which was built in 1847 (Louis C. Hunter, *Steamboats on the Western Rivers: An Economic and Technological History* [New York, NY: Dover, 2012], 23).

2. "Steamboats Leaving this Day," *Louisville Daily Courier*, February 18, 1848, 3.

INTRODUCTION

1. Paul Zweig, *Walt Whitman: The Making of the Poet* (New York, NY: Basic Books, 1984), 77.

2. Ralph Waldo Emerson famously sent Whitman a letter after reading the first edition of *Leaves of Grass*, in which he congratulated the poet on his achievement and exclaimed, "I greet you at the beginning of a great career, which yet must have had a long foreground somewhere for such a start" (July 21, 1855, *WWA*, loc. 02109). The "long foreground" has come to be a go-to expression used to describe Whitman's pre-*Leaves* poetry and prose (fiction, journalism, etc.), rendering it as (mere) biographical training ground for *Leaves*. See, for instance, David S. Reynolds, "Walt Whitman's Journalism: The Foreground of Leaves of Grass," in *Literature and Journalism: Inspirations, Intersections, and Inventions from Ben Franklin to Stephen Colbert*, ed. Mark Canada (New York: Palgrave, 2016).

3. Ed Folsom, "What New Orleans Meant to Walt Whitman," in *New Orleans: A Literary History*, ed. T. R. Johnson (New York: Cambridge University Press, 2019), 43–57.

4. Gay Wilson Allen, *The Solitary Singer: A Critical Biography of Walt Whitman* (New York: Macmillan, 1960), 91.

5. Philip Callow, *From Noon to Starry Night: A Life of Walt Whitman* (Chicago: Ivan R. Dee, 1992), 156.

6. Emory Holloway, *Whitman: An Interpretation in Narrative* (New York: Knopf, 1926), 46.

7. Justin Kaplan, *Walt Whitman: A Life* (New York, NY: Bantam Books, 1980), 143.

8. Holloway, *Whitman*, 59.

9. Zweig, *Walt Whitman*, 76.

10. Allen, *Solitary Singer*, 99.

11. "Random Recollections," *New Orleans Bulletin*, May 20, 1875, 4.

12. Ed Folsom and Kenneth M. Price, "Whitman's Life," *WWA*, whitmanarchive.org/whitmans-life/biography; Marcus Wood in his *The Poetry of Slavery: An Anglo-American Anthology, 1764–1865* (Oxford, UK: Oxford University Press, 2003), 674, describes the anecdote as a "well known" fact.

13. *WWWC* 1:457. For an image of the clipping, see Figure 9.

14. Allen, *Solitary Singer*, 94.

15. Callow, *From Noon*, 159.

16. Callow, *From Noon*, 170.

17. Jerome Loving, *Walt Whitman: The Song of Himself* (Berkeley, CA: University of California Press, 2000).

18. Callow, *From Noon*, 70. The point is echoed by Paul Zweig, *Walt Whitman*, 27.

19. James E. Miller, Jr., *Walt Whitman* (Boston: Twayne, 1990), 7.

20. Folsom, "What New Orleans Meant," 48.

21. Primarily, these are the manuscripts known by the editorial titles "1848 New Orleans," "is rougher than it was," and "wooding at night," *WWA*, med. 00725, duk. 00786, and duk. 00790.

22. Joseph Jay Rubin, *Historic Whitman* (University Park: Pennsylvania State University Press, 1973), 373n5.

23. Zweig, *Walt Whitman*, 76.

24. *LG* (1860–61), 373.

25. See Stefan Schöberlein and Zachary Turpin, "'Glorious Times for Newspaper Editors and Correspondents': Whitman at the New Orleans *Daily Crescent*, 1848–1849," *WWQR* 39 (Summer 2021): esp. 14–26.

CHAPTER 1

1. Whitman's meeting with McClure has been consistently misdated, based solely on his statement in *Specimen Days* that he had left "two days" after first encountering McClure. That departure date had, in the mid-twentieth century, incorrectly been posited as February 11. The dates were never confirmed by Whitman, but using Figure 3, we can reconstruct their departure based on contemporaneous sources (including Whitman's *Crescent* travelogue and Jeff's first letter home). That date must have been February 10, meaning "two days earlier" would have been February 8.

2. "Broadway Theatre," *New York Daily Herald,* February 8, 1848, 3. One of the performers, Mrs. Walleck, was among Whitman's favorites at the time (see "The Broadway Theatre, New York," *BDE,* November 26, 1847, 2; see also *JOURN* 2:336).

3. "The Weather," *Brooklyn Evening Star,* February 9, 1848, 2.

4. N. P. Willis, "Theatricals in New York," *Weekly National Intelligencer,* October 9, 1847, 7.

5. "John E. McClure," *DP,* May 16, 1859, 2.

6. In "Crossing the Alleghanies" (*DC,* March 5, 1848, 1), Whitman wrote that he and his brother had departed Baltimore on "Saturday" morning. According to Jeff, the two were on the Mississippi on a subsequent "Saturday" (expected to arrive in Cairo, Illinois, by night). Considering that the two deboarded in New Orleans on Friday, May 25, 1848 (all per Jeff's contemporaneous letters), and considering the timetables of the Good Intent company, advertised in New York papers and echoed by information in Walt's travelogue and Jeff's first extant letter, they could have left home no earlier than the morning of February 10.

7. See, for instance: "Latest from the Southeast," *BDE,* August 26, 1847, 2.

8. Jason Stacy, *Walt Whitman's Multitudes: Labor Reform and Persona in Whitman's Journalism and the First* Leaves of Grass, *1840–1855* (New York: Peter Lang, 2008), 75.

9. B. H. Gilley considered the *Delta* "the most militantly expansionist of the Louisiana journals" at the time; see his "'Polk's War' and the Louisiana Press," *Louisiana History* 20, no. 1 (1979): 14.

10. Tom Reilly, *War with Mexico!: America's Reporters Cover the Battlefront,* ed. Manley Witten (Lawrence: University Press of Kansas, 2010), 16.

11. "Mustang" was James Logan Freaner (1817–52), who was a personal friend of Nicholas Triste, the diplomat tasked with negotiating Mexican peace. See "Mustang," *DC,* March 5, 1848, 2. For more on Freaner's colorful career, see Alan D. Gaff and Donald H. Gaff, *From the Halls of the*

Montezumas: Mexican War Dispatches from James L. Freaner, Writing under the Pen Name "Mustang" (Denton: University of North Texas, 2019); William Anthony DePalo, *The Mexican National Army, 1822–1852* (College Station: Texas A&M University Press, 2008), 236.

12. The identity of "Alpha" remains unclear, but it was not Alexander Hamilton Hayes. "Alpha" mentions meeting Hayes in a letter to the *Delta* and later relocated to Jamaica.

13. Later, Hayes managed to get "Chaparral" (i.e., journalist John Peoples) to send letters exclusively to the *Crescent*; on Peoples and the *Crescent*, see "The American Star," *DC*, March 31, 1848, 2.

14. Reilly, *War with Mexico*, 16.

15. *PW* 2:605.

16. "Peace with Mexico," *BDE*, February 13, 1847, 2; *JOURN* 2:198.

17. "[A]n immense territory, in the northwestern and perhaps northern portions of Mexico will be 'annexed' to the United States as a result of this war. The people of the United States favor the plan, and we believe it would be right. Those regions [. . .] are comparatively unpeopled, and would be well occupied and developed by a hardy race of American republicans[, t]he Mexican population having been always sparse there"—as opposed to a "more thickly populated" Mexican south ("Peace with Mexico," *BDE*).

18. Tellingly, Whitman even spoke of the "United States of *North America*" (italics ours) when discussing the invasion of Mexico and suggested that the US might at a later date welcome a Mexico remodeled after the American republic. See "'Annexation of Mexico,'" *BDE*, November 22, 1847, 2; also *JOURN* 2:360. His time in New Orleans only hardened this belief. In late September of 1848, Whitman wrote to the *Crescent*, "That miserable Mexico must crumble [. . .] and gradually merge in the United States, there is no doubt. But all in good time" (*MHTN*, October 9, 2).

19. "Mr. Gallatin's Plan of Settling Our Dispute with Mexico," *BDE*, December 2, 1847, 2; *JOURN* 2:370.

20. "Mr. A. H. Hayes," *DP*, September 1, 1847, 2.

21. Reilly, *War with Mexico*, 150.

22. Reilly, *War with Mexico*, 150–51; *Southern Frontier Humor: An Anthology*, ed. M. Thomas Inge and Ed Piacentino (Columbia: University of Missouri Press, 2010), 268–69.

23. "Mr. A. H. Hayes," *DP*.

24. Reprinted in "Correspondence of the Picayune," *Wilmington Journal*, September 10, 1847, 2.

25. In one of its first issues, the *Crescent* would emphasize that it hoped to continue in this tradition: "Our other contemporaries [in New Orleans . . .]

may also rest assured that one of our highest gratifications, in conducting our paper, will be to preserve that spirit of courtesy and gentlemanly feeling which has hardly yet been broken at all, among the newspapers of the Crescent City. As one of our near neighbors and old friends justly says: 'There is room for us all,' without, in the least, stepping on each others' toes" ("The New Orleans Press," *DC,* March 9, 1848, 2).

26. Likely born "John Elliot Eaton McClure" to John and Catherine McClure ("Vermont Vital Records, 1760–1954," FamilySearch.com). Another co-owner, Dan Corcoran, was traveling in Europe and returned in early August 1847—he would leave the *Delta* around a year later, after political infighting.

27. "Mr. J. E. McClure," *DP,* January 1, 1845, 2.

28. "Death of an Old Friend," *DP,* November 22, 1866, 2.

29. See, for instance, "Literary Society," *DP,* December 11, 1848, 2.

30. "John E. McClure," *DP,* May 16, 1859, 2; "Young Men's Democratic State Convention," *Vermont State Paper,* January 4, 1839, 2. Locofocos were a pre-Barnburner reform wing in the Democratic party, urging a return to its Jacksonian roots. They were antimonopolist and endorsed laissez-faire doctrines. Whitman was one of them, and he maintained his sympathies for these causes into old age.

31. Fayette Copeland, "The New Orleans Press and the Reconstruction," *Louisiana Historical Quarterly* 30, vol. 1 (January 1947): 297.

32. Gilley, "Polk's War," 23.

33. A Slaveholder, "Mexican War. Domestic Grievances and Remedies," *DD,* December 16, 1847, 2.

34. See Reilly, *War with Mexico,* 55; William James Cooper, *The South and the Politics of Slavery, 1828–1856* (Baton Rouge: Louisiana State University Press, 1978), 378.

35. Reilly, *War with Mexico,* 17.

36. Reilly, *War with Mexico,* 18.

37. "Our New Press," *DD,* January 5, 1848, 2.

38. For instance, "Beta" notes, "You will have received information of the arrival of the Cambria, &c., but, as upon the subject of general news you will find the papers much more profitable than my observations"—suggesting the writer was well-acquainted with news sources and transmission speeds (Beta, "Correspondence of the Daily Delta," *DD,* August 29, 1847, 2). The whole first half of the piece contrasts Northern and Southern newspapers from a Southern perspective. The first "Beta" letter also complains about the missing telegraph line between New Orleans and New York ("Correspondence of the Daily Delta," *DD,* August 17, 1847, 2).

39. The *Crescent* openly bragged about its Hoe press when it began offering commercial printing in mid-1849 ("Crescent Job Office," *DC*, September 27, 1849, 1).

40. *PW* 1:288.

41. Typical Hoe steam presses were priced around $5,000, according to later catalogs, with the cheapest model being around $3,000. McClure lost his "promissory note" for payment when he left the *Crescent*. McClure ran an ad for the note: It was for $1,400 ("Lost," *DC*, April 27, 1849, 2).

42. "Consignees," *DP*, February 19, 1848, 3.

43. "City News," *DP*, February 24, 1848, 3.

44. "Beta" mentions the event in a way that suggests he is planning to attend (August 17, 1847), and the event itself was covered by the *Brooklyn Daily Eagle* during Whitman's editorial tenure ("The Compliment to Lieut. Marin," *BDE*, August 27, 1847, 2).

45. Thomas L. Brasher, "Whitman and the *Crescent*: A Conjecture," *Walt Whitman Newsletter* 3 (June 1957): 24–25.

46. "Mother, you remember Theodore Gould, how he has stuck it out, though sickness & death has had hold of him as you may say for fifteen years" (Whitman to Louisa Van Velsor Whitman September 8, 1863, available on WWA, loc. 00788). Multiple men shared Gould's name in the New York area at the time, but it appears the artist Gould stopped advertising his services in 1858. Gould, who also went by "Goold," has been identified conclusively by descendants as having married that year and subsequently moved with his pregnant wife to upstate New York, where he worked as a daguerreotypist. He died in Bath, Steuben County, in the early 1880s. We would like to thank Thomas A. Peters and Kathryn Davitt Peters, who shared their invaluable research on Gould with us.

47. "[untitled preface to poem]," *BDE*, March 24, 1849, 2.

48. "The Poet Gould," *BDE*, October 19, 1848, 3. Gould may have also published in the *Atlas* in 1848, a sister paper to the *Aurora* that Whitman edited prior to the *Eagle* ("[untitled news item]," *DC*, October 7, 1848, 2).

49. "The Fine Arts," *DC*, April 1, 1848, 2.

50. "Picture of Don Quixote," *DC*, August 14, 1848, 2.

51. "Picture of Don Quixote," *DC*.

52. "Selections from a Diary Written during a Sojourn in Louisiana," published in *BDE* in multiple installments in 1851 (February 15, 21, 27, and March 12).

53. E.g., "New Orleans," *New-York Times*, November 3, 1848, 4.

54. Referenced in "Lousiana Senator," *Buffalo Commercial*, February 7, 1848, 2.

55. For example, "Correspondence of the Atlas," *New York Atlas,* May 7, 1848, 1.

56. "Hall, Abraham Oakey (1826–1898)," *Vault at Pfaff's*, pfaffs.web.lehigh.edu/node/54228.

57. See, for instance, Maverick Marvin Harris, "Democratic Party," *ENCYC*, 175; William Pannapacker, *Revised Lives: Whitman, Religion, and Constructions of Identity in Nineteenth-Century Anglo-American Culture* (New York: Taylor & Francis, 2004), 26; or Matt Sandler, "Kindred Darkness: Whitman in New Orleans," in *Whitman Noir: Black America and the Good Gray Poet*, ed. Ivy G. Wilson (Iowa City: University of Iowa Press, 2014), 54.

58. For instance: "Whitman was fired from the Brooklyn *Daily Eagle* because of his free-soil politics" (Edward W. Huffstetler, "South, The American," *ENCYC*, 427).

59. Whitman, "Autobiographical Data," *WWA,* loc.05935.

60. "Impromptu Address," *BDE,* February 17, 1848, 3 (italics ours). The full text reads: "It is true, as you say / We sent *Whitman* away, / But that is a private affair; / But since you have spoken, / Know by this token, / You have not *wit, man* to spare."

61. "The Advertiser," *BDE,* July 19, 1849, 2. It is notable how closely Whitman is associated with Whig papers here—the same Whig network, it appears, that also had inside information on the planning of Johnson's new Barnburner paper in Brooklyn. The Free-Soil Party, of course, was a fusion of Whigs and Democrats.

62. "The Season in New Orleans," *BDE,* May 18, 1848, 2.

63. Brooklynite, "Effect of this War upon Mexico—Matter and Things in New Orleans," *BDE,* March 14, 1848, 2. The letter is dated March 2, 1848.

64. Dennis K. Renner, "Brooklyn Daily Eagle," *ENCYC*, 80.

65. See W., "The New Steamer Reindeer," *BDE,* August 29, 1850, 2, potentially authored by Whitman and recently rediscovered by Stephanie M. Blalock; W., "Old Times in Brooklyn," *BDE,* July 3, 1858, 2; or the unsigned "Visit to Baisley's Pond," *BDE,* June 30, 1858, 2, rediscovered and attributed by Amy Kapp. See Kapp's "A Long-Lost *Eagle* Article Puts Walt and Jeff on the Map," *WWQR* 40 (Winter/Spring 2023): 140–49. During the late 1850s, Whitman worked for the *Eagle*'s direct ideological and market competitor, the *Brooklyn Daily Times*. There are likely more Whitman pieces in the *Eagle* during these years that have yet to be discovered.

66. "Loss of the Wilmot Proviso," *BDE,* March 4, 1847, 2; also *JOURN* 2:209.

67. "Real Question at Issue!" *BDE,* October 28, 1847, 2 (italics in original); also *JOURN* 2:334.

68. "We do not recognize the distinctions of 'old hunker' or 'barnburner,'" Whitman wrote just days before the election. "We know only the name of *democratic republican* [. . . .] Let us fight with unanimity under *that* sacred name and banner—and do *our* duty to the full, whatever may be done in the rest of the state!" ("Rouse and Come Forth!" *BDE,* October 30, 1847, 2 [italics in original]; also *JOURN* 2:345).

69. "Proceedings of the democratic ratification meeting, last evening," *BDE,* June 2, 1847, 2.

70. See "Proceedings," BDE, June 2, 1847, 2, and "The Kings County Judge Case," *BDE,* June 25, 1847, 2. The *Eagle* even called for Johnson's election in its masthead; see "Democratic Republican Nominations," *BDE,* May 10, 1847, 2.

71. "Some Reflections on the Past, and for the Future," *BDE,* November 3, 1847, 2; also *JOURN* 2:347.

72. See Joseph G. Rayback, *Free Soil: The Election of 1848* (Lexington: University of Kentucky Press, 1970), esp. 76–77.

73. "Random Recollections," *New Orleans Bulletin,* May 20, 1875, 4.

74. Some of his comments to his northern friends indicate this encounter did not change Whitman's mind. Writing to the *Eagle* in early March, he still supports a lengthy occupation of Mexico to force concessions—jokingly commenting that "[n]ot all the 'senoritas,' surely, would be willing to have our good looking Yankee lads withdrawn"—and defends the invasion thusly: "The greatest error in the world is that which looks upon our descent upon Mexico, as if the case were similar to a foreign intrusion into this republic. Really Mexico is, politically, as badly mismanaged as poor old Ireland; and we are doing her the surest of benefits by stirring her up with a long pole in this way" (Brooklynite, "Effect of This War," *BDE,* March 14, 1848, 2).

75. "Old Hunkers vs. Barnburners," *Brooklyn Evening Star,* January 19, 1848, 2.

76. Anson Herrick ran the *Aurora* newspaper out of the same office from which Whitman served as its editor before the *Eagle*. The *Aurora*, and its sister publication the *Atlas*, remained on friendly terms with Whitman—even amidst similar gossip of a fallout between Whitman and Herrick. In the late 1850s, the *Atlas* would publish Whitman's "Manly Health and Training" series. As Whitman was working for the *Brooklyn Daily Times* at the time, he likely also contributed to the weekend paper in an editorial capacity (see Stefan Schöberlein, Stephanie M. Blalock, Kevin McMullen, and Jason Stacy, "Walt Whitman, Editor at the *New-York Atlas*," *WWQR* 39 [Spring 2022]: 189–204.). The letter in question is signed "Aristides," which was the pen name of an unidentified Free-Soil friend of Whitman's who was in the law

profession and who often updated local papers about Walt's professional and personal life (as late as Whitman's editorship of the *Brooklyn Daily Times* in the 1850s; see "Aristides," "The Right of Revolution," *Brooklyn Daily Times,* October 26, 1859, 3). Perhaps this fellow Brooklynite was Judge Samuel E. Johnson, financial backer of the *Freeman* and fellow Free-Soil Party activist, though concrete evidence is still wanting.

77. "Aristides," "Brooklyn Affairs," *New York Atlas,* January 23, 1848, 3. The authors would like to thank Stephanie M. Blalock for bringing this piece to our attention.

78. "A Barnburner Paper," *Long Island Farmer and Advertiser,* January 25, 1848, 2.

79. "Democracy in Kings County," *Evening Post,* January 21, 1848, 2. The piece responded to an article in the *Brooklyn Evening Star* ("Old Hunkers vs. Barnburners," January 19, 1848, 2), which named "Mr. Walter Whitman" as well as "another Brooklyn paper" to support its claim of a new paper being started. (Thanks to Jason Stacy for clarifying the origin of this clipping and identifying its sources.)

80. See also Loving, *Walt Whitman,* 143; 501n4. The *Tribune* article ("A Barnburner Paper," *New-York Daily Tribune,* January 21, 1848, 7) responded to the same *Brooklyn Evening Star* article as the New York *Evening Post,* though without quoting it. The *Brooklyn Evening Star* had a good relationship with Whitman, who republished his fiction in the pages of the Whig paper in the 1840s and who was rightly described as a source of information "from the best authority" by the *Tribune.* Notably, the same papers that spread the Barnburner paper rumors in early 1848 were those also listed by Whitman in the *Eagle* as having been "interested [. . .] in his behalf" before he, "through their good offices[,] got a handsome place in New Orleans" (The Advertiser," *BDE,* July 19, 1849, 2.

81. Johnson is often falsely named as "Samuel V. Johnson" in scholarship. He was adjudicated judge in October of 1848 after winning his election by only a handful of votes, leading to a public inquiring into his name to decide the count of unclear ballots, which led to a ruling in his favor based on the fact that he was the only Johnson in town in the legal profession ("Supreme Court," *Brooklyn Evening Star,* October 25, 1848, 2). Johnson's grave can still be visited at Greenwood Cemetery in Brooklyn.

82. "Corporation Notice. Sale of Property for Unpaid Taxes," *Brooklyn Evening Star,* January 6, 1848, 3–4. Johnson was leading a year-long legal battle over his election, which he finally won in 1848.

83. See "Supreme Court," *Brooklyn Evening Star*; also "Result in Kings County," *BDE,* June 10, 1847, 2.

84. Daniel M. Tredwell, *Personal Reminiscences of Men & Things on Long Island* (Brooklyn: C.A. Ditmas, 1912), 1:13. Future lawyer Tredwell, who appeared to blame his work at the paper for his dating woes, was not a great admirer of Whitman's, considering him "vulgar" and "coarse" as early as 1853. Notably, Tredwell's diary contains this backdated entry (likely written later and reconstructed there) for March 6, 1848: "This day ascertained that Walter Whitman formerly of the Brooklyn Eagle and Kings County, was making arrangements for establishing a new paper in Brooklyn to be called The Brooklyn Freeman. I am to have a place upon it." An entry for April 25, 1848, indicates that the "first number of the Freeman appeared to-day. Walter Whitman editor. Samuel E. Johnson, Proprietor" (Daniel M. Tredwell papers, New York Public Library, MssCol 3028, leaves 119–21). The dating is incorrect, though the notion of a one-and-a-half month run-up to print sounds feasible (that is, while the dates are false, the intervals between may well be correct).

85. In the printed version of Tredwell's diary this information is transposed onto an entry of March 12, 1848 (absent from the manuscript), in which the author intends to "[m]ake an appointment to take position on a new daily paper to be published in Brooklyn and be called 'The Brooklyn Freeman.' It is to be edited by Walt Whitman, a young man, formerly of the 'Eagle'" (Tredwell, *Personal Reminiscences,* 1:13). The subsequent entry in the print edition points to a lecture, dated by the documents to "March 16," by one Professor Mitchell on Lord Rosse's telescope. That event actually took place in early October 1848 ("Professor Mitchell's Second Lecture," *BDE,* October 13, 1848, 2), suggesting that Tredwell's notes—in print and in manuscript—are off by about seven months. If the order of the entries is correct (as appears likely), the original diary notes must have been of early October, as well, which fits the publication date of the *Freeman*: Its first issue was printed on September 9, 1848.

86. Loving, *Walt Whitman,* 115.

87. James F. Hamilton, *Democratic Communications: Formations, Projects, Possibilities* (Lanham, MD: Lexington Books, 2009), 128.

88. As Whitman wrote in "Passage to India" (1871): "The earth to be spann'd, connected by network / The races, neighbors, to marry and be given in marriage, / The Oceans to be cross'd." For more on Whitman's literary networks, see Edward Whitley's "Networked Literary History and the Bohemians of Antebellum New York," *American Literary History* 29, no. 2 (2017): 287–306.

89. John Nerone, *The Media and Public Life: A History* (Cambridge, UK: Polity Press, 2015), 56.

90. Ellen Gruber Garvey, *Writing with Scissors: American Scrapbooks from*

the Civil War to the Harlem Renaissance (New York: Oxford University Press, 2012), 31.

91. "Exchange Papers," *DC,* March 5, 1848, 2.

92. See Ed Folsom, "Co-Responding with Walt Whitman," in *The Edinburgh Companion to Nineteenth-Century American Letters and Letter-Writing,* ed. Celeste-Marie Bernier, Judie Newman, and Matthew Pethers (Edinburgh: Edinburgh University Press, 2016), 596–611. Folsom argues that "Whitman's very idea of the reader was at once of an intimate single person and a representative democratic self—a single historical person, and a representative public" (596).

93. "Serviceable Courtesy," *DC,* March 11, 1848, 2.

94. "Nothing but Dryness," *DC,* March 28, 1848, 2.

95. "[News column]," *Texian Advocate,* May 23, 1848, 2.

96. "To our Northern Contemporaries," *DC,* March 25, 1848, 2.

97. "Do you intend exchanging with us, gentlemen, or did you merely send that copy to get a puff?" ("First Rate Notice," *DC,* April 12, 1848, 2).

98. "First Rate Notice," *DC* (italics in original).

99. Leon Jackson, *The Business of Letters: Authorial Economies in Antebellum America* (Redwood City, CA: Stanford University Press, 2007), 122.

100. Jackson, *Business of Letters,* 122.

101. Jackson, *Business of Letters,* 125, 122.

102. Whitman, "[1848 New Orleans]," *WWA.*

103. For instance: Maverick Marvin Harris, "New Orleans *Crescent,*" *ENCYC,* 457.

104. In his biography, Jerome Loving, for instance, falsely suggests the term is Whitman's (*Walt Whitman,* 115). In other pieces he goes as far as claiming that "Whitman himself is on record as stating (*Uncollected Poetry and Prose,* 2:78), he served only as an exchange editor who clipped pieces from other newspapers [. . .] not as 'chief editor'" (review of Joel Myerson, *Walt Whitman: A Descriptive Bibliography, WWQR* 11 [Spring 1994]: 206–7). The words *only, chief editor,* or *exchange editor* (or *any* variation of the term *editor*) are, of course, *not* part of Whitman's account. Instead, Whitman describes activities usually reserved for editors without adding a label.

105. Reynolds, "Walt Whitman's Journalism," 50.

106. Meredith McGill, *American Literature and the Culture of Reprinting, 1834–1853* (Philadelphia: University of Pennsylvania Press, 2007).

107. For instance: "We notice that one class of papers head the French news with '*Horrible* Revolution' [. . .] while another gives it '*Glorious* Revolution'" ("[Untitled]," *DC,* April 1, 1848, 2).

108. For example, "Loss of Life and Property," *DC,* April 1, 1848, 2.

109. Indeed, even Whitman's never-printed attack on the memory of John Quincy Adams (the subject of our final chapter) was one such item, framed around "Northern contemporaries" in the press being "entirely beyond the record in their eulogies."

110. Cf. Stacy, *Walt Whitman's Multitudes*, 75.

111. "[We receive]," *Sunday Dispatch*, March 19, 1848, 2. The paper reiterated its assessment a month later, when it called "Walter Whitman, Esq., [. . . the] now editor of the New Orleans *Crescent*" (*Sunday Dispatch*, April 30, 1848, 2). The *Brooklyn Evening Star*, of course, put Whitman "in charge" of the paper ("[Mr. Walter Whitman]," *Brooklyn Evening Star*, March 15, 1848, 2), while the *Eagle* discovered "his handy work in several of its editorials" (*BDE*, March 14, 1848, 2).

112. Matt Cohen, *Whitman's Drift: Imagining Literary Distribution* (Iowa City: University of Iowa Press, 2017), 15.

113. *LG* (1860–61), 455.

114. Thomas Jefferson Whitman to his family, March 27, 1848, *WWA*, nyp.00132.

115. Thomas Jefferson Whitman to his family, March 14, 1848, *WWA*, nyp.00131.

116. *Brooklyn City Directory and Annual Advertiser for the Years 1848–9* (Brooklyn: E. B. Spooner, 1848), 225, 245.

117. See P.W.W., "Northern Correspondence," *DC*, April 25, 1848, 2. Wilson was by no means a marginal figure in the *Eagle* office. He was active in a number of social groups alongside (fellow) *Eagle* staff members, as evidenced by a "Meeting of the friends of Mrs. H. V. Lovell" that included *Eagle* printer Tombs (also mentioned in one of Jeff's letters) and *Eagle* owner Isaac Van Anden (*BDE*, December 20, 1850, 2). The *Crescent* also featured a regular "New York Correspondent" at this time, going by "Sunshine," who was very likely also connected to the paper via Whitman.

CHAPTER 2

1. "By the Public Line," *Public Ledger*, February 10, 1848, 3.

2. Walter Whitman, "My Boys and Girls," *Rover* 3, no. 5 (1844): 75; also *WWA*. Thomas Jefferson "Jeff" Whitman (1833–90) would follow in Walt's footsteps until the 1850s, when he switched from a career in printing to public works, becoming a successful waterworks engineer. See also Stephanie M. Blalock, Kevin McMullen, Stefan Schöberlein, and Jason Stacy, "'One of the Grand Works of the World': Walt Whitman's Advocacy for the Brooklyn Waterworks, 1856–59," *Technology and Culture* 65, no. 1 (2024): 237–63.

3. "Through in Forty-Eight Hours," *Evening Post,* December 29, 1847, 4. Since the line only sold tickets at Philadelphia, not in New York City (see Figure 3), the "forty-eight hour" promise only applied to the final stretch of the line; the trip took about three days in total.

4. "How the Northern Cities Compare with New Orleans," *DC,* April 17, 1848, 1. His concern with lewd men accosting women on the street was expressed in very similar verbiage in a letter, clearly identifiable as by Whitman, sent to the *Sunday Times* (Nassau Street, "Matters and Things in New Orleans," *Sunday Times*, April 2, 1848, 2); see page 50.

5. See officialdata.org. Tickets from Philadelphia to Wheeling were thirteen dollars a head, train tickets from New York to Philadelphia (via Newark) likely ran three dollars per person. Specific prices for steamboat travel are unknown.

6. McClure's portion of the paper was sold for $1,040 at the close of 1848; see page 91.

7. "Poet and Printer," *DP,* June 8, 1882, 6. The piece reprinted there, from a late-life column in the *Camden Courier*, appears to mine a now-lost manuscript draft/note that would also lead to a similar, though shorter, account published in *Specimen Days*, published in December of the same year.

8. "Excerpts from a Traveller's Note Book: Crossing the Alleghenies," *DC,* March 5, 1848, 1.

9. Nearly half of all Black persons in Cumberland at that time were enslaved. Census numbers for Cumberland in 1850 list 267 free and 220 enslaved Black persons (Seventh Census of the United States: 1850–Maryland, 221, via census.gov).

10. All of this paragraph's quotations are from "Crossing the Alleghanies," *DC,* March 5, 1848, 1.

11. Henry B. Rule, "Walt Whitman and George Caleb Bingham," *Walt Whitman Review* 16 (1969): 248–53. Bingham's painting is discussed in more detail in chapter 4; see pages 83–84.

12. "Western Steamboats—The Ohio," *DC,* March 10, 1848, 2.

13. "An Octogenarian Dead," *Wheeling Daily Intelligencer*, April 11, 1883, 4.

14. "Western Steamboats," *DC.*

15. "U.S. Mail Steamer St. Cloud," *DP,* January 6, 1848, 3.

16. "Gen. Taylor in New Orleans," *Louisville Daily Courier,* November 25, 1848, 1.

17. Thomas Jefferson Whitman to his family, February 18?–28, 1848, *WWA*, nyp.00130.

18. Nassau Street, "Matters and Things."

19. "Cincinnati and Louisville," *DC,* March 6, 1848, 3.

20. "Western Steamboats," *DC.*

21. "Another Delta City," *DC,* May 8, 1848, 2.

22. "Cairo," *DC,* May 20, 1848, 1.

23. Rubin, *Historic Whitman,* 373n5.

24. "[We see]," *BDE,* September 24, 1849, 3. Thanks are due to Stephanie M. Blalock, who brought this piece to our attention. Whitman likely used weekend papers regularly to support his meager income from working editorial posts at various dailies (which did not publish on weekends); see for instance, Stefan Schöberlein, Stephanie M. Blalock, Kevin McMullen, and Jason Stacy, "Walt Whitman, Editor at the *New-York Atlas,*" *WWQR* 39 (Spring 2022): 189–204.

25. "The Combat of Death: Or, the Cholera Against the Yellow Fever," *Sunday Times and Messenger,* June 17, 1849, 2.

26. Timothy C. Winegard, *The Mosquito: A Human History of Our Deadliest Predator* (New York: Penguin, 2020), 38; see also Kathryn Olivarius, *Necropolis: Disease, Power, and Capitalism in the Cotton Kingdom* (Cambridge, MA: Harvard University Press, 2022).

27. For example on August 11, 1847, 2: "The deaths during the last week in July, were 63, of which 38 were from yellow fever. The prevailing sickness in that city at the present time seems to be the yellow fever. We learn from the Delta, that there are many cases under private treatment, and if anything the disease is somewhat on the increase."

28. W., "Correspondence of the Sunday Times," *Sunday Times and Messenger,* May 21, 1848, 2.

29. W., "Correspondence."

30. "New Theory of Yellow Fever," *DC,* March 25, 1848, 1.

31. "Habitants of Hotels," *DC,* March 10, 1848, 2.

32. See his recommendations in "Manly Health and Training" (1858) or in pieces like "Yellow Fever," *Brooklyn Daily Times,* April 27, 1858, 2; also *WWA.*

33. "Doctor Sangrado Snipes," *DC,* June 29, 1848, 2.

34. First version of the draft, revisions and subsequent lines removed; see "Sailing Down the Mississippi at Midnight," *WWA,* nyp.00736.

35. Notably, Whitman's previous fiction printed in the *Eagle,* "The Half-Breed" (1846), was also signed "Brooklynite."

36. *MHTN,* July 27, 2.

37. Thomas Jefferson Whitman, letter, March 14, 1848, *WWA,* nyp.00130.

38. "Western Steamboats," *DC.*

39. Thomas Jefferson Whitman, letter, March 14, 1848. Jeff's account is a bit puzzling. The *Crescent* office, as per its masthead, was 95 St. Charles, which lay on the western side of St. Charles, facing Poydras. The St. Charles Hotel was on the same side of St. Charles, just a little north. Tremont House

was located on 102 St. Charles (*New Orleans Annual and Commercial Register of 1846* [New Orleans: Michel & Co, 1845], 323), which was most likely located in a large block across the street from both, framed by Gravier and Poydras streets, at the site where Natchez intersects St. Charles today. Perhaps the impression of being "adjoining" *and* "directly opposite" two structures on the same side of the street was due to the bend in St. Charles Street there, as well as perhaps a laxer use of the term *adjoining*.

40. "Death of Mr. Patrick Irwin," *Morning Star and Catholic Messenger*, April 28, 1878, 4.

41. "Fifth Ward, Second Municipality," *DC*, September 22, 1848, 2.

42. At least, this much may be deduced by the fact that Irwin was one of less than a dozen guests attending the funeral of editor Hayes in 1866 ("Funeral of A. H. Hayes," *DP*, November 24, 1866, 4).

43. "Restaurants," *DD*, August 7, 1846, 1 (italics in original). Irwin ran this ad to announce significant renovations and a new business model for the Tremont.

44. "Tremont House Restaurant," *DP*, November 2, 1843, 1.

45. "Ephraim Broadhorn," *DC*, August 10, 1848, 1.

46. Nassau Street, "Matters and Things." The letter is dated March 12. First identified by John Jay Rubin, the letter is undoubtedly by Whitman, even mentioning, by name, the steamer *St. Cloud*.

47. "Razors, Reason, and Resolution," *DC*, March 31, 1848, 2; see also "Odeon Temple," *DC*, July 16, 1851, 3, which lists "95 St. Charles Street" as "Temperance Hall." For more on Henry Smith and his temperance activism, see his *The Life and Adventures of Henry Smith, the Celebrated Razor Strop Man* (Boston: White & Potter, 1848).

48. Thomas Jefferson Whitman, letter, February 18?–28, 1848, *WWA*, nyp.00130.

49. "'The Season' hereabouts," *DC*, March 7, 1848, 2. The striking contrast of fresh oranges in winter carried through to Whitman's late life, illustrated, for instance, in his 1888 poem "Orange Buds by Mail from Florida."

50. Nassau Street, "Matters and Things."

51. Thomas Jefferson Whitman, letter, March 14, 1848 (underscored in original).

52. Whitman recalled in 1887: "Sundays I sometimes went forenoons to the old Catholic Cathedral in the French quarter" (Whitman, "New Orleans in 1848," *DP*). The result of this interest may be found in "Combat of Death." In its twist ending, it reveals the old Ohioan to be the Bishop of New Orleans, who marries the protagonist to the young maiden who saved him from disease at his house of worship—which would have been St. Louis.

53. Thomas Jefferson Whitman, letter, March 14, 1848.

54. Denise B. Bethel, "Notes on an Early Daguerreotype of Walt Whitman," *WWQR* 9 (Winter 1992): 148–53.

55. *New Orleans Annual and Commercial Register for 1846* (New Orleans: Michel & Co, 1845).

56. "Daguerreotype Portraits," *DC,* March 6, 1848, 2.

57. "Cantatrice. A Scene During the Flood at New Orleans," *Sunday Times and Messenger,* July 15, 1849, 2.

58. Jeroen Dewulf, "The Missing Link between Congo Square and the Mardi Gras Indians? The Anonymous Story of 'The Singing Girl of New Orleans' (1849)," *Louisiana History* 60, no. 1 (Winter 2019): 83–95.

59. "Novelties in New Orleans," *DC,* March 13, 1848, 3.

60. "Correspondence of the Atlas," *New York Atlas,* May 7, 1848, 1.

CHAPTER 3

1. Stanford E. Chaillé, *The Vital Statistics of New Orleans* (New Orleans: Jas. A. Gresham, 1874), 22. Moore Norman claimed over 130,000 in 1845. See *Norman's New Orleans*, 76.

2. Norman, *Norman's New Orleans,* 73.

3. Norman, *Norman's New Orleans,* 73–76.

4. "Population of the United States Decennially from 1790 to 1850," in *The Seventh Census of the United States, 1850* (Washington, DC: Robert Armstrong, 1853), ix; United States Census Bureau online, census.gov/library/publications/1853/dec/1850a.html.

5. This figure comes from Walter F. Willcox's report "The Negro Population" for the 1900 US Census, page 16, via the United States Census Bureau, www2.census.gov/prod2/decennial/documents/03322287no8ch1.pdf.

6. There is an earlier piece on slavery in the *New-York Mirror*, variously attributed to Whitman or not, titled "The Olden Time" and signed "W." (November 29, 1834, 173). A piece of fanciful antiquarianism, it discusses the centenarian "Negro Harry" and his memories of early New York. New scholarship by Nick Hentoff and Ed Folsom has cast doubt on its being authored by Whitman, however, finding good evidence that its likelier author was engraver, writer, and politician Thomas Richard Whitney. For their full discussion, see Hentoff and Folsom's "Who Is 'W.'?: Questions about Whitman's First Known Piece of Published Journalism," *WWQR* 37 (Summer/Fall 2019): 116–21.

7. "Black and White Slaves," *New York Aurora,* April 2, 1842, 2, and *WWA,* per. 00422.

8. "Franklin Evans; Or, the Inebriate: A Tale of the Times," *New World*, November 23, 1842, 22.

9. "Franklin Evans," 22–23.

10. Stephanie Blalock and Nicole Gray, "Introduction to *Franklin Evans* and 'Fortunes of a Country-Boy,'" *WWA,* anc. 02072.

11. For the former, see Amina Gautier's "The 'Creole' Episode: Slavery and Temperance in *Franklin Evans,*" in Wilson, *Whitman Noir,* 32–53. For the latter, examples include Gretchen Murphy's "Enslaved Bodies: Figurative Slavery in the Temperance Fiction of Harriet Beecher Stowe and Walt Whitman," *Genre* 28 (1995): 96–97; and Katherine Henry's "Slavery and Civic Recovery: Gothic Interventions in Whitman and Weld," in *The Gothic Other: Racial and Social Constructions in the Literary Imagination,* ed. Ruth Bienstock Anolik and Douglas L. Howard (Jefferson, NC: McFarland, 2004), 32–53.

12. "Slavers—and the Slave Trade," *BDE,* March 18, 1846, 2; also *JOURN* 1:288–89.

13. As he later would in the 1850s; see, for example, his description of a captured slave ship, the *Braman,* in his article on the "The Slave Trade" for New York's *Life Illustrated* magazine, for August 2, 1856.

14. In 1847, Whitman had even served as a secretary for the "Prison Ship Martyr's Monument" organization (see "Prison Ship Martyr's Monument," *BDE,* November 29, 1847, 2).

15. The *BDE* editorials in question are, respectively, "Slavery," August 31, 1846, 2; "Letter from Gen. Cass," January 3, 1848, 2; also *JOURN* 2:39–40, 389.

16. Wilmot Proviso, August 8, 1946, Bills and Resolutions Originating in the House; RG 233: US House of Representatives. National Archives Identifier 2127333.

17. "American Workingmen, Versus Slavery," *BDE,* September 1, 1847, 2; also *JOURN* 2:318–20.

18. Sean Wilentz, *The Rise of American Democracy* (New York: W.W. Norton, 2005), 605.

19. "American Workingmen," *BDE* (emphasis in original).

20. "American Workingmen," *BDE* (emphasis in original).

21. "American Workingmen," *BDE.*

22. See, for example, "The Opinions of Washington and Jefferson on an Important Point," *BDE,* March 11, 1847, 1; also *JOURN* 2:222–23.

23. *PW* 2:605.

24. *PW* 2:606.

25. Nassau Street, "Matters and Things."

26. *PW* 2:606.

27. *PW* 2:606.

28. *PW* 2:605.

29. Of course, more notes may have existed but are now lost.

30. "A Walk About Town: By A Pedestrian," *DC,* April 26, 1848, 2.

31. "[S]aw about a dozen stalwart sailors [. . .] Saw a negro [. . .] Saw a poor long-shoreman [. . .] Saw a shipping master [. . .] Saw him go on board a vessel [. . .] saw a man, a good old man [. . .] saw rounds of beef [. . .] saw that every luxury given to sinful man by sea and land."

32. For a particularly perceptive reading of "A Walk About Town" and of Whitman's relationship to "the Hispanized realm of midcentury New Orleans," see Kirsten Silva Gruesz's *Ambassadors of Culture: The Transamerican Origins of Latino Writing* (Princeton: Princeton University Press, 2001), specifically a subsection of chapter 4 titled "The Fertile Crescent: Whitman's Immersion in the 'Spanish Element,'" 121–36.

33. Deshae E. Lott, "Biography of William Douglas O'Connor," *ENCYC,* 447.

34. Martin Van Buren, *Inquiry into the Origin and Course of Political Parties in the United States* (New York: Hurd and Houghton, 1867), 856.

35. Thomas Jefferson Whitman, letter, March 14, 1848.

36. Phil Johnson, "Good Time Town," in *The Past as Prelude: New Orleans 1718–1968,* ed. Hodding Carter (New Orleans, LA: Pelican Publishing, 1968), 236. For a great deal more information on this topic, see also Richard Tansey's "Prostitution and Politics in Antebellum New Orleans," in *History of Women in the United States,* vol. 9, ed. Nancy F. Cott (New York: De Gruyter, 1993), 45–75.

37. "Miss Dusky Grisette," *DC,* March 16, 1848, 1.

38. "Miss Dusky Grisette," *DC.*

39. *PW* 2:606.

40. "Miss Dusky Gisette," *DC.*

41. Compare this also to the character in Whitman's *Jack Engle* of Violet Foster, a prototypical working-class mother who remains "unspoiled" by the idea of women's rights.

42. See Judith Kelleher Schafer's *Brothels, Depravity, and Abandoned Women: Illegal Sex in Antebellum New Orleans* (New Orleans: Louisiana State University Press, 2009), 4–5. Whitman himself may hint at the subject of interracial relationships in New Orleans in his "Ephraim Broadhorn" sketch for his series of "Sketches of the Sidewalks and Levee" for the *Daily Crescent*: "'Kiss who, did you say?' said Ephraim. 'Why, I'll be darned if I've seed any body in Orleans that a feller would want to kiss—such a variety of white humans, and black humans, and yaller humans!'"

43. "Ephraim Broadhorn," *DC.*

44. *WWWC* 2:283 (italics in original).

45. Whitman's late-life thinking on Creoles tends to recoil from their supposed "magnetism," sensuality, or ignorance, possibly as a way of taking

any question of his own sexuality and marginalizing it within an Other. As a result of such squeamishness, an ageing Whitman largely rejected the idea of racial amalgamation between whites and non-whites. For an illustrative, and shocking, example, see his discussion with Horace Traubel of September 8, 1888: "Did he believe in amalgamation? 'I know many who already have it done—critics, reviewers, historians—done, proved: proved as they prove most things, which is not to prove them at all. I don't believe in it—it is not possible. The nigger, like the Injun, will be eliminated: it is the law of races, history, what-not: always so far inexorable—always to be. Someone proves that a superior grade of rats comes and then all the minor rats are cleared out.' I said: 'That sounds like Darwin.' 'Does it? It sounds like me, too.' W. then proceeded: 'I have been in New Orleans—known, seen, all its peculiar phases of life. Of course my report would be forty years old or so. The octoroon was not a whore, a prostitute, as we call a certain class of women here—and yet *was*, too: a hard class to comprehend. . . .'" For the full conversation, see *WWWC* 2:283.

In this context, perhaps important to acknowledge is that Whitman's ruminations to Traubel about these magnetic, sexual, ignorant Creoles leads him to reject racial mixing for white Americans, who, in his mind, seem immune from it in a way the French and Spanish are not.

46. In his pseudonymous treatise of 1858, "Manly Health and Training," Whitman would later warn young urban (white) men against frequenting prostitutes, even as he defended the "prostitute" with "pimpled neck" in "Song of Myself."

47. "The Old Cathedral," *DC*, April 22, 1848, 3.

48. Matt Sandler, "Kindred Darkness: Whitman in New Orleans," in Wilson, ed., *Whitman Noir*, 63.

49. "Talbot Wilson" notebook, *WWA*, loc. 00141.

50. Folsom, "What New Orleans Meant," 51.

51. Folsom, "What New Orleans Meant," 51.

52. *WWWC* 1:458.

53. These quotes come from "Unruly Negroes" and "Bad Negroes," editorials that appeared in the *DC* on April 28 and May 16, 1848, respectively, both on page 3. Scholars of Whitman's periodical writings do not consider them to be his work.

54. Thomas Jefferson Whitman, letter, March 14, 1848. The complaint is of central importance to many biographical accounts of the Whitmans' time in town, though it is rarely quoted in full. See, for instance, Holloway, *Whitman*, 55; Rubin, *Historic Whitman*, 193; Loving, *Walt Whitman*, 119, 133. The latter uses the example to illustrate *both* Whitmans' objection to the hypocrisy of Southern life.

55. Cited in James B. Bennett, *Religion and the Rise of Jim Crow in New Orleans* (Princeton, NJ: Princeton University Press, 2005), 143.

56. Bennett, *Religion and the Rise of Jim Crow*, 143. Bennett is quoting a visitor here.

57. Amy R. Sumpter, "Segregation of the Free People of Color and the Construction of Race in Antebellum New Orleans," *Southeastern Geographer* 48, no. 1 (2008): 19.

58. Sumpter, "Segregation of the Free People of Color," 19.

59. The quote from *The Eighteenth Presidency!* may be found in Walt Whitman's *Poetry and Prose*, ed. Justin Kaplan (New York: Library of America, 1982), 1346.

60. *MHTN,* August 28, 2.

61. *LG* (1855), 58.

62. "Slave-Labour Grown Sugar—Free-Labour Grown Sugar—Emancipation in the British West Indian Colonies," *National Anti-Slavery Standard,* March 16, 1848, 1. The article is a reprint from the New York *Daily Globe.*

CHAPTER 4

1. "The Sabbath," *DC,* March 6, 1848, 2.

2. "Celebration of St. Patrick's Day," *DC,* March 18, 1848, 2.

3. As Jeff wrote in his letter of March 14, "I suppose I shall see all the fun I am going to night to see Mr Collins" (Thomas Jefferson Whitman, letter, March 14, 1848).

4. "Right opposite here," Jeff wrote in the same letter, "they are fixing it up for a balloon ascension on next Sunday" (Thomas Jefferson Whitman, letter, March 14, 1848).

5. "The Balloon Blow Up," *DC,* April 10, 1848, 2.

6. "'Mardi Gras' in New Orleans," *Alexandria Gazette,* March 23, 1848, 2.

7. "Mardi Gras," *DC,* March 8, 1848, 2.

8. For second-story location, see "To Rent," *DP,* February 19, 1850, 1, which also lists the owner of the house, an Odd Fellow. The property was put up for sale in 1888, its description ("across from the Phoenix Hotel") suggesting it may still have been the same antebellum office building; see "Positive Sale, Withoimit," *DP,* January 8, 1888, 3.

9. The following two paragraphs borrow from Schöberlein's previously published introduction to *Walt Whitman's New Orleans: Sidewalk Sketches and Newspaper Rambles* (Baton Rouge, LA: LSU Press, 2022).

10. "George W. Reeder," *DC,* December 27, 1848, 2; "Internments," *DC,* December 27, 1848, 3.

11. "The Irish League," *DC,* September 4, 1848, 2.

12. "Gen. Taylor's Nomination and Election," *DD,* November 20, 1848, 4. In this capacity, Reeder was considered to have been the first person to suggest the presidency to Taylor ("The Question Settled," *Buffalo Courier,* December 1, 1848, 2). For a sample of one such sketch, see his poem, spoken by a newspaper carrier, under A Carrier [G. W. Reeder]: "Carrier's Address," *DP,* January 2, 1848, 4.

13. "Seeing the Responsible Editor," *State Times,* August 28, 1874, 7; Whitman, "[1848 New Orleans]," *WWA.*

14. Larue's father was a close friend of the father of James Fenimore Cooper and lived in the same place; Larue's middle name was, then, likely an homage to the novelist or his father. Larue spent his adolescence in St. Louis and moved down to New Orleans in 1836, where he associated himself with the *Picayune* before ultimately joining the *Crescent*; see "Our Old and Mediæval Bar," *DP,* June 5, 1887, 9.

15. "First District Court," *DC,* June 21, 1848, 3.

16. Larue served on the finance committee ("Louisiana Legislature," *DC,* March 9, 1848, 1).

17. "Mortuary," *Galveston Daily News,* August 8, 1894, 2. Consequently, Larue was "incessantly disputing about politics" with William Walker, when the filibustering firebrand joined the *Crescent* following Whitman's departure. See "Random Recollections," *New Orleans Bulletin,* May 20, 1870, 4.

18. "The Great Meeting at the St. Louis," *Weekly Delta,* April 17, 1848, 6.

19. Whitman, "[1848 New Orleans]," *WWA.*

20. See "Da Ponte," *Lamb's Biographical Dictionary of the United States,* vol. 2 (Boston: James H. Lamb Company, 1900), 342. Lamb's piece provides an incorrect birth year, which appears to have been 1829, not 1825 (see "The Death of Da Ponte, The Grandson of Mozart's Librettists," *American Art Journal,* August 18, 1894, 330).

21. Cornelia E. Durant Da Ponte (1804–65).

22. See "Jack Waterways," *DP,* October 7, 1842, 2.

23. Paul Foos, *A Short, Offhand, Killing Affair: Soldiers and Social Conflict During the Mexican-American War* (Chapel Hill: University of North Carolina Press, 2003), 52.

24. Stretching from his first weeks in New Orleans to the late summer in New York, "Sketches of the Sidewalks and Levee," with its seventeen thousand words total, stands as one of Whitman's more sustained newspaper endeavors, rivalling his "Letters from a Travelling Bachelor" (nineteen thousand words) and surpassing his "Sun-Down Papers" series (ten thousand words).

25. "Western Steamboats," *DC.*

26. The following pages are based on Schöberlein and Turpin, "'Glorious Times.'"

27. *LG* (1855), 23.

28. Henry B. Rule makes a convincing case for Whitman's call for an "American artist" in the *Crescent* as inspired by Bingham ("Walt Whitman and George Caleb Bingham," *Walt Whitman Review* 15 [1969]: 248–53).

29. Brian Luskey, *On the Make: Clerks and the Quest for Capital in Nineteenth-Century America* (New York: New York University Press, 2010), 6.

30. Jason Stacy, "Clerk Trouble: Masculinity, Consumerism, and Whitman's Print Culture," in *Critical Insights: Walt Whitman*, ed. Robert Evans (Hackensack, NJ: Salem Press, 2019), 4–5.

31. Luskey, *On the Make*, 3, 17. See also Ruth L. Bohan, "Vanity Fair, Whitman, and the Counter Jumper," *Word & Image* 33, no. 1 (2017): 57–69.

32. "John J. Jinglebrain," *DC,* March 28, 1848, 1.

33. Luskey, *On the Make*, 12, 98, 187.

34. "John J. Jinglebrain," *DC* (italics in original).

35. Luskey, *On the Make*, 112.

36. "Boston Mercantile Library Association," *DC,* March 6, 1848, 1.

37. Luskey, *On the Make*, 112.

38. See Zachary Turpin, "Introduction to Walt Whitman's 'Manly Health and Training,'" *WWQR* 33 (Spring 2016): 147–83.

39. "Samuel Sensitive," *DC,* July 15, 1848, 1.

40. *Henry the Fourth, Pt. 2*, II.ii.22.

41. "Samuel Sensitive."

42. Final two quotes are from the second installment of "Samuel Sensitive," in *DC,* May 2, 1848, 1.

43. Stacy, "Clerk Trouble," 13.

44. As Jason Stacy eloquently summarizes, in light of the clerking debate, "*Leaves of Grass* [. . .] becomes one more means by which Whitman, like his readers, used print to make themselves into the men they wanted to be" ("Clerk Trouble," 15).

45. *Norman's New Orleans and Environs* (Baton Rouge: LSU Press, 1973 [1845]), 76.

46. As he wrote in his piece from March 10 on hotel dwellers, which serves as a set-up for "Sketches": "When we have a pen, virgin so far as ink is concerned—any quantity of satin paper with gilded edges, and a few gallons of cologne, we shall endeavor to describe the peculiarities of those chosen mortals who will live above board—or, at least above the bar-room" (W., "The Habitants of Hotels," *DC,* March 10, 1848, 2).

47. Late in life, Whitman told one of his disciples, John Addington

Symonds, that he had "had six children—two are dead—One living southern grandchild, fine boy, who writes to me occasionally." Whitman rather rashly wrote Symonds as much after nearly a decade of pestering on the latter's part regarding the homosexual nature of "Calamus." The poet immediately added, "I am fain to hope the pages themselves are not to be even mention'd for such gratuitous and quite at the same time entirely undream'd & unreck'd possibility of morbid inferences—[which] are disavow'd by me & seem damnable" (John Addington Symonds to Walt Whitman, September 5, 1890; *WWA,* loc. 05155). Stories of mysterious children in the South may have started early in Walt's life: "The Combat of Death," the 1849 story possibly authored by him, centers on a Northern bachelor miraculously rediscovering a long-lost, mixed-race daughter (a Spanish dancing girl).

48. "Selections from my Journal, Written During a Sojourn in Louisiana," *BDE,* February 21, 1851, 1.

49. As Jonathan Ned Katz reminds us, "We may refer to early-nineteenth century men's acts or desires as gay or straight, homosexual, heterosexual, or bisexual, but that places their behaviors and lusts within our system, not the system of their time." Instead, we should wish to "locate [such intimacies] within the erotic and emotional institutions of their own time" and recognize in the "evidence of extremely intense, complex desires" between men elements of "what we today recognize as erotic feelings and acts" (*Love Stories: Sex Between Men before Homosexuality* [Chicago: University of Chicago Press, 2001], 9, 6).

50. "Death of an Old Friend," *DP,* November 22, 1866, 2.

51. This is also confirmed by Whitman's various accounts pointing to McClure as the person handling payment both before and at the close of his tenure at the *Crescent.*

52. "[Untitled]," *DP*, March 1, 1860, 3.

53. Auguste (Augustus) Titus (1828–73), going by "Indicator."

54. "A New Year Epistle to M. of N.Y," *DC,* January 1, 1848, 1.

55. "The Crescent," *DC,* March 7, 1849, 2.

56. "Lost Item," *DC,* April 26, 1849, 2.

57. "The 'New Eureka,'" *DP,* June 26, 1850, 2.

58. See, for instance, Brady Harrison's *Agent of Empire: William Walker and the Imperial Self in American Literature* (Athens: University of Georgia Press, 2004), 155, or his "Mercenary Romances: Masculinity, William Walker, and U.S. Imperialism," *Journal of Men's Studies* 4 (1996): 325.

59. "Died," *DP,* February 20, 1857, 4.

60. See, for example, "New Orleans Daily Crescent," *WWA,* per.00163, or Loving, *Walt Whitman,* 115.

61. "[Untitled]," *DP,* March 1, 1860, 8.

62. "Death of an Old Friend," *DP,* November 22, 1866, 2.

63. "Sudden Death," *DP,* November 22, 1866, 8.

64. "Funeral of A. H. Hayes," *DP,* November 24, 1866, 4.

65. "Funeral of A. H. Hayes," *DP*. It should be noted that Whitman's old landlord, Irwin, was also present.

66. Katz, *Love Stories*, 9.

67. For an overview, with a particular focus on Collyer's trouble with the law, see Jack W. McCullough, *Living Pictures on the New York Stage* (Ann Arbor, MI: UMI Research Press, 1983), 19–36.

68. Ettore Rella, *A History of Burlesque* (San Francisco: Works Program Administration/City of San Francisco, 1940), 10–12.

69. Rachel Shteir, *Striptease: The Untold History of the Girlie Show* (New York: Oxford University Press, 2004), 15–17.

70. In David Monod, *The Soul of Pleasure: Sentiment and Sensation in Nineteenth-Century American Mass Entertainment* (Ithaca, NY: Cornell University Press, 2016), 99.

71. Monod, *Soul of Pleasure*, 98.

72. "A Question of Propriety," *DC,* March 14, 1848, 2.

73. Some of the more titillating tableau titles mentioned were "Lady and the Devil" (*DC,* May 3, 1848, 2), "Adam's first sight of Eve" (*Weekly Crescent,* May 10, 1848, 2), and "sublime scenes of Paradise" (in Monod, *Soul of Pleasure*, 98).

74. "Model Artists," *DC,* July 29, 1848, 2. The "Sable Melodists" were minstrel performers.

75. Rella, *A History*, 12. A different, perhaps less plausible, take is Shteir's: "'Dr.' Collyer's living pictures became popular in part because in sending up high art, they mocked the British, who were by this point much hated" (15).

76. Monod, *Soul of Pleasure*, 99.

77. As Whitman's former Brooklyn paper bemoaned, "We understand that a troupe of so-called 'model artists' intend giving a few exhibitions in this city. We trust the authorities will, if they have the power, prevent any such disgraceful show within the limits of Brooklyn. Dr. Collyer, who first introduced this class of entertainment in New York, was comparatively chaste in his exhibitions, but the success which followed his experiment has brought out others much less scrupulous. 'Model artists' are now to be seen in almost every filthy groggery in our sister city. The best of them but slightly clad and the lowest of them scarcely wearing any covering at all" ("Model Artists," *BDE,* February 4, 1848, 2). Clearly, Whitman, who was on his way out at the *Eagle*, did not write this comment. The situation in New York continued to escalate, leading to a number of well-publicized brawls and a mass arrest of "model artists"

(not associated with Collyer). For more on the latter, see "The Model Artists," *DP,* March 31, 1848, 2.

78. "[News items]," *New Orleans Weekly Delta,* March 6, 1848, 8.

79. "The Manager of the Models," *DC,* April 7, 1848, 3.

80. Monod, *Soul of Pleasure*, 101.

81. Covered by Whitman as "General Taylor at the Theatre" (*DC,* May 9, 1848, 2).

82. "The Model Artists," *Buffalo Morning Express,* August 16, 1848, 2.

83. "Philadelphia Correspondence of the Delta," *DD,* July 3, 1848, 1.

84. "Dr. Collyer in Boston," *DD*, September 18, 1848, 6. Collyer was famously prone to filing libel suits, which in turn invited mockery by the press: "The 'Model Artists,' having sued a Western editor, for libel, that gentleman expresses a hope that they will gain their *suit*, as they certainly need one among them" (*DC*, July 21, 1848, 2).

85. "Henry Clay," *Pittsburgh Post,* February 26, 1848, 2.

86. "Amusements," *DC,* March 30, 1848, 3.

87. During Whitman's editorship, the *Eagle* was silent on the troupe; after his departure, the paper became one of Collyer's leading critics in Brooklyn. A more drastic trend may be observed in the *Sunday Times*, in which Whitman may also have been involved: Prior to his departure the *Times* supported Collyer; afterward, it filled its pages with pearl-clutching outrage.

88. "Model Artists," *DC,* March 6, 1848, 2.

89. Of course, Collyer was also known to offer payment for puffs, which sometimes backfired: Later that year, the *Cincinnati Gazette* successfully took him to court for nonpayment for a positive review ("Dr. Collyer," *DC,* August 11, 1848, 2).

90. "A Question of Propriety," *DC.*

91. "St. Charles Theatre," *DC,* March 20, 1848, 1.

92. "A correspondent asks us if he can with propriety take the female members of his family to see the Model Artists. We answer *yes*, by all means" ("Take the Ladies," *DC,* March 23, 1848, 1).

93. "Correspondence of the Sunday Times," *Sunday Times,* May 21, 1848, 2. The letter is dated May 12.

94. Monod, *Soul of Pleasure*, 101.

95. "Model Artists at Pittsburg," *Alexandria Gazette,* February 21, 1848, 2.

96. "Morality and Model Artists," *Weekly Delta,* May 22, 1848, 1.

97. "A Mistake: Or, the Model Artists," *Weekly Delta,* March 6, 1848, 1.

98. One of whom died an accidental death during Whitman's tenure, prompting a sentimental farewell by Walt: "Death of a Juvenile Model Artist," *DC,* April 1, 1848, 2. The piece is strongly reminiscent of Whitman's

contemporary fiction: "Beautiful child! no one ever looked at him without feeling the better; for there is something in the loveliness of children that has a singularly calming and purifying effect upon the mind. His glossy white hair, fine as the choicest silk—his large blue eyes—the heavenly fairness and sweetness of his face—are before our mind at this moment." Note how the piece emphasizes the morally purifying effect of observing the boy's body.

99. *LG* (1855), 14.

100. *LG* (1860–61), 363. Of course, the location of the "City of Orgies" is generally identified as Manhattan. Yet the suggestive resonance of the "shifting tableaus" remains. The Model Artists performed in New York prior to visiting New Orleans. The *Eagle* would lead the charge against their risqué performances in town—but only *after* Whitman departed its editorial chair in January 1848. Never outright defending the troupe to rural Brooklyn's more conservative readership, Whitman nonetheless refused to participate in the public outcry while in charge of the *Eagle*.

101. Katz discusses an analog to such a male-male erotic space in his analysis of Abraham Lincoln's somewhat notorious habit of telling dirty jokes and smutty stories when in the company of male associates (*Love Stories*, 5–6). That masturbation may have been common is underscored by a comments in the *Sunday Times and Messenger*: "What struck us as remarkable was that almost every man came in solitary and alone, and was enveloped in an exceedingly roomy cloak, a goodly portion of which he wore over his face; yet the night was quite a warm one" ("The New Mania," *Sunday Times and Messenger*, January 30, 1848, 2).

102. Emily Banta, "Agonistic Audiences: Comic Play in the Early National Theater," *American Literature* 92, no. 3 (2020): 430, 433. A note of thanks is due to Daniel Couch and Michelle Sizemore for bringing Emily Banta's work to our attention at the 2024 C19 conference in Pasadena.

103. Banta, "Agonistic Audiences," 430, 435. Lawrence W. Levine's groundbreaking *Highbrow/Lowbrow: The Emergence of Cultural Hierarchy in America* (Cambridge, MA: Harvard University Press, 1990) reminds us that the "theater, like the church, was one of the earliest and most important cultural institutions established in frontier cities" (18). The drama on the stage was then an "expressive form that embodied all classes within a shared public space" (68), and it consequently became a powerful metaphor for the Jacksonian state. As Levine notes by example of Shakespeare, the texts performed were regarded as "property of those who flocked to see them" (72), which gave them the right to interfere or even intervene if performers or performances caused offense or consternation. See also Nigel Cliff, *The Shakespeare Riots: Revenge, Drama, and Death in Nineteenth-Century America* (New York: Random House, 2007).

104. Alexis de Tocqueville, *Democracy in America*, trans. Arthur Goldhammer (New York: Library of America, 2004), 564.

105. *LG* (1860–61), 368.

106. *LG* (1855), 258.

107. "General Taylor at the Theatre," *DC*.

108. Mary Ann Clawson, "Fraternal Orders and Class Formation in the Nineteenth-Century United States," *Comparative Studies in Society and History* 27, no. 4 (1985): 672.

109. "Died," *DP*.

110. *Proceedings of the Grand Commandery of Knights Templar and Appendant Order of the State of Louisiana* (New Orleans: Isaac T. Hinton, 1864), 16.

111. "S W M," *DP*, February 28, 1855, 5.

112. "George Washington Lodge," *DP*, May 14, 1869, 4.

113. For more on the Union, see Billy H. Wyche, "The Union Defends the Confederacy: The Fighting Printers of New Orleans," *Louisiana History* 35, no. 3 (1994): 271–84.

114. "The Irish League," *DC*.

115. "Gubernatorial," *Weekly Delta*, December 11, 1848, 1.

116. "Gubernatorial," *Weekly Delta*.

117. "Grand Fancy Dress and Mask Ball," *DP*, February 9, 1860, 6.

118. Mary Ann Clawson, *Constructing Brotherhood: Class, Gender, and Fraternalism* (Princeton: Princeton University Press, 1989), 161–63; Mark C. Carnes, *Secret Ritual and Manhood in Victorian America* (New Haven: Yale University Press), 7.

119. Ryan M. Hall, "A Glorious Assemblage: The Rise of the Know-Nothing Party in Louisiana" (master's thesis, Louisiana State University and Agricultural and Mechanical College, 2015), 24.

120. Hall, "A Glorious Assemblage," 24–26; Tyler Anbinder, *Nativism and Slavery: The Northern Know Nothings and the Politics of the 1850s* (New York: Oxford University Press, 1992), 167.

121. Vincent J. Bertolini, "Fireside Chastity: The Erotics of Sentimental Bachelorhood in the 1850s," in *Sentimental Men: Masculinity and the Politics of Affect in American Culture*, ed. Mary Chapman and Glenn Hendler (Berkeley: University of California Press, 1999), 19.

122. "A Night at the Terpsichore Ball; by 'You Know Who,'" *DC*, May 18, 1848, 1.

123. "Who shall wear Motley?" *DC*, April 3, 1848, 2.

124. "Hard Lines," *DP*, February 16, 1840, 4.

125. "Shall the Bachelor be Taxed?" *Louisiana Review*, September 23, 1891, 4.

126. "The following most owdacious [*sic*] proposition has been put forth in the assembly [. . .] by a married gentleman, of a complexion of sinister

yellow—the father of fourteen children, (without saying anything about the future.) Thirteen of these children are girls. . . . Bachelors, awake! arouse! or be forever fallen—into the payment of seven dollars!" ("[Untitled]," *BDE,* October 30, 1847, 2).

127. "Taxing Bachelors," *DP,* February 28, 1840, 8.

128. Thomas Jefferson Whitman, letter, March 14, 1848.

129. "Firemen's Celebration," *DC,* March 5, 1848, 3.

130. Cf. Thomas O'Connor, *History of the Fire Department of New Orleans* (New Orleans, 1895).

131. O'Connor, *History*, 673.

132. Clawson, "Fraternal Orders"; Carnes, *Secret Ritual,* 3–6.

133. *MHTN,* October 9, 2.

134. The abbreviation was a common target for ridicule: "A New Order—The frequent overflows of the modern [city of] Cairo has given rise to a new order, or secret society, in that aquatic town, called S.O.I.N., which admits no one that cannot swim. Their device, or great seal, is a web-foot and a whisky bottle, upon a muddy ground. What it means we don't know—but the initials stand for Swim Over In Nudity. Its paper don't say whether ladies are received as members" (*Port Allen Observer,* May 14, 1859, 2).

135. For instance, "Masonic," *DC,* March 9, 1848, 2; or "Grand Lodge," *DC,* March 28, 1848, 2.

136. "Odd Fellows," *DC,* March 22, 1848, 4.

137. "Sons of Temperance," *DC,* March 6, 1848, 2.

138. *JOURN* 2:492.

139. *WWWC* 6:63.

140. Ami Pflugrad-Jackisch, *Brothers of a Vow: Secret Fraternal Orders and the Transformation of White Male Culture in Antebellum Virginia* (Athens: University of Georgia Press, 2011), 30.

141. Carnes, *Secret Ritual,* 11.

142. Carnes, *Secret Ritual,* 11. On the symbolism of "riding the goat," see William D. Moore, "Riding the Goat: Secrecy, Masculinity, and Fraternal High Jinks in the United States, 1845–1930," *Winterthur Portfolio* 41, nos. 2/3 (Summer/Autumn 2007), esp. 161–69.

143. Carnes, *Secret Ritual,* 12.

144. Carnes, *Secret Ritual,* 18–23.

145. E. Willis, *Renunciation of Odd Fellowship* (Boston: W. S. Damrell, 1846), 20.

146. Willis, *Renunciation,* 23.

147. David S. Reynolds, *Walt Whitman's America: A Cultural Biography* (New York: Knopf, 1996), 121.

148. Moore, "Riding the Goat," 165.

149. Whitman, *Every Hour, Every Atom: A Collection of Walt Whitman's Early Notebooks and Fragments*, ed. Matt Miller and Zachary Turpin (Iowa City: University of Iowa Press, 2020), 239.

150. Pradeep A. Dhillon, "Cosmopolitanism Patriotism Educated Through Kant and Walt Whitman," in *Cosmopolitanism: Educational, Philosophical and Historical Perspectives*, ed. Marianna Papastephanou (New York: Springer, 2016), 105–14.

151. Whitman, *Every Hour, Every Atom*, 247.

152. *MHTN*, July 25, 2.

153. *MHTN*, October 10, 2 (italics in original).

154. "A Question of Propriety," *DC*.

155. "Nauseating," *DC*, March 29, 1848, 2.

156. "'Age Cannot Wither Her,'" *DC*, March 6, 1848, 2.

CHAPTER 5

1. "The Stage," *BDE*, August 17, 1846, 2; also *JOURN* 2:19–29.

2. "Mr. Collins—The Irish Comedian," *DC*, March 9, 1848, 2. In a later letter back to the *Crescent*, Walt still considers Collins "very popular, and really [. . .] better than any Irish comedian at present among us" (*MHTN*, October 7, 2).

3. "Crossing the Alleghanies," *DC*. Although Ronald Wallace's assertion that Whitman's first meaningful "exposure to popular humor" was in New Orleans is an exaggeration, the poet's peculiar fascination with framing his Southern experience through humor is hard to deny. See Ronald Wallace, *God Be With the Clown: Humor in American Poetry* (Columbia: University of Missouri Press, 1984), 58.

4. The following pages have been adapted from Schöberlein and Turpin, "'Glorious Times,'" 14–26.

5. Schöberlein and Turpin, "'Glorious Times,'" 3–5, 14–26.

6. The typical time between letters mailed by "Manhattan" from New York City and their publication in the *Crescent* was ten to fifteen days.

7. The Tremont House rented out rooms above its "bar-room," next door to the St. Charles, that frequently saw violent fights; see, for instance, "A Row," *DP*, February 6, 1852, 4.

8. W., "Habitants of Hotels."

9. Nassau Street, "Matters and Things."

10. "Daggerdraw Bowieknife," *DC*, March 23, 1848, 1.

11. McDraw votes in elections and, from this habit, acquires moderate

wealth. In this, and other regards, he foreshadows Whitman's character Barney Fox in his 1852 novel *Jack Engle*.

12. Loving, *Walt Whitman*, 122.

13. Another passage worth contrasting to Grisette is Whitman's 1856 sketch of a sex worker for *Life Illustrated*: "Dirty finery, excessively plentiful; paint, both red and white; draggle-tailed dress, ill-fitting; coarse features, unintelligent; bold glance, questioning, shameless, perceptibly anxious; hideous croak or dry, brazen ring in voice; affected, but awkward, mincing, waggling gait. Harlot." ("New York Dissected," *Life Illustrated*, August 16, 1856, 125; also *WWA*).

14. Loving, *Walt Whitman*, 122.

15. "Mrs. Giddy Gay Butterfly," *DC*, April 12, 1848, 1. Compare this to Martha's father in *Jack Engle*, who recalls, "[M]y home was not worthy the name; I had no home. Although parents cared enough for me to spend money liberally, and give me an almost unlimited indulgence that way, yet they did not furnish me what is most wanted from parents—good example, good counsel and a true home-roof. I was boarded, almost from the beginning, away in the country" ("Life and Adventures of Jack Engle: An Auto-Biography," ed. Zachary Turpin, *WWQR* 34 [Winter/Spring 2017]: 340). Here we have the same logic of providing the material but not the emotional familial support—coupled with a premature injection into the outside world. Similar character elements are contained in Inez's backstory as well.

16. "Mrs. Giddy Gay Butterfly," *DC*.

17. Paumanok, "Letters from a Travelling Bachelor," *New York Sunday Dispatch*, October 28, 1849, 1; also *WWA*.

18. "Franklin Evans; or, the Inebriate: A Tale of the Times," *New World*, November 23, 1842, 7; also *WWA*.

19. Walt Whitman, "The Shadow and the Light of a Young Man's Soul," *Union Magazine of Literature and Art* 2, no. 6 (1848): 281; also *WWA*.

20. "Miss Virginity Roseblossom, Spinster," *DC*, July 25, 1848, 1.

21. Loving, *Walt Whitman*, 120.

22. The author observed that Jinglebrain "*dawdles* about, as Fanny Kemble would say, until dinner." Kemble was known, and at times ridiculed, for her spirited expressions like "dawdles." Also see Faye E. Dudden, *Women in the American Theatre: Actresses and Audiences, 1790–1870* (New Haven: Yale University Press, 1994), 44.

23. See Whitman's "Letters from New York," *National Era*, November 14, 1850, 1. See also Susan M. Meyer, "Actors and Actresses," *ENCYC*, 4. Likewise, see his references to Kemble in his "Manhattan" letters: "On the Park stage we first saw Fanny Kemble" (*MHTN*, August 14, 1848, 3; cf. *PW* 2:592, 695).

24. "Ephraim Broadhorn," *DC.* As Halleck puts it, "Theirs is a pure republic, wild, yet strong, / A 'fierce democracie,' where all are true / To what themselves have voted—right or wrong— / And to their laws denominated blue" (*The Poetical Works of Fitz-Greene Halleck* [New York: D. Appleton & Co., 1848], 97). Ephraim echoes these politics: He sees himself as "a 'dimocrat,' a one of the b'hoys," Tantalizingly, these political musings have the author of Ephraim Broadhorn end the sketch as well as the whole series with a direct political quote from one of the authors of the Missouri Compromise: Pinkney's plea to respect the "the unsophisticated good sense and noble spirit of the American people" makes an early states' rights argument (claiming that each new state should be allowed the same right to decide to be a slave-state or not).

25. Quoted in James Grant Wilson, *The Life and Letters of Fitz-Greene Halleck* (New York: D. Appleton, 1869), 493.

26. Wilson, *Life and Letters,* 492.

27. For instance, the "Williamsburgh Word Portrait" series he likely authored for the *Brooklyn Daily Times* in the late 1850s.

28. Jay Charlton, "Bohemians in America," *Danbury News* (pre-1883), via the *WWA,* med. 00575). On Whitman and Pfaff's, see also Stephanie M. Blalock, *"GO TO PFAFF'S!": The History of a Restaurant and Lager Beer Saloon* (Bethlehem, PA: Lehigh University Press, 2014).

29. John W. M. Hallock, *The American Byron: Homosexuality and the Fall of Fitz-Greene Halleck* (Madison: University of Wisconsin Press, 2000), 170.

30. *WWWC* 4:8.

31. *WWWC* 2:252.

32. *WWWC* 7:388.

33. *MHTN,* October 21, 2. The letter is dated October 10, 1848, and describes seeing John Van Buren speak at a Free-Soil mass meeting at the Park Theatre on the evening of October 9, 1848.

34. Lauren Berlant, *The Female Complaint: The Unfinished Business of Sentimentality in American Culture* (Durham, NC: Duke University Press, 2008), 146.

35. "The meeting was addressed by Dr. Boyd, Walter Whitman, John S. Noble, Mr. Lester and one or two others. [. . .] A resolution was presented, instructing delegates to vote for Martin Van Buren. This brought out the eloquence of a number of gentlemen whom we have known for many years as prominent loco-focos" ("Free Soil Meeting," *Brooklyn Evening Star,* August 7, 1848, 2).

36. Richard Chase, *Walt Whitman Reconsidered* (New York: William Sloane Associates, 1955), 73, 72.

37. Constance Rourke, *American Humor: A Study of the National Character* (New York: Doubleday Anchor Books, 1935), 142 (emphasis ours).

38. Ronald Wallace echoes his mistake, noting Whitman's "popular" humor in New Orleans but failing to meaningfully contextualize it (*God Be With the Clown*, 58–59).

39. Fitz-Greene Halleck, "An Address," in *The Poetical Writings*, 329.

40. Emily Banta, "Comic Feelings: Theater Discourse in the Early United States," paper presented at C19 Conference (Pasadena, CA), March 14, 2024. The authors would like to thank Emily Banta for sharing her comments with us.

41. Walt Whitman, "New Orleans in 1848," *DP,* January 25, 1887, 3.

42. Emily Banta, "Agonistic Audiences: Comic Play in the Early National Theater," *American Literature* 92, no. 3 (2020): 433.

43. Banta, "Comic Feelings."

44. Banta, "Agonistic Audiences," 432 (italics ours).

45. "The Presidential Campaign," *DC,* April 26, 1848, 2.

46. "Day after the Election!" *DC,* April 5, 1848, 3.

47. Banta, "Agonistic Audiences," 448.

48. Floyd Stovall, for instance, calls this specific claim "not convincing" and panned the whole book for being idiosyncratic and his "criticism [. . .] confessedly personal" and therefore inherently limited ("*Walt Whitman Reconsidered* by Richard Chase [review]," *American Literature* 27, no. 3 [1955]: 431–32). The book had no significant impact on Whitman studies.

49. Chase, *Walt Whitman*, 59, 60.

50. Chase, *Walt Whitman*, 60.

51. *LG* (1855), 4.

52. "Ephraim Broadhorn," *DC.*

53. Bernard Hirschhorn, "Political Views," *ENCYC,* 531.

54. In *American Oratory, Or Selections from the Speeches of Eminent Americans* (Philadelphia: Desilver, Thomas, 1836), 331.

55. *MHTN,* October 10, 2.

56. See Walter Grünzweig, "'Solidarity of the World': Walt Whitman as an International Poet," in *The Oxford Handbook of Walt Whitman*, ed. Kenneth M. Price and Stefan Schöberlein (New York: Oxford University Press, 2024), 550–51.

CHAPTER 6

1. For context, see Christopher Clark, *Revolutionary Spring: Europe Aflame and the Fight for a New World, 1848–1849* (New York: Crown, 2024), esp. 169–64.

2. Nassau Street, "Matters and Things."

3. ["A mightier power"], *DC,* April 1, 1848, 2. Jerome Loving rightly argues that this piece was likely authored by Whitman.

4. "Prospects of War," *DC,* April 17, 1848, 2.

5. "A French Revolution," *DC,* March 25, 1848, 2. The paper on that day responded to doubters by saying that "we are not disposed to discredit the news altogether. There may have been an *emeute* [*sic*] in Paris, it may have even assumed a formidable character, it may possibly have assumed the dignity of a revolution."

6. *PW* 1:189.

7. "Sympathy with France," *DC,* May 3, 1848, 2.

8. Timothy Mason Roberts, *Distant Revolutions: 1848 and the Challenge to American Exceptionalism* (Charlottesville: University of Virginia Press, 2009), 44.

9. Roberts, *Distant Revolutions,* 56.

10. Larry J. Reynolds. *European Revolutions and the American Literary Renaissance* (New Haven: Yale University Press, 1988), 14.

11. The poem "may be viewed as an updated version of 'The Old World,'" according to Loving (*Walt Whitman,* 132).

12. Loving, *Walt Whitman,* 132.

13. The *London Pioneer* (vol. 2, no. 101: 784) of 1848 attributes it to "Dr. Bowring." See also "Libertas (from the *London Morning Chronicle*)," *Lancaster Examiner,* December 23, 1830, 4.

14. "The Old World," *DC,* April 28, 1848, 4.

15. Walter Whitman, "Resurgemus," *New-York Daily Tribune,* June 21, 1850, 3.

16. Reynolds, *European Revolutions,* 133–38.

17. See, for instance, Betsy Erkkila, *The Whitman Revolution: Sex, Poetry, and Politics* (Iowa City: University of Iowa Press, 2020), 239n2.

18. "The editors of the *Crescent,* who welcomed European revolutions, were otherwise delighted to think the revolutions rendered, 'it certain that Mexico cannot receive any assistance from England'" (Loving, *Walt Whitman,* 129).

19. "John C. Larue," *DP,* November 18, 1856, 2.

20. Speculation based on Larue's last name, his Francophile political leanings, as well as his familiarity with French history, culture, and language.

21. "John C. Larue," *The South-Western,* November 26, 1856, 2.

22. Whitman, "[1848 New Orleans]."

23. "Young Men's Free Library Association," *DP,* January 30, 1846, 2.

24. "Gubernatorial," *New Orleans Weekly Delta,* December 11, 1848, 1.

25. "To the Public," *DP,* August 26, 1837, 2.

26. "[J. C. Larue], *DD,* February 8, 1846, 2

27. Reilly, *War with Mexico,* 31.

28. "The American League," *DC,* April 14, 1848, 2. Walker was the organization's president, Larue a vice president. It pledged to aid "determined resistance by the Irish nation to British encroachment until the gem of the ocean shall take its place among the nations of the earth."

29. "[J. C. Larue]," *DD.*

30. "Gubernatorial," *DC,* December 11, 1848, 1.

31. "Our Old and Mediæval Bar."

32. "To the Hon. John C. Larue," *New Orleans Weekly Delta,* November 11, 1850, 3.

33. "The Crescent," *New-Orleans Times,* April 20, 1869, 2.

34. "To the Hon. John C. Larue."

35. "Public Meeting," *Mississippi Free Trader,* November 22, 1839, 2.

36. "Crescent," *New-Orleans Times.*

37. John C. Larue and Thomas J. Durant, "Prospectus of *The Southerner,*" *Mississippi Free Trader,* March 27, 1838, 1.

38. "Our Old and Mediæval Bar."

39. ["A mightier power"].

40. Roberts, *Distant Revolutions,* 56.

41. Mark A. Lause, *The Antebellum Crisis and America's First Bohemians* (Kent, OH: Kent State University Press, 2009), esp. 85–103.

42. "Russia," *DC,* May 6, 1848, 2.

43. "England and Its Revolution," *DC,* May 12, 1848, 2 (emphasis ours).

44. "French Politics–Communism," *DC,* May 30, 1848, 2. See also "Socialism–Fourierism–Communism," likely also authored by Larue, which echoes the same argument and concludes "[Fourierism and Communism], it must be conceded, are seductive as well to the reason as to the senses, and we cannot therefore be surprised that their doctrines have taken a firm hold upon the minds of the laboring classes in France. Those men enjoy few of the benefits, while they sensibly feel all the evils and defects of the present state of society, and it is but natural that they should have become fascinated by theories which propose to relieve them of their miseries and elevate them to a position of comparative happiness and comfort" (*DC,* July 25, 1848, 2).

45. "Revolutionary Movements," *DC,* April 18, 1848, 2.

46. "Our Old and Mediæval Bar."

47. "Germany–Prussia," *DC,* April 19, 1848, 2.

48. "Russia," *DC,* May 6, 1848, 2.

49. "The Progress of Liberty," *DC,* May 16, 1848, 2.

50. "To the Public," *DC,* March 23, 1848, 2.

51. At least, his recently reconstructed Geography Scrapbook attests as much. See "Whitman's Cultural Geography Scrapbook," eds. Matt Cohen,

Kevin McMullen, Caterina Bernardini, Ashlyn Stewart, and Caitlin Henry, *WWA,* owu.00090.

52. "Meeting of the Germans," *DP*, April 18, 1848, 2.

53. "The Italian Meeting," *New Orleans Weekly Delta,* April 24, 1848, 2.

54. The resulting article is "Celebration of St. Patrick's Day," *DC,* March 18, 1848, 2.

55. "Great Meeting at the St. Louis in Honor of the French Revolution," *DC,* April 12, 1848, 2.

56. The reporter clearly presents himself as a non-French outsider attending the event and takes no clear stance on the contentious events of the evening, opting for a humorous style more common for Whitman's peeps than Larue's ultra-radicalism. There are also numerous errors in the piece that a French expert like Larue would likely have avoided: The assassination took place in 1835, not 1836, and the name of the assassin is listed incorrectly as well. Whitman also referred to the French as "Galls" in other editorials for the *Crescent.*

57. William H. Coleman, *Historical Sketch Book and Guide to New Orleans and Environs* (New York: William H. Coleman, 1885), 134.

58. In what is likely one of his first editorials, Whitman boasts about "the French opera at the Orleans Theatre, with its magnificent troupe" ("Novelties in New Orleans," *DC,* March 13, 1848, 3).

59. Coleman, *Historical Sketch Book*, 134.

60. "The French Banquet," *New Orleans Weekly Delta,* April 17, 1848, 1 (emphasis in original).

61. "The Grand Banquet in Honor of the French Revolution," *DC,* April 17, 1848, 2. The event took place on April 15.

62. "[The New Orleans]," *Richmond Enquirer,* April 25, 1848, 2.

63. "The Grand Banquet in Honor of the French Revolution," *DC,* April 17, 1848, 2.

64. "The Grand Banquet."

65. Stacy, "Clerk Trouble," 11.

66. Reynolds, *European Revolutions*, 19.

67. "[Lamartine]," *DC,* October 10, 1848, 3.

68. In Larue's micro-essays on European revolutions, published during Whitman's tenure, Lamartine's name is mentioned a mere handful of times. Unlike Whitman, Larue seems to have had some aversion to the "Great Men" theory of history.

69. "Lamartine," *DC,* May 18, 1848, 2.

70. "French Character—Lamartine's 'Girondists,'" *DC,* March 16, 1848, 2 (italics in original). Of course, Whitman had reviewed the book for the *Eagle*, where he called it "the most dramatic work we ever read—too dramatic,

perhaps, for the higher purposes of history" ("The French Revolution," *DE,* August 10, 1847, 2).

71. See Jason Stacy, "Washington's Tears: Sentimental Anecdote and Walt Whitman's Battle of Long Island," *WWQR* 27 (Spring 2010): 213–26.

72. "The Man of His Country and of the Age!" *DC,* April 27, 1848, 1.

73. "Lamartine," *DC.*

74. "[We have received]," *DD*, February 28, 1847, 2.

75. "Democratic State Convention," *DC,* March 16, 1848, 2.

76. "Happy Are We," *DC,* March 16, 1848, 2 (italics in original).

77. *MHTN,* November 13, 2.

78. Manhattan, "Herr Hecker—Macready, &c," *MHTN*, October 19, 1848, 2. The letter is dated October 9, 1848.

79. Betsy Erkkila, "Whitman, Marx, and the American 1848," in *Leaves of Grass: The Sesquicentennial Essays*, ed. Susan Belasco, Kenneth M. Price, and Ed Folsom (Lincoln: University of Nebraska Press, 2008), 52–53.

80. "In [England] there is already no need of revolutions: for the mighty progress of unfettered public opinion is gradually achieving reforms—and haply will in a method of peace and quiet, remove the wrongs under which her people yet labor" ("Abroad," *BDE,* February 11, 1847, 2; also *JOURN* 2:195).

81. *WWWC* 1:221.

82. "The Presidential Campaign," *DC,* April 26, 1848, 2.

83. *MHTN,* August 14, 3.

84. "[The attack]," *BDE,* April 20, 1847, 2; also *JOURN* 2:252.

85. *MHTN,* July 25, 2.

86. *MHTN,* October 14, 2.

87. Sabine Freitag, *Friedrich Hecker: Two Lives for Liberty*, vol. 1, trans. Steven Rowan (St. Louis: St. Louis Mercantile Library, 2006), 168.

88. Rayback, *Free Soil,* 220. The platform read: "*Resolved,* That the free grant to actual settlers, in consideration of the expenses they incur in making settlements in the wilderness, which are usually fully equal to their actual cost, and of the public benefits resulting therefrom, of reasonable portions of the public lands, under suitable limitations, is a wise and just measure of public policy, which will promote in various ways the interests of all the States of this Union; and we therefore recommend it to the favorable consideration of the American people" (see presidency.ucsb.edu/documents/free-soil-party-platform-1848).

89. "Then let them come and welcome! say we; and the more the better," he wrote in 1847 ("The Latest Raw Head and Bloody Bones," *BDE*, January 22, 1847, 2; also *JOURN* 2:173).

90. Grünzweig, "Solidarity of the World," 550–51 (emphasis in original).

91. "Socialism–Fourierism–Communism," *DC*, July 25, 1848, 2.

92. Eric Foner, *Free Soil, Free Labor, Free Men: The Ideology of the Republican Party Before the Civil War* (New York: Oxford University Press, 1995).

93. W., "The Trist Treaty," *DC*, March 11, 1848, 2. Note that Whitman had signed his "Mississippi at Midnight" poem "W." just a few days prior, which can clearly be tied to Whitman through manuscript evidence. Additionally, the specific charge of Mexican "semibarbarism" was also echoed in Whitman's earlier *Eagle* writings (see *JOURN* 2:328–29).

94. For several instances, see *WWWC* 2:522, 6:292, or 7:34.

95. "The Contents of the Pillow-Case," *DC*, April 11, 1848, 2. The term is a pun referencing the Hellenic deity via Sterne's *The Life and Opinions of Tristram Shandy, Gentleman.* See also Esther Shephard, "Possible Sources of Some of Whitman's Ideas in Hermes Mercurius Trismegistus and Other Works," *Modern Language Quarterly* 14 (1953): 60–81.

96. "The French Revolution and Mexico," *DC*, April 1, 1848, 2.

97. "The Treaty: Who Made It?" *DC*, March 18, 1848, 2.

98. "Paredes in Mexico," *BDE*, September 18, 1847, 2; also *JOURN* 2:329.

99. "The Mexican Treaty," *DC*, March 20, 1848, 2.

100. "Who Will Have Yucatan?" *DC*, April 8, 1848, 2.

101. "The Ratification of the Treaty," *DC*, May 31, 1848, 2.

102. "The Republic of Sierra Madre," *DD*, October 20, 1848, 2.

103. "The Next Slavery Foray," *New-York Daily Tribune*, August 9, 1848, 1.

104. *PW* 2:605. On Peoples and Kinney, see "The Corpus Christi Humbug," *DD*, October 2, 1848, 2.

105. *MHTN*, August 24, 2.

106. *MHTN*, September 14, 2.

107. See Eric Foner, "Racial Attitudes of the New York Free Soilers," *New York History* 46, no. 4 (1965): esp. 315.

108. *MHTN*, October 9, 2.

109. Cf. Friedrich Kittler, *Discourse Networks 1800/1900*, trans. Michael Metteer and Chris Cullens (Stanford, CA: Stanford University Press, 1990), 3. Kittler famously claims that "German Poetry," by which he means German Romanticism, "begins with a sigh." "The sigh," the media theorist notes, "is the sign of the unique entity (the soul) that, if it were to utter another signifier or [. . .] any other signifier whatsoever, would immediately become its own sigh of self-lament."

110. *MHTN*, July 25, 2.

111. *MHTN*, October 19, 2.

112. *LG* (1860–61), 367.

113. Cited in: "Introduction to the Brooklyn Freeman," 9, Noverr Papers,

Louisa H. Bowen University Archives and Unique Collections, University of Southern Illinois-Edwardsville. The "Introduction" was likely written by Herbert Bergman, an icon of Whitman journalism research, around 1981.

The cited piece was published in the *Brooklyn Daily Advertiser* of September 24, 1849, following Whitman's departure from the *Freeman*. It was clearly part of his puffery campaign in the papers during in his post-*Freeman* period of freelancing, which his contemporaries have noted. This suggests the *Advertiser* as a potentially overlooked journalistic outlet in Whitman's late 1840s journalism. At the very least, the series "Sketches of Distinguished Animals," which the Whitman portrait piece is from, deserves more scrutiny. The *Advertiser*, a Whig paper, was a staunch supporter of Whitman's *Freeman* and frequently praised him personally. There was even rumor of its editors ensuring the *Freeman* was awarded a contract to print the city's corporation notices, which caused the *Eagle* to publicly charge the *Advertiser* with "fostering, and coaxing into life Mr. Whitman's paper [and] open[ing] its columns to Mr. W's grievances" (["We can assure"], *BDE*, July 21, 1849, 2). The only extant issues of the *Advertiser* from this time are housed in the Brooklyn Public Library and are now inaccessible to researchers due to their fragile nature.

114. See also Roberts, *Distant Revolutions*, esp. 69–72.

115. "Paredes in Mexico," *BDE*.

116. *PW* 1:93. For the Mexican perspective on the war, see Timothy J. Henderson, *A Glorious Defeat: Mexico and Its War with the United States* (New York, NY: Hill and Wang, 2007).

117. *MHTN*, September 5, 1848, 2. The letter is dated August 24, 1848.

118. For a representative overview, see Walter Grünzweig, "Imperialism and Globalization," in *Walt Whitman in Context*, ed. Joanna Levin and Edward Whitley (New York: Cambridge University Press, 2018), 249–58.

CHAPTER 7

1. Ed Folsom and Kenneth M. Price, "Whitman's Life," *WWA*, whitmanarchive.org/whitmans-life/biography#orleans.

2. Loving, *Walt Whitman*, 138.

3. Holloway, *Whitman*, 65.

4. Holloway, *Whitman*, 65.

5. "May!" *DC*, May 1, 1848, 2.

6. Rubin, *Historic Whitman*, 202.

7. In August he would write to the *Crescent*: "Dysentery and cholera infantum are carrying off from twelve to twenty persons daily; most of the deaths

of the former disease too are children. This is about as bad as your yellow fever, isn't it?" (*MHTN,* September 5, 2).

8. Loving, *Walt Whitman*, 138–39.

9. Whitman, "[1848 New Orleans]," *WWA,* med.00725. The notion that Jeff was overworked is belied, at least in part, by Jeff's own correspondence. In his letter of March 27, the last extant from their time in New Orleans, he notes that "[m]y work is good and light. I have such a part of the mail (and I can do it most over night) and then I have nothing to do for the rest of the day (I generally get through with it about two o'clock) but stay in the office."

10. Wages for 1851 are listed in the United States Department of Labor's Bureau of Labor Statistics, *History of Wages in the United States from Colonial Times to 1928* (Washington, DC: US Government Printing Office, 1934), 349.

11. This is a rough estimate, as we only know the costs to Wheeling, which was twenty-six dollars for both. Travel down the Mississippi appears to have run between ten and fifteen dollars per person.

12. Thomas Jefferson Whitman, letter, March 14, 1848.

13. See assessor's fees listed for Walter Whitman in, for example, the *Brooklyn Evening Star,* March 22, 1849, 4, and *BDE,* April 11, 1849, 4.

14. This steamer, incidentally, may have helped supply the *Daily Crescent* and its now-departing editor with exchange papers. See an editorial notice in *DC,* October 28, 1848, 2, second column, thanking "the obliging clerk of the Pride of the West for later papers."

15. "Promoted from the Ranks," *John-Donkey,* May 13, 1848, 309. News between New Orleans and New York took about ten days based on the dates on Whitman's "Manhattan" correspondence.

16. "Yucatan," *DC,* June 26, 1848, 2.

17. See "Dixoniana," *DC,* October 4, 1848, 2. A number of accounts may be found of Dixon's final years in New Orleans, such as "Reminiscences of Players," by one "Dr. Kane" in the *St. Louis Republican* (reprinted in *DP,* November 3, 1882, 3), in which Dixon is fondly, and more or less accurately, called "the father of negro minstrelsy." For a more recent scholarly account, see Dale Cockrell's *Demons of Disorder: Early Blackface Minstrels and Their World* (New York: Cambridge University Press, 1997).

18. Walt Whitman, ["wooding at night"], *WWA,* duk.00790.

19. Both quotes are from the final version of "Our Old Feuillage," found in *LG* (1891–92), 139–40.

20. *PW* 2:606.

21. "The Cure," *Brooklyn Daily Times,* September 30, 1857, 2; also *WWA.*

22. *LG* (1855), 29, 19, 39.

23. “Death of Captain J. J. Warman, the River Pilot,” *Public Ledger,* October 28, 1880, 4. Warman piloted the steamer according to an advertisement for the *Pride of the West* (*DD,* May 27, 1848, 3).

24. “A Race on the Mississippi in 1841,” *Opelousas Courier,* February 28, 1874, 3.

25. Whitman, [“wooding at night”].

26. “Port of St. Louis,” *St. Louis Republican,* June 5, 1848, 3. While arrival times are not listed, it is likely that the position on the port arrival announcement reflects the results of the race. The *St. Louis Daily Union* of the same date also lists the *Grand Turk* before the *Pride of the West.* The authors would like to thank Amy L. Waters at the State Historical Society of Missouri for her kind assistance with this query.

27. Taylor made this statement in the so-called “Allison letter” of April 22, 1848; see Rayback, *Free Soil,* 155.

28. *MHTN,* August 10, 2.

29. *PW* 2:608.

30. *PW* 2:608.

31. Though, of course, Herbert Bergman has pointed out that a “Chicago” poem in the Toronto *World* of December 8, 1884, signed “Walt Whitman,” decries the democratic potential of Chicago being dragged down by immigrants and “diseased niggers” suppressing wages. It ends: “Blood is the bans [bane?] of the hustling prosperity that now attends you and an adept pig-sticker is the embodiment of thy manhood!” (Herbert Bergman, “‘Chicago,’ An Uncollected Poem, Possibly by Whitman,” *Modern Language Notes* 65, no. 7 [1950]: 478–81). The poem certainly mimics Whitman but does not sound like the poet in 1884.

32. *PW* 2:608.

33. *PW* 2:608.

34. “Affecting Calamity,” *Milwaukee Daily Sentinel,* June 9, 1848, 3. Hinckley’s husband, Roger Gibson Hinckley (1805–81), subsequently moved his family to California, where Hinckley Basin and Hinckley Creek in the Forest of Nisene Marks State Park near Santa Cruz still bear the family name (see California State Parks, *The Forest of Nisene Marks State Park, Preliminary General Plan* [March 2023], 39; parks.ca.gov/pages/21299/files/tfnm prelimgp-draft eir.pdf). The child in question may have been “Benjamin Hinkley,” who was stillborn on March 27, 1844, and is buried in Racine, Wisconsin. The child is not mentioned in the news item about Hinckley’s death. In any case, this detail suggests that Whitman discussed the incident with fellow passengers and inquired into the cause for her suicide. Another paper even states: “Her derangement,

it is said, was caused by the death of her three children" ("Affecting Calamity," *American Freeman,* June 14, 1848, 2). This, most certainly, was untrue.

35. "Casualties," *Poughkeepsie Journal,* June 24, 1848, 2.

36. *LG* (1890–91), 390.

37. *PW* 2:609.

38. *PW* 2:609.

39. *PW* 2:609.

40. *LG* (1855), 39.

41. *PW* 2:609.

42. *PW* 2:610.

43. Samuel E. Johnson, "Subscribers' list for Brooklyn newspaper," Library of Congress (Charles E. Feinberg Collection), hdl.loc.gov/loc.mss/ms004014.mss18630.01610.

44. The first letter to the *Crescent* was mailed two days after the Freeman planning meeting of July 11, 1848; cf. Johnson, "Subscribers' list."

CHAPTER 8

1. The *Freeman* was expanded into a daily in April 1849 (Bergman, "Introduction," 5).

2. Jon Panish, "Brooklyn Freeman," *ENCYC*, 82.

3. Allen, *Solitary Singer*, 87.

4. For more on Johnson, see his obituary: "In Memoriam," *BDE,* February 7, 1870, 4.

5. "Died," *BDE,* February 3, 1870, 3.

6. Evan M. Johnson, *"The Communion of Saints": A Discourse Delivered in St. Michael's Church, Brooklyn, N.Y., on Sunday, the 26th of March, A.D. 1848* (Brooklyn: Eagle Printing Office, 1848), 17.

7. The elder Johnson figures prominently in Craig D. Townsend's illuminating *Faith in Their Own Color: Black Episcopalians in Antebellum New York City* (New York: Columbia University Press, 2005); see esp. 135–40.

8. Prithi Kanakamedala, *Brooklynites: The Remarkable Story of the Free Black Communities that Shaped a Borough* (New York: New York University Press, 2024), 140–41.

9. Johnson, "Subscribers' list."

10. Rubin, *Historic Whitman*, 210.

11. Jason Stacy, *Walt Whitman's Multitudes: Labor Reform and Persona in Whitman's Journalism and the First* Leaves of Grass, *1840–1855* (New York: Peter Lang, 2008), 101.

12. These are contained in the Daniel M. Tredwell papers at the New York Public Library (MssCol 3028).

13. Daniel M. Tredwell, *Personal Reminiscences of Men and Things on Long Island*, vol. 2 (Brooklyn: C.A. Ditmas, 1912), 212; Emory Holloway, "Conversation with Daniel M. Tredwell—April 12, 1921," Noverr Papers, Louisa H. Bowen University Archives and Unique Collections, University of Southern Illinois-Edwardsville. Tredwell, also spelled "Treadwell," died in November of 1921. Tredwell is listed as living at 174 Nassau Street in 1850 (Henry R. and William J. Hearnes, *Brooklyn Directory and Yearly Register for 1849 and 1850* [Brooklyn: Lees and Foulkes], 325). Tredwell's recollection is fuzzy, and he mixed up dates; perhaps his salary started at a later point (he continued to work at the paper until at least the 1850s).

14. "The Brooklyn Freeman," *Brooklyn Freeman,* September 9, 1848, 1 (italics in original); Library of Congress.

15. "The Great Fire in Brooklyn," *DC,* September 20, 1848, 2.

16. Perhaps not coincidentally, Whitman would later become a staunch proponent of improving Brooklyn's water supply. See Blalock, McMullen, Schöberlein, and Stacy, "'One of the Grand Works.'"

17. "The Great Fire in Brooklyn," *DC,* September 20, 1848, 2.

18. Gay Wilson Allen, "Whitman Biography in 1992," in *Walt Whitman: The Centennial Essays*, ed. Ed Folsom (Iowa City: University of Iowa Press, 1994), 5.

19. Schöberlein and Turpin, "'Glorious Times.'"

20. "Every one conversant with New York politics must be aware that the young democracy have four-fifth of their party with them, and most of the ambition, talent, and desire for spoils, too. If there be any truth in signs, John Van Buren will cut a larger 'figure' before the good folk of this land, than ever his papa did" (Sunshine, "Northern Correspondence," *DC,* March 5, 1848, 1). A later letter reveals "Sunshine" as an anti-Taylor Whig ("Northern Correspondence," *DC,* March 17, 1848, 2). This suggests "Sunshine" might be a voice from Whitman's Whig support network in New York or Brooklyn. Given the pen name, an association with the New York *Sun* also seems plausible; Whitman had published fiction with the *Sun* in the 1840s and served as its police reporter in 1843.

21. Foner, *Free Soil, Free Labor, Free Men.*

22. "Political Rumors and Speculations," *DC,* June 29, 1848, 2.

23. For more on this destabilization, the reader is encouraged to consult James McPherson's *Battle Cry of Freedom: The Civil War Era* (New York: Oxford University Press, 1988), esp. 6–144, as well as William E. Gienapp's *The Origins of the Republican Party, 1852–1856* (New York: Oxford University Press, 1987) and Philip S. Foner's *History of Black Americans: From the*

Compromise of 1850 to the End of the Civil War (Westport, CT: Greenwood Press, 1983), among many others.

24. "How Things Have Been Managed in Kings County," *Brooklyn Freeman,* September 9, 1848, 1, Library of Congress (italics in original).

25. *LG* (1855), iii.

26. "A New Brooklyn Paper," *Brooklyn Evening Star,* September 5, 1848, 2.

27. "A Good Bye," *BDE,* September 11, 1849, 2.

28. "A Good Bye," *BDE.*

29. In spite of its good circulation and the consistent editorial attention it received from other newspapers in New York, only two issues of the *Freeman* are extant today: the very first (vol. 1, no. 1; September 9, 1848), kept today in the archives of the New York Public Library; and an issue of the *Daily Freeman* published on May 30, 1849 (vol. 2?, no. 22), which resurfaced at auction in 2016, before being purchased by an anonymous buyer. Scattered reprintings of single *Freeman* items also exist.

30. "[Editorial]," *DC,* July 24, 1848, 2.

31. *LG* (1860–61), 404.

32. See also, Kimo Reder, "Whitman's Metro-Poetic Lettrism: The Mannahatta Skyline as Sentence, Syntax, and Spell," *WWQR* 35 (Summer 2017): 88–114.

33. Stacy, *Walt Whitman's Multitudes,* 75.

34. *MHTN,* July 27, 2.

35. For ease of reading, we have referred throughout to the full set of these letters as the "Manhattan" letters, including those attributed to "Manahatta."

36. *WWWC* 4:473.

37. Rachel A. Shelden and Erik B. Alexander, "Dismantling the Party System: Party Fluidity and the Mechanisms of Nineteenth-Century U.S. Politics," *Journal of American History* 110, no. 3 (2023): 421.

38. Michael J. Dubin, *Party Affiliations in the State Legislatures: A Year by Year Summary, 1796–2006* (Jefferson, NC: McFarland, 2007), passim, cited in Shelden and Alexander, "Dismantling the Party System," 431.

39. Walt Whitman, "Party Allegiance," *Brooklyn Daily Times,* December 12, 1857, 2; also *WWA.*

40. For an in-depth discussion of the formation of the Free-Soil Party, particularly the basic facts of the nomination and delegation process, see Rayback, *Free Soil,* esp. 131ff.

41. *MHTN,* August 21, 3.

42. "The Evening Post," *BDE,* August 8, 1848, 2.

43. "Free Soil Meeting," *Evening Star,* August 7, 1848, 3.

44. This Tredwell is unrelated to the Tredwell in the *Freeman* office.

45. Mr. Barney objected to the label, writing to the *Eagle* a few days later (and making a great point for Shelden and Alexander's claims about party fluidity): "I have for several years struck from the democratic tickets those nominees whom I considered recreant to the cause of freedom, and have sometimes substituted in their places sound men. But I have never voted a whig ticket. If you had called me a *democratic* Abolitionist, I should not have complained. Respectfully yours, Hiram Barney" ("To the Editor," *BDE*, August 11, 1848, 3).

46. "The Free Soil meeting," *BDE*, August 7, 1848, 2.

47. "Free Soil Meeting," *Evening Post*, August 7, 1848, 3.

48. "The Buffalo Convention," *BDE*, August 10, 1848, 2.

49. "Free Soil Meeting," *Brooklyn Evening Star*, August 29, 1848, 2.

50. *MHTN*, August 21, 3.

51. Cf. Wilentz, *Rise of American Democracy*, 531. The *Crescent* in 1848 explains it thusly to its readers: "The Barnburners are by no means addicted to the crime of arson [. . .]. On the contrary, being mostly farmers, they are rather a barn-building and barn-preserving race [. . . . B]eing rather radical in their political notions, they on more than one occasion attacked the old usages of the party to root out what they considered abuses" ("Barnburners and Old Hunkers," *DC*, May 31, 1848, 2).

52. *MHTN*, August 21, 3 (italics in original).

53. *MHTN*, August 21, 3.

54. See for instance, Martin Klammer, "Free Soil Party," *ENCYC*, 237.

55. Whitman had already put himself in opposition to the ruling caste of the Democratic Party in early 1842 (then as a so-called Locofoco), writing, for instance, in the *Aurora* that: "Tammany leaders will not have the fearlessness decidedly to repudiate the move it has taken—for fear of losing the votes of those under the control of the priests. It remains to be seen whether the whole democratic party are to be led by the nose, by this manœuvre of a clique of jesuits" ("Organs of the Democracy," *New York Aurora*, March 29, 1842, 2). Here, he is referring to the party's courting of the Irish vote. But the logic of Whitman's engagement with leadership is already fully extant: the leaders are few, rich, and self-interested—and the noble core of Jefferson's party was abandoned in favor of spoils and power.

56. Wilentz, *Rise of American Democracy*, 531–32.

57. "Party Names in New York," *United States Almanac and Political Register for 1859* (New York: Parsons and Chapin, 1859), 43.

58. "Another Delta City," *DC*, May 8, 1848, 2; "Cairo," *DC*, May 20, 1848, 1.

59. The appointment was a consolation attempt by the Polk administration (Rayback, *Free Soil*, 67).

60. Wright was a Barnburner and a Wilmot man—and by dying in 1846, he became a martyr to the Free-Soil movement. Whitman spoke of the "crushing effect" Wright's death had on fellow radicals, and Wright's memory figured prominently in the Free-Soil split: "A Barnburner delegate," for instance, "called on the convention to do justice to Silas Wright," in a 1847 meeting with Hunkers and was sneered at by an opponent, "whereupon another Barnburner leapt atop a table and declaimed that, though it might be too late to do Wright justice, 'it is not too late to do justice to his assassins'" (Wilentz, *Rise of American Democracy*, 609). A Free-Soil paper like Buffalo's *Republic* ran the phrase "Remember Silas Wright" as part of the presidential ticket in its masthead, even reprinting his "parting admonition" in support of nonextension (August 8, 1848, 2).

61. *MHTN,* October 9, 2.

62. Charles W. McCurdy, *The Anti-Rent Era in New York Law and Politics, 1839–1865* (Chapel Hill: University of North Carolina Press, 2003), 124–25.

63. The first issue of the *Crescent* was printed on March 5, 1848—the only Sunday issue it ever put out. Given Whitman's arrival in late February one might speculate there was a production snag, delaying the first issue, perhaps making the piece seem less than timely.

64. "The People and John Quincy Adams" (c. March 1848), proof sheet with corrections and notations, Library of Congress (Charles E. Feinberg Collection), hdl.loc.gov/loc.mss/ms004014.mss18630.00848.

65. "The People and John Quincy Adams."

66. As Betsy Erkkila has framed it, "The ideas [Whitman] taught—independence, freedom, equality, local sovereignty, and minimal government—were an urban version of Jeffersionian republicanism [. . .]. But in Whitman's vision of a harmonious society of artisans, farmers, and laborers owning homesteads in fee simple, his association of virtue with the laboring classes, and his emphasis on the interactive values of independence and cooperation, freedom and community, Whitman's ideal republic also reflected the artisan republicanism of the city workers among whom he was raised" (*Whitman the Political Poet* [New York: Oxford University Press, 1989], 27).

67. Rayback, *Free Soil,* 423.

68. Rayback, *Free Soil,* 251–52.

69. Edward Lillie Pierce, *Memoir and Letters of Charles Sumner*, vol. 3 (London: Sampson Low, Marston, 1893), 160.

70. *MHTN,* July 29, 2 (italics ours).

71. *MHTN,* August 7, 2.

72. Compare this to Whitman's critique, in the *Freeman*, of the *Brooklyn Daily Eagle*, which he decries as run by "men [who] have 'managed' themselves

into office, and in to the control of the democratic party here" (via reprint in *Brooklyn Daily Advertiser* of April 25, 1849, in Bergman, "Introduction," 5).

73. "Free Soil Platform," *Free Soil Banner,* November 3, 1848, 2; Indianapolis Public Library Digital Collections.

74. *MHTN,* October 14, 2.

75. *MHTN,* August 25, 2.

76. Karen Karbiener describes the discovery of the newspaper ad by Margaret Guardi in her "Even the Brooklyn Boy Needs a Break: Walt Whitman's Summer Fling in Greenport," *Gotham Center,* October 25, 2016, gothamcenter.org/blog/even-the-brooklyn-boy-needs-a-break-walt-whitmans-summer-fling-in-greenport.

77. *MHTN,* August 21, 3.

78. Wilentz, *Rise of American Democracy*, 623–24.

79. See for instance, "Buffalo Convention, Anticipated Proceedings," *BDE,* August 5, 1848, 2; "Benj. F. Butler and Frederick Douglass," *BDE,* August 14, 1848, 2. The latter piece casts half of the convention as Douglass sympathizers and accused all of "fraternizing" with exemplars of "negro 'smartness'"; the former plays up the split over abolitionism by imagining an exchange between a Barnburner "sore head," out for revenge (but hiding it under Jacksonian rhetoric) with a proper Ohio abolitionist.

80. *MHTN,* August 21, 3 (italics in original).

81. Both quotes are from Shelden and Alexander, "Dismantling the Party System," 437.

82. Whitman served in this position alongside Democratic firefighter Stephen A. Dodge (c. 1822–1917) and normal school principal Albert D. Wright (1814–54). See "Free Soil General Committee for Brooklyn," *Brooklyn Freeman,* September 9, 1848, 2; Library of Congress (Charles E. Feinberg Collection), hdl.loc.gov/loc.mss/ms004014.mss18630.02494. For ward boundaries, see "Map of the city of Brooklyn, L.I." (New York, NY: M. Dripps, 1850), Library of Congress, lccn.loc.gov/2013593137.

83. "Our Enmity to the South," *Brooklyn Freeman,* September 9, 1848, 1.

84. "Ephraim Broadhorn," *DC.*

85. "Our Enmity," *Brooklyn Freeman.*

86. *MHTN,* October 7, 2.

87. *MHTN,* October 3, 2.

88. "John Van Buren—The New York Free Soilers," *DC,* October 21, 1848, 2 (italics in original).

89. George Lippard, *The Quaker City, Or, The Monks of Monk-Hall: A Romance of Philadelphia Life, Mystery, and Crime*, vol. 1 (Philadelphia: T.B. Peterson, 1845), 328.

90. Whitman signed the only extant business letter from that time as "Walter Whitman Publisher 'Freeman' 106 Myrtle avenue, Brooklyn L.I." (Walt Whitman to George and Charles Merriam of G. & C Merriam Company, April 17, 1849, *WWA*, prc.00152). City directories for 1850 (*Hearnes' Brooklyn City Directory for 1850–1851* [Brooklyn, NY: Lees & Foulkes, 1850], 384) and 1851 (*Hearnes'* [1851], 449) listed both Walt and his father at this address—in the latter volume, Walt Whitman's job description was given as "printing office and store" (likely a reference to his involvement with the *Salesman and Travelers Directory for Long Island*). The *Hearns'* directory of 1849 (345) did the same, but described the younger Whitman as "editor Brooklyn Freeman Fulton c Middaugh h 106 Myrtle." Whitman later recalled, "I built the building which is at 106 Myrtle avenue. Afterward I added an extension to it in the rear yard, where I did job printing in connection with my building enterprises" (F. B. S., "A Visit to Walt Whitman," *BDE*, July 11, 1886, 10; also in *WWA*). The building was demolished in the early twentieth century. The later "Freeman Building" at Fulton Street was erected after Whitman's tenure, when the *Freeman* had turned Whig.

91. Bergman, "Introduction," 4.

92. *MHTN*, November 13, 2.

93. *MHTN*, November 13, 2.

94. "Presidential Election of 1848: A Resource Guide," *Library of Congress Research Guides*, Library of Congress, guides.loc.gov/presidential-election-1848.

95. This gave the *Delta* ample opportunity for mockery: "The Free-Soil party of New Orleans polled one whole vote yesterday in the First Ward, Second Municipality. [. . .] We congratulate the Free-Soilers upon the promising prospects of that party in this State" ("Free-Soil Vote," *DD*, November 9, 1848, 2).

96. Klammer, "Free Soil Party."

97. The previously mentioned caricature of Whitman—likely a puff written by himself—in the *Brooklyn Daily Advertiser* of 1849 read: "[W]hen 'Old Bullion' [Benton] sits in state in the White House—in [. . .] 1852,—he will, no doubt, 'do something for him,'—because [Whitman] was the first to nominate him, for President of these United States" (cited in Bergman, "Introduction," 9). Even if the sketch wasn't written by Whitman during his post-*Freeman* period of self-promotion, the claim must be his.

98. "Thos. H. Benton," *Brooklyn Daily Times*, April 21, 1858, 2; also in *WWA*. As the *Advertiser* puff portrait suggested, Whitman likewise considered himself a bit of a political animal.

99. Ken Mueller, *Senator Benton and the People: Master Race Democracy on the Early American Frontier* (Ithaca, NY: Cornell University Press, 2014).

100. Mueller, *Senator Benton*, 234.

101. The piece is quoted in the *Brooklyn Advertiser* of June 5, 1849, and reproduced, in parts, in Bergman, "Introduction," 6–7.

102. Cf. "Ephraim Broadhorn," *DC.*

103. *MHTN,* November 13, 2.

104. *MHTN,* November 13, 2.

105. Samuel F. Cogswell was a practical printer, previously employed at the *North Hempstead Gazette* ("Editorial Change," *Brooklyn Evening Star,* July 13, 1848, 2). Perhaps he was, like Daniel Tredwell, a budding legal professional in the 1840s; he later became Commissioner of Deeds before succumbing to an accidental opium overdose in 1858 ("Inquest," *Brooklyn Evening Star,* January 5, 1858, 3). Shortly before taking over at the *Freeman,* he was appointed secretary of the Democratic Whigs of Brooklyn's Second Ward ("Second Ward," *Brooklyn Evening Star,* April 6, 1849, 2).

106. "Plain Answers to Plain Questions," *Brooklyn Daily Advertiser,* September 27, 1849, 2; via manuscript copy by Herbert Bergman, housed in Noverr Papers, Louisa H. Bowen University Archives and Unique Collections, University of Southern Illinois-Edwardsville.

107. Walt Whitman to John Parker Hale, August 14, [1852], *WWA,* nhh.00001.

108. "Presidential Election of 1852," *Library of Congress Research Guides.*

109. Schuyler C. Marshall, "The Free Democratic Convention of 1852," *Pennsylvania History: A Journal of Mid-Atlantic Studies* 22, no 2. (1955): 153.

110. *LG* (1891–92), 359.

111. Erkkila, *Political Poet*, 51–52.

112. *LG* (1855), iv.

CONCLUSION

1. *WWWC* 8:375.

2. *LG* (1855), 55.

3. "The People and John Quincy Adams," Library of Congress.

4. *WWWC* 5:358.

5. *WWWC* 6:347.

6. *WWWC* 5:93.

7. *WWWC* 6:111–12.

8. *MHTN,* July 25, 2.

9. The piece is available in reprint as "Poet and Printer," *DP,* June 8, 1882, 6.

Index

THE IOWA WHITMAN SERIES

The Afterlives of Specimens: Science, Mourning, and Whitman's Civil War
BY LINDSAY TUGGLE

Conserving Walt Whitman's Fame: Selections from Horace Traubel's "Conservator," 1890–1919
EDITED BY GARY SCHMIDGALL

Constructing the German Walt Whitman
BY WALTER GRÜNZWEIG

Democratic Vistas: The Original Edition in Facsimile
BY WALT WHITMAN, EDITED BY ED FOLSOM

"The Disenthralled Hosts of Freedom": Party Prophecy in the Antebellum Editions of Leaves of Grass
BY DAVID GRANT

Every Hour, Every Atom: A Collection of Walt Whitman's Early Notebooks and Fragments
EDITED BY ZACHARY TURPIN AND MATT MILLER

The Evolution of Walt Whitman
BY ROGER ASSELINEAU, FOREWORD BY ED FOLSOM

Intimate with Walt: Selections from Whitman's Conversations with Horace Traubel, 1888–1892
EDITED BY GARY SCHMIDGALL

Leaves of Grass, 1860: The 150th Anniversary Facsimile Edition
BY WALT WHITMAN, EDITED BY JASON STACY

Life and Adventures of Jack Engle: An Auto-Biography: A Story of New York at the Time in which the Reader Will Find Some Familiar Characters
BY WALT WHITMAN, INTRODUCTION BY ZACHARY TURPIN

"The Million Dead, Too, Summ'd Up": Walt Whitman's Civil War Writings
INTRODUCTION AND COMMENTARY BY ED FOLSOM
AND CHRISTOPHER MERRILL

A Place for Humility: Whitman, Dickinson, and the Natural World
BY CHRISTINE GERHARDT

The Pragmatic Whitman: Reimagining American Democracy
BY STEPHEN JOHN MACK

Selected Letters of Walt Whitman
EDITED BY EDWIN HAVILAND MILLER

Song of Myself: With a Complete Commentary
BY WALT WHITMAN, INTRODUCTION AND
COMMENTARY BY ED FOLSOM AND CHRISTOPHER MERRILL

Supplement to "Walt Whitman: A Descriptive Bibliography"
BY JOEL MYERSON

"This Mighty Convulsion": Whitman and Melville Write the Civil War
EDITED BY CHRISTOPHER STEN AND TYLER HOFFMAN

Transatlantic Connections: Whitman U.S., Whitman U.K.
BY M. WYNN THOMAS

Transnational Modernity and the Italian Reinvention of Walt Whitman, 1870–1945
BY CATERINA BERNADINI

Visiting Walt: Poems Inspired by the Life and Work of Walt Whitman
EDITED BY SHEILA COGHILL AND THOM TAMMARO

Walt Whitman: The Centennial Essays
EDITED BY ED FOLSOM

Walt Whitman: The Correspondence, Volume VII
EDITED BY TED GENOWAYS

Walt Whitman and the Class Struggle
BY ANDREW LAWSON

Walt Whitman and the Earth: A Study in Ecopoetics
BY M. JIMMIE KILLINGSWORTH

Walt Whitman and the Making of Jewish American Poetry
BY DARA BARNAT

Walt Whitman, Where the Future Becomes Present
EDITED BY DAVID HAVEN BLAKE AND MICHAEL ROBERTSON

Walt Whitman and the World
EDITED BY GAY WILSON ALLEN AND ED FOLSOM

Walt Whitman's Reconstruction: Poetry and Publishing between Memory and History
BY MARTIN T. BUINICKI

Walt Whitman's Selected Journalism
EDITED BY DOUGLAS A. NOVERR AND JASON STACY

Walt Whitman's "Song of Myself": A Mosaic of Interpretations
BY EDWIN HAVILAND MILLER

Walt Whitman's Songs of Male Intimacy and Love: "Live Oak, with Moss" and "Calamus"
EDITED BY BETSY ERKKILA

Whitman among the Bohemians
EDITED BY JOANNA LEVIN AND EDWARD WHITLEY

A Whitman Chronology
BY JOANN P. KRIEG

Whitman & Dickinson: A Colloquy
EDITED BY ÉRIC ATHENOT AND CRISTANNE MILLER

Whitman East and West: New Contexts for Reading Walt Whitman
EDITED BY ED FOLSOM

Whitman and the Irish
BY JOANN P. KRIEG

Whitman Noir: Black America and the Good Gray Poet
EDITED BY IVY G. WILSON

The Whitman Revolution: Sex, Poetry, and Politics
BY BETSY ERKKILA

Whitman's Drift: Imagining Literary Distribution
BY MATT COHEN

Whitman's Southern Sojourn: Rediscovering the Poet in New Orleans, 1848
BY STEFAN SCHÖBERLEIN AND ZACHARY TURPIN